T0345674

Undoing Impunity

Undoing Impunity
Speech after Sexual Violence

V. GEETHA

ZUBAAN SERIES ON SEXUAL VIOLENCE AND IMPUNITY
IN SOUTH ASIA

IDRC | CRDI
International Development Research Centre
Centre de recherches pour le développement international

zubaan

Zubaan
128 B Shahpur Jat, 1st floor
NEW DELHI 110 049
Email: contact@zubaanbooks.com
Website: www.zubaanbooks.com

First published by Zubaan 2016

This project was undertaken with financial support provided by the
International Development Research Centre, Canada

10 9 8 7 6 5 4 3 2 1

ISBN 978 93 84757 77 9

Zubaan is an independent feminist publishing house based in New Delhi
with a strong academic and general list. It was set up as an imprint of India's
first feminist publishing house, Kali for Women, and carries forward Kali's
tradition of publishing world quality books to high editorial and production
standards. *Zubaan* means tongue, voice, language, speech in Hindustani.
Zubaan publishes in the areas of the humanities, social sciences, as well as in
fiction, general non-fiction, and books for children and young adults under
its Young Zubaan imprint.

Printed and bound at Raj Press, R-3 Inderpuri, New Delhi 110 012

To Mythily Sivaraman
for her heeding of social suffering and injustice
with love and gratitude

Contents

Part III

Zubaan Series on Sexual Violence and Impunity in South Asia

An Introduction

URVASHI BUTALIA, LAXMI MURTHY AND
NAVSHARAN SINGH

The Sexual Violence and Impunity project (SVI) is a three-year research project, supported by the International Development Research Centre (IDRC), Canada, and coordinated by Zubaan. Led by a group of nine advisors from five countries (Bangladesh, India, Nepal, Pakistan, Sri Lanka), and supported by groups and individuals on the ground, the SVI project started with the objectives of developing and deepening understanding on sexual violence and impunity in South Asia through workshops, discussions, interviews and commissioned research papers on the prevalence of sexual violence, and the structures that provide impunity to perpetrators in all five countries.

The project began with some key questions and concerns. We noted that recent histories and contemporary political developments in South Asia had shown an exponential increase in sexual violence, particularly mass violence. And yet, even as such violence had increased across the region, so had the ever-deepening silence around it.

Why, for example, had the end of 25 years of violent conflict in Sri Lanka in May 2009 not resulted in an open and frank discussion about sexual violence as a weapon of war? Why had the International Crimes Tribunal (ICT) of Bangladesh, set up in 2009 to investigate and prosecute suspects for the genocide committed in 1971 by the Pakistan army and their local collaborators, paid such little attention to the question of mass rape, despite it being widely acknowledged that it had happened and many women having spoken out about it? Why did discussions on Kashmir in India or Swat in Pakistan, simply ignore the question of sexual violence? Why was caste violence, violence against sex workers and men and transgender persons barely spoken about?

Nor was silence the only issue here. Crucial to maintaining the silence was—and is—the active collusion of states in providing impunity to perpetrators, sometimes under the guise of protective laws and special powers to the armed forces, at others under the guise of nationalism. So heavily were the odds stacked against women that, until recently, very few had dared to speak out. Backed by culture, and strengthened by the state, and often with the active collusion of non-state actors, impunity then, remained largely unchallenged.

We asked ourselves if these conditions were specific to the South Asian region. Elsewhere in many parts of the world, we noted, rape was increasingly being discussed and accepted, not only as a weapon of war, but also as a crime against humanity and as an instrument of genocide. The 1998 Akeyesu judgment by the International Criminal Tribunal for Rwanda (ICTR) provided a clear definition of rape and delineated its elements as a crime against humanity and as an instrument of genocide. In the International Criminal Tribunal for the former Yugoslavia (ICTY) jurisprudence pioneered the approach that used acts of rape and other forms of sexual violence to include elements of other international crimes such as torture, enslavement, and persecution, which previously had not been litigated in the context of gender violence.

The Special Court for Sierra Leone (SCSL) brought into jurisprudence on violations of international humanitarian law a particular form of sexual violence prevalent in the conflict in Sierra Leone—forced marriages . In this case, forced marriage was distinguished from sexual slavery or sexual crimes and argued as a crime against humanity. Building on the progressive development of the case law for sexual and gender-based violence under ICTR, ICTY and SCSL, the Rome Statute of the International Criminal Court (ICC) includes rape and forms of sexual violence as part of the crimes of genocide, crimes against humanity, and war crimes, and specifically enumerates rape, forced prostitution, sexual slavery, forced pregnancy, enforced sterilization and prosecution on account of gender as specific crimes punishable under the statute.

The progressive thinking developed in the course of these trials brought sexual violence into the mainstream of international jurisprudence (something that was largely invisible until the 1990s) such that it became part of the collective knowledge to which women's movements worldwide have contributed enormously. In South Asia a comprehensive and critical analysis of existing jurisprudence on sexual violence is a newly emerging area of scholarship, and a solid community of practice is still to emerge in this field. There are many dimensions of sexual violence—ranging from conceptual clarity on definitions of sexual violence, to legal, medical and forensic understandings of evidence gathering and monitoring and more—that remain inadequately explored.

South Asia has much to learn from advancements elsewhere. How do our countries expect a 'return' to peace (and we need to question the composition of such a peace) without addressing the question of the large-scale and calculated attack by perpetrators on women and the systematic violation of their right to bodily integrity and autonomy? How can this question be addressed without including rape and sexual violation squarely within definitions of crimes against humanity? What are the glaring silences of our domestic laws and policies? What do they have to say about the endemic sexual violence and rape driven by caste, ethnicity and religion? How can we think creatively about questions of reparation beyond the ways states in the region have done by ghettoizing women in rehabilitation camps where they remain stigmatized and marked as raped women, to be separated from others, as we saw in India following the partition of 1947 and post-1971 relief measures in Bangladesh.

As feminist activists and academics we were—and continue to be—concerned about the growing violence and the serious and continuing lack of accountability on the part of states and governments, the failure to address the impunity enjoyed by perpetrators, the absence of effective mechanisms to provide justice and reparations, and the virtual indifference to the psychological damage suffered by victims, survivors and their families and communities. We feel that our collective inability and unwillingness to address the profound impact of such violence is a serious impediment to peace and justice in our region.

Our discussions began in January 2012, when a group of women from South Asia came together in a meeting facilitated by a small IDRC grant, to begin the process of thinking about these issues. We were concerned not only at the legal silences around the question of sexual violence and impunity, but also how deeply the 'normalization' of sexual violence and the acceptance of impunity, had taken root in our societies.

It became clear to us that women's movements across South Asia had made important contributions in bringing the issue of sexual violence and impunity to public attention. And yet, there were significant knowledge gaps, as we have pointed out earlier. However, an absence of adequate literature on the subject did not mean that there was nothing available. South Asia has a rich literary and scholarly tradition and indeed there is a fair amount of writing on sexual violence, and while impunity is not necessarily directly addressed in these writings, concern about it is implicit in most of them. We felt it was important to systematically understand the nature of impunity, and what legal, social and cultural norms states draw upon to enable and allow impunity for the perpetrators and to silence the demands for accountability. We thought, too, that it was important to document the lesser-known ways in which women, and sometimes communities, create structures to deal with the trauma and dislocation caused by sexual violence. These stories had remained largely unknown. In much of caste violence in India for example, or in cases of feudal or tribal instances of retribution and punishment, the violation of women's bodies is an accepted way of establishing male superiority. And because these hierarchies of caste and tribe are so embedded even in the 'minds' of our secular, modern states, the victims/survivors often find solutions of their own, creating ways of ensuring some sense of justice.

It was out of these concerns that the SVI project grew. Over a period of time, we contacted scholars and researchers, conducted research, held several country meetings and a series of methodology workshops and, step by step, the project brought together a community of young researchers (we had consciously planned to stay away from established and overstretched scholars), more than 85 per cent of whom are, we are proud to say, under the age of 40. Our workshops focused on unpeeling the layers of impunity for sexual violence, on writing skills, on questions of ethics in researching subjects as sensitive as sexual violence, on the nature of evidence, on working with states and more.

During the time that the project has been under way, the region has witnessed many changes—in the public domain, a changed public discourse, as well as legal reform as a result of feminist and human rights' activism. These critical moments found resonance in the ongoing research—and indeed many of our researchers were centrally involved in working for these changes—and pointed to directions for future work.

The gang-rape and subsequent death of a young student in Delhi in December 2012 culminated in mass public anger, and generated public debate and feminist interventions. The testimonies of feminist activists to the Justice Verma Committee, constituted to recommend amendments to the criminal law for sexual assault against women, were an outcome of decades of intense engagement of the women's movement in India. The occasion provided a moment of deep reflection on the questions that activists were already grappling with. It also led to serious questioning within the movement: why, for example, did caste rape, or rape by the army, not result in the same kind of outrage, the same explosion of anger as the incident of 16 December 2012 had done? In the open discussion with the Verma Committee, feminist activists' testimonies did not remain confined to amendments in the law but demonstrated a remarkable understanding as they presented the continuum of violence against women from home to communities to the frontiers of the nation states where women's safety and bodily integrity were threatened in the name of protection of the borders.

In a small but significant step towards challenging impunity, on 6 September 2015, an army court martial awarded life sentences to six of its personnel found guilty in the 'fake encounter' case of April 2010 when the army killed three youths in the Machil sector of Kupwara district of Indian-administered Kashmir on the grounds that they were foreign militants. Even though the accused were not tried in a civil court, and the appeal process is ongoing, this conviction is significant since this is the first time army personnel in Kashmir have been handed life-terms on these charges.

Over in Sri Lanka, a significant judgment was the Jaffna High Court sentencing, on 7 October 2015, of four soldiers to 25 years of rigorous imprisonment, compensation and reimbursement of legal fees for the 2010 gang-rape of a woman at a resettlement camp in Viswamadhu, Kilinochchi. Assigning culpability and ensuring strict punishment of the security personnel involved has been possible only with the sustained intervention of activists.

Undoubtedly, accountability has been a fraught issue across South Asia, especially when it comes to war crimes. December 2012 saw vehement protests in Bangladesh by the right-wing Jamaat-e-Islami supporters and their student wing, Bangladesh Islami Chhatra Shibir, demanding the disbanding of the ICT of Bangladesh set up three years earlier to investigate and prosecute suspects for the genocide committed in 1971 during the Bangladesh Liberation War by the Pakistani Army and their local collaborators, Razakars, Al-Badr and Al-Shams. The vigorous counter protests, of those pressing for accountability and an end to impunity culminated in the 'Shahbag movement'—a popular student movement for justice for war-time crimes. The gazette notification recognition, on 12 October 2015, recognizing 41 Birangonas (war heroines) as freedom fighters for their contribution in the country's Liberation War in 1971 has been more than 40 years in the coming, but an official recognition that can be viewed as reparation for the stigma and suffering these women were made to face in addition to the sexual violence perpetrated on them.

In Sri Lanka, still staggering under the history of ethnic conflict and the Eelam war that ended in 2009, the report of the Office of the High Commissioner for Human Rights (OHCHR) released in September 2015 concluded that there were reasonable grounds to believe that war crimes and/or crimes against humanity had been committed with regard to a variety of abuses, including sexual violence and other forms of torture; unlawful killings by all sides; forced recruitment of adults and recruitment of children as fighters by the LTTE and enforced disappearances. The report recommended several legal, justice and security sector reforms and the establishment of an ad hoc hybrid justice mechanism integrating international judges, prosecutors, lawyers and investigators. In a move demonstrating the political will of the new regime to redress war-time human rights violations, a consensus resolution co-sponsored by Sri Lanka was passed on 1 October 2015 by the UN Human Rights Council encouraging the Government of Sri Lanka to implement its recommendations.

Following the end of Nepal's 10-year insurgency in 2006, while the Truth and Reconciliation Commission (TRC) made rape a crime for which amnesty cannot be granted, the 35-day statute of limitations for reporting of rape makes it virtually impossible for war-time rapes to go to court. Additionally, the TRC gave effective amnesty to those alleged to have been responsible for gross human rights violations and gives broad powers of reconciliation to the TRC, with the result that victims will be forced to give up their right to justice as part of the reconciliation process with the commission empowered to undertake mediation between victims and perpetrators even in the case of rape.

Over the three-year period since this project began, there have been amendments in the criminal law in India and the definition of sexual assault has expanded, we have gained considerable grounds in our understanding on impunity for sexual violence and consequently are better able to speak about it and to fight for justice. It is noteworthy that during the recent targeted violence in Muzzafarnagar in India in 2013, seven Muslim women who were brutally gang raped and sexually assaulted by men belonging to the other communities, filed writ petitions for protecting their right to life under Article 21. In a landmark judgment in March 2014, recognizing the rehabilitation needs of the survivors of targeted mass rape, the Supreme Court of India ordered that a compensation of INR 500,000 each for rehabilitation be paid to the women by the state government.

The Occupy Baluwatar movement of December 2012 in Nepal, which some see as the ripple effects of the Delhi protests against sexual violence and demands for justice, had sexual violence and impunity at its centre. One of the major outcomes of the movement was the 27 November 2015 amendment broadening the definition of rape, bringing same-sex rape and marital rape into the ambit of law.

In Pakistan too, small steps forward were taken in the shape of a parliamentary panel approval in February 2015 of amendments in the anti-rape laws, supporting DNA profiling as evidence during the investigation and a prohibition on character assassination of rape victims during the trial.

The eight volumes (one each on Bangladesh, Nepal, Pakistan and Sri Lanka, two on India, and two standalone books on impunity and on an incident of mass rape in Kunan Poshpora in Indian-administered Kashmir) that comprise this series, are one of the many outcomes of this project. The knowledge built on the subject through workshops, discussion fora, testimonies and interviews is part of our collective repository and we are committed to making it available to be used by activists, students and scholars. Of the 50 papers that were commissioned, nearly all came in. Along the way, we tragically lost two of our co-travellers, our advisor, Sharmila Rege and our young Sri Lankan researcher, Priya Thangarajah. Both Sharmila and Priya had been central to this project, bringing their considerable knowledge, their activism, their commitment to the work in hand. True to the feminist spirit of collectivity, their friends and colleagues rallied round to complete the work they had begun.

It is our hope that these volumes will begin the process of opening up the question of sexual violence and impunity in South Asia. The essays in these volumes, as well as the two standalone volumes address many of the issues we have raised above, and yet, significant gaps remain. We have not been able to adequately address questions of sexual violence and caste, the question of male and transgender sexual violence, or violence on queer communities. We need to gather more evidence about sexual violence on sex workers, on agricultural workers, in urban workspaces and more.

We can only say with some satisfaction that through this collective endeavour, through putting our heads together, a fairly solid beginning has been made, layers have started to be uncovered and speech is beginning to replace silence. This systematic effort has allowed us to give this critical issue the focused attention that it deserves.

Creating a community of researchers and activists, building a common understanding resting on a shared history but not guided by national interests of the countries can make a significant move towards peace building in a region fractured by political, religious and ethnic divides. This series of books and other resources are being launched with the hope they will inspire the next generation of scholars and activists to build on this knowledge, and broaden and deepen it to end impunity for sexual violence.

Prologue

The Recognition of Suffering

In 2011, a Sessions court in Tamil Nadu made history. It delivered a verdict in a case that had been dragging on for 19 years and had to do with violence inflicted on the villagers of Vachathi—a modest-sized adivasi hamlet—by personnel of the Tamil Nadu Forest department and local policemen. Two hundred and sixty-nine men were pronounced guilty, including top officials of both departments. While 269 men had participated in the State action, 54 had died over the years. In effect, 215 men were sentenced to imprisonment.

The violence that marred lives and futures in Vachathi was part of a long, relentless and tortured campaign that the Tamil Nadu government had launched against Veerappan, an ostensible sandalwood smuggler. In this instance, it was alleged that some villagers from Vachathi were in the employ of Veerappan and that the Forest and Police departments had been notified that there were hidden logs of sandalwood in the village. As Forest and Police department officials sought to 'recover' the sandalwood logs, a predictable sequence of events unfolded. An adivasi man was questioned, thrashed and then assaulted brutally. When others gathered around him and argued with the police, a scuffle ensued and a forest official was injured. The enraged raiders left, vowing retaliatory action. The men of the village knew what that meant and some fled into the forested hills. Towards the evening the police and forest officials returned. They beat up whoever they found, destroyed standing crops in the fields, slaughtered and fed on fowl belonging to the village, polluted wells in the neighbourhood, vandalized homes…Eighteen women, including girls who were barely into their teens, were subject to verbal and violent sexual assault. Along with some men, they were arrested and taken away to the nearest police station where they were all subject to further humiliation.

Even as the Vachathi incident gained public visibility, the government of Tamil Nadu hastened to justify the actions of its men. From then on, and at every stage, this case saw gross prevarication on the part of government on every aspect. From refusing to acknowledge that an atrocity had been committed by its personnel to refusing to commit itself to reparations owed to its hurt citizens, successive governments in this southern state exhibited indifference with impunity. But the Sessions court judgment answered nearly two decades of government inaction with a resounding affirmation of justice. In addition to sentencing a staggering number of State personnel to various terms of imprisonment, the Court ordered that compensation was still owed to the victims of this infamous attack.

How had this verdict come about? For one, the Communist Party of India–Marxist (CPM) prosecuted the case, assisted by a team of dedicated lawyers. Their collective effort ensured that witnesses felt protected—a very important task in cases such as this, where intimidation is used routinely to compromise witness testimonies. Secondly, when investigation of the case was entrusted to the Central Bureau of Investigation (CBI)—on the plea that investigating agencies in the state of Tamil Nadu were under political pressure—it went about its job relentlessly and meticulously. Thirdly, and most important, the villagers of Vachathi and especially its women stood their ground with dignity and courage. When the verdict was announced, the sense of quiet victory the villagers experienced was evident in the poignant scene of several of them breaking down: those who were but children when the incident happened and had since grown up, married and had children themselves, expressed their satisfaction with the judgment. However, they were not exultant, and neither were they sentimental. They accepted that justice had been done unto them, after a fashion and their dignity shone through the expressions on their faces.

***

The Vachathi judgment sentenced the perpetrators of violence on the basis of the Prevention of Atrocities against Scheduled Castes and Tribes Act (or the PoA Act), 1989 and sexual violence was marked for special attention in the final judgement. As in other instances which have witnessed police action of this kind, sexual violence was part of a continuum of specific and enumerable acts that included torture, bodily humiliation (of both men and women), displacement of people from their homes and forced confinement. Such action, punitive and gratuitous, is constitutive of governance in fraught situations—as we see in Kashmir and in Manipur (see chapter 12 for more details).

Yet none of this led to passive acquiescence. The women of Vachathi fought back. Braving stigma and shame, they stayed with an impossibly long trial process. They acted on their account as well as on account of their village, and of a way of life that had all but been destroyed. This is quite remarkable: across the world, victims of sexual violence, whether in times of war or civil conflict, or even in 'normal' times, have testified to the fear they experience when they have to speak of what had happened to them. Fear of being marked as raped women, of having to reckon with rapists still at large in the community, the sheer terror at having to recall what is best forgotten and most of all, the stigma of being considered 'dishonoured' have prevented women from speaking out, bearing witness, and approaching the courts, except when there is an enabling context or supportive forum. In this case, the women found it possible to 'speak' because of the sustained and concerted action of a political party, a women's organization affiliated to that party, the investigating agency and the courts.

Members of the CPM-affiliated Tamil Nadu Tribal People's Association were the first to visit Vachathi a few days after the incident. They spoke to whoever was willing to testify and submitted a memorandum to the District Collector and Chief Minister, detailing the extent of violence, destruction, arrests and assault. Mythily Sivaraman, a prominent leader of the CPM-affiliated All India Democratic Women's Association (AIDWA), wrote to the State Commission for the Scheduled Castes and Scheduled Tribes seeking its intervention. Following a High Court Order that supported this demand, P. Bamathi visited Vachathi and filed a report on behalf of the Commission, which among other things called attention to local government's indifference and the destruction caused by the police raid. Around the same time, a team comprising advocates, intellectuals and students, put together by the People's Union of Civil Liberties (PUCL), also came to find out the facts of the matter. Their report confirmed the details of what had transpired at Vachathi.

Yet the Tamil Nadu government continued to deny allegations of violence by its officers and insisted that sexual assault did not take place. Undaunted, the eighteen women who had been assaulted filed a complaint alleging sexual violence had been committed against them. In retrospect, they noted that they were impelled to do so, not only because they had the support of the CPM, but also because they were haunted by the injustice and humiliation they and their fellow villagers were subject to. From a position that can only be described as precarious, they acted, and kept faith with the law, however demanding that proved to be. It is as if their very precarity demanded that they act.

As the case became mired in legal details, the CPM filed a petition in the courts asking for the case to be transferred to the CBI, on the grounds that they did not trust local police to be impartial. They also demanded compensation from the government for loss of homes, livelihood and dignity. Three years after the event, the CBI was called in by a court order. Slowly and in the face of sustained campaigning by the victims of Vachathi and their supporters, which resulted in enabling court orders, the government made reparations, but reluctantly and without admitting to a sense of their responsibility. Even after the CBI completed its investigation and indicted more than 200 officers of the state, court proceedings continued to be delayed for a few years until 2002, when decisive action was taken. A petition was filed in court seeking appointment of a special Prosecutor under the Prevention of Atrocities (PoA) against Scheduled Castes and Tribes Act, 1989. Only from that point onward did the trial proceed at a somewhat even pace, but the path to justice was anything but easy.

The importance of invoking the PoA Act in this instance cannot be exaggerated. The Act may be regarded as perhaps one of the most important pieces of legislation in independent India. Its very text constitutes an indictment of our social order and insists on our recognizing quotidian acts of humiliation and violence for the horrific crimes that they are. It may be said that in this instance, recognition of the pain and humiliation produced by our civic inhumanity is mandated by this Act, even if it is not always applied or taken note of by local police and sometimes even local courts. I will return to discussing the Act's importance in a subsequent section of this prologue.

***

In spite of the sustained support that the victims of Vachathi had, and their own determination to stay with the legal struggle, the State did all it could to 'mis'recognise the tragedy its actions had made happen. It was particularly insistent in denying sexual assault had taken place; and refused to grant that its officials were capable of brutality towards citizens whose rights they were constitutionally enjoined to protect. For its part, the CPM continued to foreground State indifference and inaction, as if to say that the impunity which it exhibited was particularly deplorable because it denied the suffering inflicted by its own agencies on hapless citizens. While holding the State culpable in the eyes of the law, it also facilitated social recognition of imposed hurt and suffering.

That it achieved this is significant—made evident in the manner in which it mediated public memory and kept alive the story of a crime that, like many others, might well have been forgotten or cast to the very edges of our collective memory. Given the often winding path to justice in the Indian context, such forgetting is not exceptionable. Besides, the State has an investment in ensuring that we forget, especially where its own acts of violent commission are concerned. One of the means through which the State does this is by refusing to take responsibility, not only for the act but for the pain such an act causes. Whatever may be pronounced in autopsy and post-mortem reports, and whatever may be the actual marks of hurt, these are never allowed the eloquence that they deserve. Rather they are papered over, made to disappear under a pile of unintelligible words, to do with the law, forensic science and routine government procedure. With respect to Vachathi, social recognition preceded the relentless legal battle that was fought. If members of the CPM had not visited the place, and by their physical presence assured the villagers that they deserved justice, and their own assistance in securing it, there would have been no legal battle. It was that moment of recognition, of injustice and suffering, which earned the trust of the villagers. On the other hand, once the legal struggle was set in motion the CPM ensured that the vile incidents that happened in the fateful summer months of 1992 were not forgotten.

Yet one cannot be too sanguine about the relationship between social recognition and the possibility of justice. Social recognition of suffering may or may not produce legal victories in all instances.

After all, the law is governed by protocols and precedents that rely as much on evidentiary details as it does on an understanding of the human predicament. Perhaps what such recognition achieves is what may be described as ethical affect; and whatever consequence this has for the doing of justice, it certainly is consequential as far as the sufferer is concerned. Bearing legal and social witness in the cause of those who have suffered helps affirm a horrific reality that the victim imagines only she can really ever know or understand. In turn, such affirmation implicates in a common humanity those who have suffered as well as those who do not want such suffering to go unacknowledged.

Auschwitz survivor and writer Primo Levi has pointed out how he had a recurrent dream of himself trying to recount what he had experienced in the death camps and not being listened to: 'I cannot help noticing that my listeners do not follow me. In fact, they are completely indifferent: they speak confusedly of other things among themselves, as if I was not there. My sister looks at me, gets up and goes away without a word.' He further notes: 'My dream stands in front of me, still warm, and although awake I am still full of its anguish... Why does it happen? Why is the pain of every day translated so constantly into our dreams, in the ever-repeated scene of the unlistened-to story?' (Levi, 1959: 66).

The impossibility of securing a hearing for things said and done that are beyond the pale of what we consider human or normal leaves victims of such inhumanity helpless in the face of something that resists communication. Therefore those who listen, acknowledge and are prepared to bear witness on behalf of victims, help lighten and even dissolve the latter's burdened memory. The 'alone'ness of suffering is somewhat mitigated as pain finds a hearer—and if that in turn finds a legal resonance, the chances of securing justice are that much higher.

This is particularly the case with victims of sexual assault, which is seldom taken seriously as a crime even under what we may consider 'normal' circumstances. Or if it is considered a heinous act, it is because it is seen as staining the woman's reputation, her very being, and by that token a crime that ricochets on her family and community. I will come back to discussing this widely prevalent attitude but for now, I want to reiterate the fact that the eighteen women of Vachathi were not taken seriously by the police or their defendants, and were in fact mocked—both when the crimes were committed and when they complained. This is what marks the CPM's recognition of that vile act as decisive and sensitive. Acting on a writ petition filed by A. Nallasivan, CPM Rajya Sabha member, seeking a writ of mandamus, the Madras High Court, through an important ruling, paved the way for a CBI investigation. A substantial section of this judgment has to do with the denial by the Tamil Nadu government—via a counter-affidavit filed by the Secretary of the Department of Environment—that the women of Vachathi were raped by the defendants, in this case, officers of the state. The judgement notes that Nallasivan's affidavit had explicitly called attention to acts of sexual violence and 'gravest humiliation'; it examines counter-claims—that such acts did not take place—in the light of this affidavit, and at the end of a long discussion on what the police are required to do, by way of filing a first information report, observes that State denial in this instance is not 'unbiased'. The judgement also records its dismay at the police—for 'trying to burke or evade investigation of the alleged offences'. The clarity with which State denial is dismissed as unworthy is significant—a fine instance of well-exercised judicial discretion on the one hand, and on the other hand, a recognition of the strength of A. Nallasivan's affidavit, which stated quite unequivocally that the writ petition was being launched in the public interest 'on the footing that the abovesaid villagers, on their own, are in no position to pursue their grievances'. Speaking on behalf of victims, who are precarious in their being and situation, the affidavit encodes civil responsibility of a particular kind: it stands testimony to citizens' efforts to not only heed but also represent the grievances of the disenfranchised and bear witness to their salience.

***

I have dwelt somewhat on the implicit significance of recognition of suffering because in a fundamental sense, it is such recognition that challenges and illuminates the contours and details of State impunity. Further, it positions impunity as not merely a legal or political conundrum, but as resolute refusal on the part of State personnel to be part of shared humanity. For, apart from setting itself above law and the realm of justice, State impunity refuses to either recognize or take responsibility for the hurt it causes, and actually relishes its authority to be that way. This relish is most evident in the State's elaborate and completely fantastic justifications of wrong-doing. Paradoxically, this move to fabricate reasons for its actions is indicative of the State's illegality, of the fact that it has lost its sovereign character and remains set in authority chiefly on account of its enormous power to both cause hurt and disclaim responsibility for acts that result in suffering.

Conversely, as must be evident from what I have said above, those who challenge impunity take responsibility, in a legal as well as ethical sense: their search for justice happens within the horizon of the law, but it is their ethical indignation that overwrites the language of legality and speaks in the name of the aggrieved and the innocent. In doing so, they do two things: they foreground the essential immorality of the State, its refusal to be bound by shared norms of what it means to be human; and by the same token, underscore the justice claims of the affected to be, essentially, serious ethical claims.

It would be useful to return to a consideration of the PoA Act at this point. It seems to me that this Act comes closest in identifying the intertwined and indissoluble nature of moral and justice claims. Writing of the genesis of the Act, P. S. Krishnan, responsible for piloting it through Parliament, notes that violence meted out to dalits and adivasis is not at the behest of those who are 'criminals' in the ordinary sense of the word: the purveyors of violence act in an unjust and criminal fashion, being part of a social order that allows this, and worse, considers the suffering of those who are hurt by such crimes as being inconsequential, even as it upholds the privileges of those who cause hurt. To point to the criminality of a social order that enables and sanctions such habitual cruelty, the Act lists a range of crimes. These are not generic acts of violence; rather each is a distinct expression of perverse, deliberate cruelty directed against one who is perceived as a social inferior, in fact a non-person: compelling him or her to eat human faeces, despoiling his water source, wrecking her home, to name a few.

This elaborate listing of atrocities is not accidental. It is clearly meant to shock us out of the moral torpor that caste society routinely produces and make us take note of what is obviously visible, but seldom granted attention. Equally important, we are forced to ask the question: who or what sort of person would indulge in the commission of such atrocities? In other words, the Act forces us to account for human venality and so commits us to an ethical position regarding suffering and hurt, on the one hand, and injustice on the other, even before it is put to specific use. On the other hand, such a position can only be acted on, in a legal and public sense.

***

If the obverse of impunity is the recognition of suffering, and the expression of ethical affect, what other public forms may this assume? That is, apart from the filing of petitions, affidavits and representing the affected in courts of law, what else might such recognition achieve?

The relationship of wrong-doing to the suffering it causes has become central to contemporary quasi-judicial processes, such as those set in motion by Truth Commissions across the world. These commissions are viewed—and view themselves—as enabling forums that enable victims to speak and express what until now had remained buried or suppressed. They are constituted in contexts where terrible crimes have taken place but have not been viewed as such, or understood in those terms; often these Commissions are set up after the events they are meant to judge are already distant memory or at least forgettable for any number of reasons. In this sense, they are about securing justice for past crimes, but more importantly, they are also conceived as efforts that will illumine what has been kept in the dark. Truth Commissions thus are about coming to terms with stubborn pasts that will not go away but insist on being released from the thralldom of imposed silence and official forgetting; or they are about a time when impunity was exercised habitually and naturalized, as in South Africa during the apartheid era. In fact, even before they commence their hearings, such Commissions come with a mandate to acknowledge and endorse the claims of justice and morality, and it is their incipient recognition of what they are about to interrogate—acts against humanity—that grant them ethical charge.

The act of speaking out in a context that guarantees quiet and sympathetic reception may or may not serve the ends of justice, but truth-telling answers to a deep-felt need amongst those who have endured violence to explain their case, and brings to light crimes that otherwise would remain hidden from history and the future. Bearing witness to their own fate, in however broken, fragmentary and incomplete a manner, those who testify both indict and invite perpetrators into a possible conversation, in the hope that the latter would, at the end of it all, admit to their acts of injustice; which admission, for many victims, is absolutely essential if there is to be forgiveness, reconciliation and justice. As a victim of sexual violence and witness to acts of torture and murder by the Khmer Rouge in Cambodia states, it is not merely her speaking aloud that matters; her story has to be heeded and followed by an admission of guilt, otherwise there can be no moving forward from silenced and thwarted memories of suffering towards some sort of co-existence with those who have wrought havoc and yet continue to live alongside their victims.

While much depends on how Truth Commissions function, they do possess this common feature: they are not structured to merely heed and notate tales of suffering, but are committed to establishing the legal and ethical basis for justice battles. Often, Commissions have a clearly defined mandate, complete with dates and territory defined. Their jurisdiction is also likewise defined: what they are expected to prosecute and what is not theirs to consider are set out in advance. In processing affidavits, evidence, and listening to defendants' pleas, they function as courts do: listen to witness testimonies, sift through evidence, and engage in painstaking interrogation of details and facts.

While justice may not be done on the scale that would appear fair to victims, and not all perpetrators are brought to justice, the grave admonition such Commissions deliver helps to frame and limit the exaggerated authority that impunity arrogates to itself. As Slavenka Drakulic, who sat in on some of the trials held under the auspices of the International Criminal Tribunal convened at The Hague to prosecute persons accused of crimes against humanity in the former Yugoslavia, points out, sentencing of the kind she was witness to was not likely to foster remorse or cause societies that have yielded criminals such as these into self-introspection. Yet the ethical force of such sentencing cannot be doubted.

***

In this brief prologue I have tried to define a line of hope that connotes all that impunity would like destroyed, including our capacity for empathy, for trusting that justice must and will triumph and our determination that power and authority must be accountable, not only to the law, but to an ethical sense of what it means to be human, a sense that we have evolved historically through struggle, revolution and sacrifice. This line of hope, to which victims, survivors and witnesses hold on, is what binds us in a common humanity. In what follows, I hope to examine and illuminate what keeps us within this bind and what causes it to snap.

In other words, this enquiry into sexual violence and impunity is not only about the nature of State authority, but about what thwarts and indicts it. It seems to me that unless we 'remember' the history of this thwarting, even as we do keep alive the memory of State and social violence, we would be doing grave injustice to our capacity for hope and faith in justice.

REFERENCES

Anderson, Katrina. 2004. 'Turning Reconciliation on Its Head: Responding to Sexual Violence Under the Khmer Rouge', *Seattle Journal for Social Justice*, 3 (2): 785–832.

Dorairaj, S. 2011. 'Justice for Vachathi', *Frontline*, 28 (22). http://www.frontline.in/static/html/fl2822/stories/20111104282203200.htm (accessed 25 October 2014).

Drakulic, Slavenka. 2004. *They Would Never Hurt a Fly: War Criminals on Trial at The Hague*, London: Abacus.

Krishnan, PS. 2009. 'Atrocities against Dalits: Retrospect and Prospect', *Combat Law*, September-December, p. 7–11.

Levi, Primo. 1959. *If this is a Man*, New York: Orion Press.

A. Nallasivan vs. State Of Tamil Nadu And Others 1995 CriLJ 2754.

Thomas, Suresh. 2012. 'We had to beat up our Oor Gounder, *Fountain Ink*, June. http://fountainink.in/?p=2100 (accessed 25 October 2014).

Part 1

Part I

1

Speaking about Sexual Violence

The link between sexual violence and impunity appears given. For many of us concerned with, or working on, issues to do with sexual violence in South Asia, what could be more self-evident? That this is a crime, a violation that is systematically misrecognized; that both perpetrator and the criminal justice system that is meant to investigate the crime are prone to blame the victim; that justice if and when it is delivered is almost always partial, inadequate and delayed: while enough and more has been written on all these matters, we don't need the comforting bind of scholarship to assert what we know as concerned citizens and dismayed feminists.

We know too that this indifference to sexual assault is not merely a matter of State recalcitrance to prosecute a vile crime or an extraordinary effect of the perfectly ordinary workings of the criminal justice system in our contexts. We are all too aware that there exists immense tolerance for sexual violence against women in the social and cultural worlds we inhabit, which is not always evident, belied as it is by the dramatic horror that accompanies all discussions of it. Across our geographies, the social meanings invested in the violated woman's body on the one hand and her so-called 'character' on the other precede and frame understanding and prove decisive in determining what she deserves: justice or the horrific violence she was subject to. In itself, sexual violence is not seen as problematic.

This might appear a harsh characterization, but it is not an inaccurate one. Writing of how rape has come to be viewed as 'normal' in Nagaland in India, Dolly Kikon notes that long decades of harsh militarization in the region (from the 1950s) have fostered an understanding of rape as a fundamental dividing line between the cruelty of the Indian Armed Forces and the resistance of the Naga people. Rapes committed by soldiers with impunity have thus come to stand in for 'rape' as such, and elided other sorts of sexual violence, such as they existed and continue to exist within Naga homes, rival insurgent groups and on the streets. It has been possible to 'overlook' these other forms of sexual violence, suggests Kikon, because they are not viewed as catastrophic for the victim, and instead understood in terms of what 'men' do and what in some instances women 'incite' them to do; that is, women, by their demeanor and behavior 'ask' to be assaulted. Thus, Naga women's bodies materialize value only in the context of an embattled Naga identity; in contexts where questions of identity are not germane, the harm done to these bodies is naturalized as something 'that happens' and is allowed neither the dignity of rational analysis nor passionate anger that can challenge such hurt. Further, observes Kikon, the impunity enjoyed by the armed forces in the region, sanctified by legislation such as the Armed Forces Special Powers Act (AFSPA) has meant that soldiers who rape are not punished, and this has actually produced a wider culture of non-accountability with respect to rape, and 'normalized' it.

The moral character of the victim, her symbolic value for her community or nation being crucial to an understanding of rape— not only in Nagaland, but elsewhere as well—the hurt that victims suffer emerges as less important or noteworthy than the 'dishonour' the act imposes on them, and by implication on their families, kin, communities and the social or national worlds they are part of. Depending on how they view dishonourable acts, or rather on what they consider dishonourable, societies classify acts of sexual violence as either wrong or in the nature of things. This social logic mocks accountability, and does not make for an empathetic view of suffering; even where it mandates punitive social action against those who have committed violent sexual acts, it does so on its own terms, with questions of honour and identity defining the limits of accountability. States, for their part, are not immune to considerations of honour and dishonour, as is evident in how they respond to sexual violence. As we shall see, criminal justice systems typically draw on such notions to take cognizance of a crime or ignore it and to view the victim with sympathy or with disbelief.

State and society are thus interlinked in a warped yet logical unity, broken intermittently by the long arc of justice struggles that succeeds in challenging sexual violence against women; either by insisting on a just rule of law, or by initiating a social revolution, or at least a social churning. In all such instances, as we shall see in the pages to come, it is intelligible speech that challenges the stubborn indifference to sexual hurt which impunity cultivates and feeds on. Yet, the conditions that make speech possible are uneven and varied, and the act of speaking is almost always fraught. In this event those who speak out, whether victim-survivors, witnesses or those who act on their behest, find themselves having to not only make words mean, but to ensure that they stay in place, and do not break under pressure. The outcome of such efforts is contingent on the historical moment and immediate circumstance—and this is what renders speech after sexual violence a wager, whose outcome one cannot anticipate—and yet one has to risk such speech.

Sadly, with respect to sexual assault, even justice struggles keenly invested in the act of witnessing and speech-making are uneasy about what is said. In her essay on the brutal sexual torture of Ila Mitra—communist activist renowned for her role in the great Tebhaga struggle in undivided Bengal—by the police of the newly created state of Pakistan, Kavita Panjabi calls attention to the conditions that made it possible for Ila Mitra to speak of rape. Her testimony was elicited by the Communist Party (the Communist Party of India), which saw in her a witness whose testimony could indict the violent anti-communism of the newly born Nation-State. She spoke up, no doubt on account of loyalty to the party and the cause that she so dearly loved and accepted, yet it could not have been easy to speak of a deeply distressing experience that confounded one's sense of the social and the private and shattered one's sense of worth and dignity.

Ironically, no indictment followed: the Pakistani authorities denied that such torture as described by Ila Mitra had actually taken place, and described her testimony as falsehood. They noted that she had retracted her earlier confession (sic)—extorted from her when she was brutally injured and in custody—and accused her of adopting the 'not uncommon strategy' of alleging police torture to attract sympathy. Ultimately Ila Mitra was set free, that is, her sentence was 'suspended' for six months and she was 'allowed' to go away for medical treatment. But no justice was done to her. She left Pakistan for India and suffered a nervous breakdown thereafter. However, she held on to a line of memory, of struggle and comradeship she shared with the adivasi Santhals who, like her, had endured torture in addition to dying in prison, but would not show her up, just as she endured sexual violence but would not betray them. This enabled her to claim her political space and work in the years to come.

In the years that followed, Ila Mitra was hailed as a leader who braved torture, but the brutal sexual violence inflicted on her remained unspeakable, so much so, that years later, she wondered if she actually testified in the manner she did. To quote Kavita Panjabi, 'There was a deep tension between Ila's subjectivity and the Communist Party's political strategy that was discernible even 50 years after the event. Unease and silences continued to punctuate her political confidence when I met her in 1997. Ila Mitra's narrative, while predominantly one about the sacrifice of the

Santhals, her own political commitment and struggle for survival, was nevertheless also underlined by silences and distortions of memory that signal ambiguities revealing the impact of both State violence and the repressive frameworks of the Communist Party.'

Panjabi's point is that questions of honour and female worth, which arise typically in the context of sexual violence, may be temporarily suspended in the interest of a 'higher' cause, but that does not mean they have been creatively and critically addressed. Felt pain and trauma on account of sexual assault sit uneasily with notions of honour that structure the experience, and an incommensurable distance separates these from political notions of justice. The Communist Party's strategy did not—and could not be expected to—reckon with how each of these affected the other, and in the event it was left to Ila Mitra to square them all, and at substantial cost to her psychic health.

Yet, we ought not to undervalue the party's insistence that Ila Mitra speak of rape. At the very least, it appeared to have wanted to politicize the act, in that the party saw in it an expression of malefic and cruel political intent. In most other contexts, sexual violence visited on women combatants or militant women has remained hidden from history, or at best seen as a shameful sexual crime. When the Truth and Reconciliation Commission (TRC) was set up in South Africa to address crimes committed during the apartheid years, sexual assault did not figure on this list and only after women's groups argued and insisted that sexual crimes needed to be heard did the Commission arrange for supplementary hearings. Ironically, this rendered rape, particularly as experienced by women active in politics, as a 'female' problem and not a political harm that was visited on the politically active woman. Rape was not defined as an instrument of political torture and remained an act of 'sexual' violence. In the Tebhaga instance, rape was political torture, but the Communist Party did not possess a register that would enable it sustain such an understanding and it

passed into public memory as an unspeakable act, horrific because
it was sexual.

With respect to the TRC hearings, South African feminist Louise
du Toit points out that the non-admission of rape as a political
crime meant that a significant historical opportunity was lost, to
name and recognize how male sexual aggression, in itself deeply
political, can also be used to particular political ends, to abuse,
humiliate and refuse political personhood to dissident women:
'During, and as a vital part of, the struggle, women's sexuality
was shamefully activated through rapist torture and consequently
used to strip away their political identity, their dignity and their
sense of self. There were deliberate attempts to tap into women's
sense of responsibility for dependent others and to shame them
sexually and morally. Women's bond with children or foetuses
was exploited to expose their "true", sexualised identity as one of
extreme vulnerability' (Du Toit, 2009: 19). This being the case, the
TRC could have set new standards, argues du Toit, to prosecute
sexually violent crimes, and even if reconciliation was to be urged,
it could have yet explored how and through what delicate means
this was possible (or not). It did not do this, and in any case rape
victims did not come forth visibly for a variety of reasons. Fear,
shame, and anxiety—that their present positions in families and
society could be compromised if they dared tell the truth—sealed
many mouths.

This is what happened in Bangladesh as well. When Pakistani
soliders raped an unprecedented number of women during the
liberation struggle in Bangladesh, they drew on everyday sexual
politics, which conferred sexual authority and aggression on men
to achieve particular political ends. Sadly, in the new nation that
emerged, the political nature of the crime was not acknowledged,
as it ought to have been. The victim-survivors of rape were granted
the status of national heroines, but by the same token, viewed as
sexual martyrs—neither questions of justice nor reparations were

debated or acted upon until feminists insisted on bringing these concerns to the fore. Meanwhile, those who experienced assault kept silent, and were bereft of a language that went beyond notions of honour and sacrifice.

It is evident that sexual violence against women comes up against an impasse that, to be sure, is different in different places and times, but which nevertheless structures speech about the crime. Who or what produces such an impasse is the question. To review the examples furnished above: clearly, as Kikon's observations make clear, one may speak of sexual violence as an act of gross injustice, when the perpetrator is a representative of a reviled 'enemy' State, or of an 'enemy' community; however it is not easy to name the aggressor if he is of the same family or community as the victim. Sexual violence is conceivable as political torture under certain circumstances, yet the effects of such aggression, the sustained trauma and anomie they produce are not 'speakable', or for that matter, 'hearable', beyond the immediate occasion that foregrounds either, as is evident from Kavita Panjabi's prescient remarks on the Ila Mitra story. Sexual violence remains an inexorably sexual crime, even when it is deployed in political circumstances, because it is viewed as something that has to do with 'being (shamefully) female' and therefore can only be an afterthought, something that can be discussed, if need be, but not foregrounded, in debates about systematic racial discrimination and violence, as is evident from the South African TRC hearings on the subject. It may be acknowledged, but not therefore addressed or challenged; rather it is invoked only to be relegated to the margins of collective memory, as happened in Bangladesh, where victims of sexual violence were redefined as martyrs to the national cause.

In each of these instances, reflective and sustained speech about sexual violence is stalled for rather specific reasons, but there appears to be also a general disquiet that inhibits such speech, and this has to do with the nature of the crime itself. It is as if, stained by the crime committed on her person, the victim is never allowed the dignity of a sufferer; meanwhile, and by the same token, the perpetrator remains forever in shadow, visible and challenged in some contexts, allowed his cruel authority in others, yet never fully punished; or even when brought to justice, it is not always for reasons that have to do with the victim's sense of hurt and justice or the venality of the crime itself. Evidentiary arguments sometimes prove more salient than an acknowledgement of the severity of the violation. In any case, the severity of the crime is leavened, so to speak, by inarticulate shame that compromises the victim and coded speech that translates the crime into other than what it is.

I would like to therefore begin my exploration of sexual violence and impunity with some thoughts on how we may understand this impasse, which exists almost as a defining line, constituting the very conditions of speech.

***

Before I proceed, I would like to insert a caveat. Social and State understanding of sexual violence is overdetermined by meanings invested in the purity or otherwise of the female body, to be sure. But that does not mean that sexual violence has only to do with how female body and character are repeatedly defined and redefined. For victims of sexual violence include human persons of every kind, including men, children and transgender and queer people. While one could stretch the argument about gender and honour to 'explain' violence against all categories of human persons, such reasoning does not help us understand violence committed against children. This deserves consideration on its own terms, and so must await a different argument. While I do refer to sexual assault of children in the book, I do so to clarify legal and social arguments about rape. In my understanding, the question of children, sexual assault, hurt and trauma needs its own book.

***

Though sexual violence in our contexts appears as something that 'happens' as it were, yet we realise all too often that one cannot talk about it in public, except in certain specific ways. Let me start with that most public of public spaces, the legal domain, where discussions of sexual violence may legitimately be had, and in a purposive way. But is it indeed easy for us, as feminists, as sensitive and empathetic social actors to flag legal discussions in the spirit we wish to discuss them? As Pratiksha Baxi notes in her rigorous study of rape trials, as they unfolded in particular trial courts in Ahmedabad in India in the 1990s, sexual violence, particularly rape, is considered a dirty secret that may be spoken of only in medico-legal terms. She points out that when she discussed her research with lawyers and others in court premises, many looked askance at her, as if she was contaminating herself: for what sort of woman would actually dare to speak of rape? The victim, and all those, particularly other women, who dare to speak of such matters in public become soiled, as it were, by their association with the act, which is insistently characterized as compromising a woman's character—even if she had resisted it. Subsequently, Baxi realized that one may speak of rape in a given public register, and this is how men—and a few women—speak of it, in their 'professional' capacities, as lawyers and doctors.

Yet, as she makes clear, and as those who have witnessed rape trials know, this professional-public manner of speaking is seldom 'neutral': within courts of law, both prosecution and defence insist that truth is in the details of assault and that the victim speak of these. Such testimony forces her to not only relive the moment of violence, but also endure the close questioning that accompanies it. Such questioning often betrays voyeurism that has not only to do with wanting to 'know' the truth. Often, it is social prurience on display, calculated to produce horror and self-torment on the one hand, and establish the veracity and moral worth (or the lack of it) of the victim, on the other. As this process unfolds, the victim's demeanour and sexual character emerge as pertinent to the prosecution of justice often backed by what is considered 'scientific' evidence. Only in rare cases, and I shall return to this later, (Chapter 9), have judges recognized the trauma that a court trial can induce in the victim, and re-arranged court proceedings so that she is not additionally disempowered or humiliated when she speaks up.

The medical domain is no less problematic in how it conceptualizes sexual assault. Along with legal strictures, medical pronouncements mark the violated body as being either 'truthful' and therefore deserving of justice; or 'dissembling' and therefore not credible enough to insist on justice claims. For it is doctors who decide if assault is actually rape, if the male organ has penetrated far enough or only partially, if her hymen was intact or otherwise, if her genitalia showed wounds... Through posing and addressing these questions doctors do not merely establish evidence of hurt; concomitantly, they establish the conditions for either believing or not believing a victim's testimony. If the hymen is ruptured as of old, or if the vagina betrays elasticity, the woman is marked as 'used to sexual intercourse' and that becomes an important consideration for treating her complaint as valid or not. A sexually active woman's body is thus made witness to its own undoing—for, if she is used to sex, how may one judge whether she was raped or if she consented to sex? The presumption at work in such reasoning has nothing to do with medical science: a sexually active woman, especially if she is not a wife, is morally irresolute and therefore not to be believed if she claims she has been assaulted.

Such presumption has a long social history and not only in common sense. As Baxi points out, it has been sanctified as scientific truth, through examples cited in medical textbooks that often repeat what were said in earlier textbooks, while adding select bits from contemporary debates. Thus ideas honed in particular historical contexts, and dependent on the discursive concerns of the medical discipline such as it was at those moments, have been passed on, and acquired value through repeated citations.

As for the larger and more amorphous public domain, whether media or public discussion forums: these spaces have recourse to a register that again and again objectifies the female body and reifies the violence it has suffered. Objectification in this instance is different from what we find in legal and medical discourses. Law and medical science invoke the expertise associated with their domains to translate their prejudicial understanding of femaleness and female sexuality into 'neutral' statements; on the truth or otherwise of a traumatized witness's claims. In the larger public domain, sexual prejudice works differently. It is not folded back into truth claims, based on expert knowledge. Rather, it serves to objectify and insistently sexualize the traumatized female body: as one that is either always already vulnerable to sexual assault, or inherently deserving of it.

We are familiar with those who think the latter: with the irresponsible and tasteless remarks habitually made by those who insist that 'women asked for it' or that a woman cannot be raped 'without her consent'. Such responses are legion, and tiresome, and found across cultures—and have been rightfully condemned by feminists. The others, those who view women's bodies as essentially vulnerable and deserving of male protection: their opinions and stance pose a different sort of problem for feminists, for those outraged by rape and violence are also trapped by what bothers them. Even as they register protest they find it hard to get beyond the lurid details of violence, beyond the invocation of horror. Part of the problem, of course, is the manner in which sexual violence is positioned in popular consciousness: as spectacle, which invites voyeurism, and encourages it. This has become all the more so in the age of social media—when repeated references to acts of sexual violence, each of which feeds on what has gone before, often in vivid and vicarious detail, make it impossible to break out of the stranglehold of the spectacle.

I cannot but recall here the tendentious and worrisome repetition—and graphic portrayal, through a YouTube video—of a tale of violation that unfolded in Tamil social media, during the last days of the civil war in Sri Lanka (2009). This had to do with the alleged rape and murder by Sri Lankan state soldiers of Isaipriya, a young Tamil journalist. Anger and denunciation notwithstanding, the persistence with which this news was traded and spoken of— chiefly amongst men, with men addressing each other—betrayed ghoulish relish. It was as if her extreme suffering and death rendered their nationalist cause all the more credible.

This sense of 'relish' is not exceptional—only in more mundane instances, bereft of the charge of political ideology, it dons other guises. For one, it exists as the obverse of moral horror, yet inseparable from it. What cannot be countenanced, and is forbidden, is yet guiltily made present through repeated and indignant citation. In the event, the traumatized female body dematerializes and circulates—as rumour, in print, and in virtual space—as if it were a fetish, inspiring pity no doubt, but by that token also becomes an object, to be protected, guarded and concealed.

There is another sort of relish that we find in our cultures, which confounds rape with illicit desire. Here too, the act is marked as transgressive and problematic, but yet it is viewed as an 'acceptable' marker of the sexual. That this is not too fantastic an argument is evident from what a researcher studying young women's attitudes to love and marriage in Chennai city (in the mid-2000s) had to say. She noted that she was shocked to note how 'rape' was understood as a form of sexual attention, and how girls who did not believe themselves to be attractive, noted casually and without self-consciousness that they did not expect to be raped. It was as if the ideal woman was one who was 'rapeable'; as if she was the one that men desired and wished to protect. Another researcher noted how young men just as casually remark that so-and-so cannot expect to cry rape and be believed, since she is not attractive enough to warrant being raped.

***

In this context, it is important to attend to how, in our various contexts, we process the 'sexual' and the 'violent' that together constitute the act: as we have seen, some of us cannot get beyond the 'sexual' part; and there are others who balk at the violence and find it difficult to transcend the terms of what they combat. Most of us, including those who consider themselves feminists, do not often situate sexual violence in the context of sexual and social cultures and arrangements, which define, regulate and 'manage' female sexuality. Nor do we always ask ourselves if sexual violence is indeed separable from other forms and experiences of violence that define the everyday in our cultures. These questions will remain with us through this narrative, but for now, I would like to remark rather briefly on the relationship between sexual violence and everyday acts, whether of sex or of violence. For, it seems to me, that the impasse that attends speech about sexual violence has to do with how we understand this relationship.

In the immediate aftermath of the horrific gang rape of a young woman in Delhi, India in 2012, some amongst the hundreds of protesters who gathered on the streets seeking justice demanded the rapists be hanged to death. Such a demand is neither novel nor specific to this instance, but that it should emerge in and through protests that were fuelled by widespread and clearly spontaneous expressions of empathy and solidarity for and with the victim, makes me want to pause. In the face of extreme violence, we either confuse justice with retribution, or we are so bewildered by the outrage that our understanding is both guided and limited by that experience of angry shock.

Significantly, in the instance of the Delhi rape, dalit feminists from across the country responded with critical anger and acumen to precisely this sense of outrage. They noted, not without a sense of anguish, that sexual violence against dalits does not ever incite such a response, either on the streets or in the media. In effect, they drew attention to the habitual, routine mockery of dalit women's bodies, and their equally routine violation. At stake here were everyday acts, born out of everyday circumstances, all of which ought to be considered outrageous, but are not, and are instead 'normalized'. I will return to this question in the pages to come. For now, I would like to utilize the critique advanced by dalit feminists to pose a somewhat different question: what meanings would an analysis of the 'outrageous' everyday yield?

Let us look at another instance of sexual violence—this took place in Mumbai in 2013—and the questions that the prosecution of the case raised for young feminist lawyers. Reporting on the case of a young woman journalist who was subjected to brutal gang-rape in Mumbai city, a team of young lawyers from the feminist law group Majlis noted that they had to reckon with her trauma at testifying as well as the sorrow-ridden female kin of the perpetrators, who were poor, vulnerable, and from a minority community. The presence in court, of these women, cast the perpetrators in a different light— their brutality notwithstanding, they emerged as social beings, anchored in familial and community spaces, which are, themselves, shaped by the casual violence, deprivation and discrimination that underwrite their everyday.

It seems to me that grasping this fact, of sexual violence as an act that unfolds within and along a continuum of the 'outrageous' everyday, pushes us to speak of it in a manner that goes beyond a register haunted by trauma and shame and captive to the spectacle of violence. In effect, we are pushed to ask questions, to do with the etiology of violence, the making of social evil, the relationship between contexts that shape criminal acts, and the intentionality of the act itself... in short we are pushed to account for what appears exceptional in terms of the everyday and in ways that are consequential for the prosecution of justice. As feminists, we may wish to pay attention to our speech-making such that we enable into existence public debates that work against the grain of sentimental or for that matter misogynistic objectification of the traumatized female body.

***

If sexual crimes are anchored in the violence and injustice that mark everyday life, justice as much as culpability needs to be reimagined. For now it ceases to be a measure that is secured in and through judicial procedure alone, and anticipates transformation of everyday selves and contexts. We are required therefore to evolve a conception of justice that has not only to do with reparations and punitive action, but which addresses, imaginatively, the victim-survivor's ineffable sense of hurt and loss, and impaired dignity, which do not go away easily or even over a long period of time.

Now, none of this is strictly new, and in fact might appear the stuff of feminist common sense. After all, feminists across the world have fought long and hard, and with much resilience, for well over a century to mark sexual assault as a crime against bodily integrity and personhood. With respect to law and more generally medico-legal procedures and protocols that are part of the criminal justice system, they have insisted on better standards of proof, witness protection, an understanding of sexual assault as a denial of women's right to life and dignity... Both legal and medical practices in this context have been overhauled and newer approaches defined. Locally and globally, manuals have been produced, policies drafted and reforms in law and practice brought about. Today international justice protocols recognize sexual violence in conflict situations as a crime against humanity.

A lot of this has happened because we have chosen to recognize what women experience and endure, and paid heed to their suffering. In other words, as feminists we have identified and acted on other ways of speaking about sexual assault. Further, we have also insisted that while we are for justice, we are not for retribution and set ourselves against seeking capital punishment for rapists. And lastly, we have not balked at pointing to routine instances of sexual abuse, shaming and humiliation that women endure. What are we, then, demanding of ourselves?

In this context, I wish to recall what a Cambodian survivor of sexual assault during the Khmer Rouge years (1974–77) had to say about her understanding of violence and justice.

Like countless others in her country she was subjected to gross acts of violence, including rape, by soldiers of the Khmer Rouge. When the stage was set for a truth and reconciliation process in Cambodia in the early 2000s, she agreed to be part of it, but in a tangential way: she assented to the making of a documentary film on her life and her journey towards justice and peace. In the event, the film came to represent in condensed fashion an individual's reconciliation with her past and her perpetrators.

At the beginning of the film—*The Rice Fields of Kampuchea*—Tang Kim (as she is called in her film) expresses anger, and declares that she wants her perpetrators to suffer as much as she did. As the film progresses, she steps back from her initial response and notes that she might forgive those who harmed her, provided they acknowledge what they had done, and confess to their crimes publicly. Towards the end of the film, we find her entering a Buddhist monastery—away from the din of a world that might or might not comprehend her search for peace. The monastery becomes her shelter, from whose precincts she surveys the world. The documentary features her bearing witness, and shows her angry, reflective, yielding and demanding in turn. She does not provide a blueprint for reconciliation, but points to both its difficulty and necessity. Like other Cambodians—notably the journalist who made *The Enemy of the People*, yet another documentary that engages with forgiveness, even as it demands accountability—Tang Kim returns to the question of violence, and not only because her memory is captive to it, but because she wants to go beyond it. She wants remorse from those who had hurt her and others like her, an acknowledgement of wrongdoing. As she remarks in the film 'If they admit their actions, it would be up to me to forgive them or not' (Anderson, 2009: 785).

Tang Kim sought peace and justice several decades after she had been hurt and her life destroyed: while her memory of that time was sharp, the passage of years had rendered the details of violence distant. Yet, the import of that violence, what it sought to achieve—an annihilation of an entire way of life in anticipation of an unimaginably rigid and cruel utopia—was not erased in her mind, and she wanted those who embarked on it to own up to what they did. This was necessary not only for those who stood to judge them, but also for those whose lives had been destroyed by the violence. Accountability was an essential condition for reconciliation and peace—and for the remaking of a destroyed ethical universe. Violence, Tang Kim and others like her make clear, has to explain itself, and perpetrators must be made to express remorse. Significantly, she does not close the door on forgiveness; to her it is neither possible, nor is it impossible. It remains a conundrum, but not one that cannot be contemplated; neither can it be dismissed away.

The story of Tang Kim is instructive: it sets up a tense dialogue between the politics of recognition and the will to compassion. In the event, we find ourselves in a threshold space, where we can reflect on the practice of justice and rights, and ask some rather fundamental questions. Some of these have to do with the victim-survivor: do we adequately 'recognize' suffering? What makes for healing speech after sexual violence? Who must speak and how and to whom? Other questions have to do with justice and survival in the wake of trauma: how do we define accountability, beyond what is sanctioned by the letter of the law? What do we want for the perpetrator, if at all, beyond justice? Most important, how do we engage with issues of remorse and forgiveness, reconciliation and co-existence, in contexts where sexual violence has been directed at entire communities of women?

Keeping these questions in focus, this book examines the many ways in which as feminists, democrats, socialists and citizens in search of justice, victim-survivors and their supporters have 'spoken' in the wake of sexual violence. It seems to me, to restate an argument I have outlined in the prologue, impunity needs necessarily to be seen in its thwarted moments, rather than in the habitual arrogant mode that it expresses itself. I propose to identify such moments in the modern history of India and wherever it appears relevant in the history of modern South Asia. In the chapter that follows I argue my case for taking a historical lens to the subject at hand.

REFERENCES

Agnes, Flavia, Audrey D'Mello and Persis Sidhva. 2014. 'The Making of a High Profile Rape Trial', *Economic and Political Weekly,* July 19, XLIX (29): 37–41.

Anderson, Katrina. 2004. 'Turning Reconciliation on Its Head: Responding to Sexual Violence Under the Khmer Rouge', *Seattle Journal for Social Justice,* 3 (2): 785–832.

Baxi, Pratiksha. 2014. *Public Secrets of the Law: Rape Trials in India,* New Delhi: Oxford University Press.

Channel 4. 2013. Video footage, reporting and discussion on the rape and murder of Isaipriya. https://www.youtube.com/watch?v= kjgX9FxR20gl (accessed 27 October 2015).

Du Toit, Louise. 2009. *A Philosophical Investigation of Rape—The Making and Unmaking of the Feminine Self,* London: Routledge.

Kikon, Dolly. 2016. 'Memories of Rape: The Banality of Violence and Impunity in Naga Society' in U. Chakravarti (ed.), *Fault lines of History: The India Papers Volume 1 (Zubaan Series on Sexual Violence and Impunity in South Asia)*, New Delhi: Zubaan.

Kowtal, Asha and Jenny Rowena. 2013. 'State expects dead Dalit girl to prove she was violated and killed?' *Savari*, August. http://www.dalitweb.org/?p=2078 (accessed 27 October 2015).

Mohsin, Amena. 2016. 'History of Sexual Violence, Impunity and Conflict: The Bangladesh Context' in H. Hossain and A. Mohsin, (eds.), *Of the Nation Born: The Bangladesh Papers (Zubaan Series on Sexual Violence and Impunity in South Asia)*, New Delhi: Zubaan.

Panjabi, Kavita. 2016. 'Between "Honour" and Justice: Rendering the Law Ineffective' in U. Chakravarti (ed.), *Fault lines of History: The India Papers Volume 1 (Zubaan Series on Sexual Violence and Impunity in South Asia)*, New Delhi: Zubaan.

2

Sexual Violence, Sexual Politics and the Question of History

The female body to which sexual harm has been done is viewed not as unjustly destroyed or prevailed upon, but rather as a problem. The hurt and violence inflicted appear less important than the all-consuming question: why was she subject to such an act? Other questions follow: did anything in her presence—her clothes, the way she dressed—warrant such a response? Was she well-behaved and discreet or did she seek to attract men, provoke their attention through word and deed? What sort of a woman had she been, until that moment? These 'generalized' queries into her being and behaviour lead on to further and more technical questions (as I have pointed out earlier): are there injuries on the woman's body that indicate she had resisted and therefore suffered harm? Is her hymen intact or flexible? Is it freshly torn? Is there evidence of the man's penis 'fully' entering her or only partially? Answers to this set of questions are got from considering forensic evidence and through the notorious 'two-finger' test.

It is as if the crime can only be admitted to have taken place, if and when all these questions are addressed to the satisfaction of interlocutors involved in the criminal justice proceedings, the police, forensic experts, advocates and the judge. Prosecution and justice are in fact contingent on getting the 'right' set of answers—

that is, on establishing that the woman was in fact an innocent victim and not a manipulative promiscuous woman. In earlier judicial reasoning in India—which perhaps is still extant in some of the trial courts—the victim of sexual assault was termed an 'accomplice' to the crime, and her testimony was therefore suspect in the eyes of the court, unless it was corroborated. That is, a woman speaking of the violation she suffered was not an adequate or reliable witness—the very fact of her 'involvement' in the crime compromised her veracity. Even before her sexual and moral character came to be examined, she was shadowed by untruth. While such reasoning has become rare, the principles that underlay it have not been abandoned.

Such confounding of the victim's moral character with the harm done to her person serves impunity well; even the barest consideration that the woman is somehow to blame for the assault she has been subjected to, is enough to exonerate, affirm and sanction violence against her. States in fact do all of this: as far as rape is concerned, across the world, conviction rates are low. More often than not, victims are blamed for what happens to them. Finally, such reprobate reasoning comes in handy, when the State commissions sexual crimes, or looks the other way when its men commit them (subsequent chapters in this book engage with all these aspects of State practice, across South Asia.)

How may we understand this play of violence, morality, justice and impunity? Feminists across the world have debated this matter for decades: in the public sphere, in legal contexts, and in the context of campaigns against sexual violence. It is evident from the vast array of available information and arguments that the condoning of sexual violence has to do with the specific ways in which women's bodies are marked and defined in a given context and culture. Such marking differentiates women into good and bad, and maps this distinction on to other differences, to do with status groups, clans, castes, classes and races. I provide two examples of how such marking works.

***

My first example is from Pakistan.

Across the world and for centuries, rape was viewed as a crime against property. Since women were considered no better than chattels, belonging to fathers, brothers and husbands, an act that threatened or lowered the value of a woman's body signified loss of value to the men that headed or felt themselves responsible for the family in question. In the face of such perceived and real harm to valuable 'goods', due compensation was expected to be paid. The value of such compensation was measured by the alleged moral character of the woman in question; that is, her chastity defined her worth. Such practices were extant in many parts of the world until recently.

However, they have not entirely disappeared and continue to be in place in cultural contexts where women are viewed as objects of transaction between clans and communities, and crimes against them are settled through carefully calibrated monetary or land payments. In Pakistani feminist Rubina Saigol's words, in such contexts, women exist as 'mobile symbols and signs of honour… Their own bodies are thus commodified as they can be given in exchange, delivered as peace offering, sold, bought or otherwise transferred. Their value is calculated in both symbolic and material terms in an economy which is deeply steeped in economic and political relations of power, hierarchy and competition.'

Writing of Mukhtar Mai who was subjected to punitive rape, as compensation for allegedly 'illicit' sexual relationships a young man from her clan had with a young woman from another clan, Saigol notes: 'If a tribe feels that it has been dishonoured, the restoration of its honour is possible when an equivalent act is performed upon the accused. However, in this notion of crime and punishment the culpability is transferable to a female relative of the accused person. The punishment can be carried out on a woman merely on the basis of her relationship with the offender. The custom of transferable culpability is almost never applied on the male relatives of the accused, especially in cases involving illicit sexual relations.'

It is perhaps this linking of honour to compensation (and justice) that haunts our criminal justice systems, and underlies the anxiety they evince with respect to the woman's bodily status. However this may be, we may want to understand this historical legacy in terms of how it has compromised women's civic status. Rubina Saigol's account of the 'justice' meted out to Mukthar Mai indicates that women are not merely possessions; equally they are non-persons in a civic sense. Violence rendered unto their bodies is mere public affirmation of this fact, and encodes value in a perverse sort of way—that women can be damaged renders them valuable to kin and community and by that same token devalues or renders non-existent their civic value, their existence as persons who are entitled to rights and dignity. The law can have no bearing on their lives, and the State often ends up backing custom and practice—not only because it is politic to do so, but also because it actually imagines that secular law need not apply or may be easily overlooked in domestic and intimate spheres.

In fact, as has been argued by feminists from the Maghreb and West Asia, in certain historical and geographical contexts, the State enters into a 'kinship' contract with its male citizens. To secure the consent of various social groups in the national project, post-colonial Nation-States in North Africa and West Asia 'agreed' to the continued existence of patriarchal kin arrangements, which enabled male heads of clans and families to manage and regulate matters to do with property, conjugality and progeny. Among other things, this meant that families and the extended kin network regulated female choices and interests—to be sure in the name of care and protection, but the exercise of authority was often coercive.

Enmeshed in these benevolently despotic relationships women found themselves placed beyond the pale of civic life and citizenship. Meanwhile, acts of discrimination or violence against their persons could be ignored with impunity by the State.

***

My second example is from Indian history.

Historically, in all societies, there existed groups of persons who were denied civic status—those held to be low-born, those ranked low in the social order, those who are considered racial others, economic dependents, slaves... Yet, women are non-persons in a rather specific sense. Indian feminist historian Uma Chakravarti notes how, under what she defines as 'Brahminical Patriarchy' and which marked social arrangements in various parts of India in the earliest periods of its history, female nature—*strisvabava*—was deemed inherently unstable and dissolute. She observes that, in this worldview, women acquire the right to be counted as moral persons in spite of their nature only through their pursuit of what was considered appropriate behavior and action, referred to as *stridharma*. This required them to be chaste, monogamous and submissive to their husbands and kinsfolk. *Stridharma* however was not for everyone, but only the 'pure' and 'high'-born—which, in the Indian instance, comprised women from priestly and royal groups—could hope to avail of this dharmic path; others, either because they belonged to social groups that were considered low-born or were marked as public women, could not hope to redeem their fallen nature. In this scheme of things, chastity was a class—and caste—virtue: only a woman conscious enough to know its value would and could guard her person from possible violation; as for the rest, they actually stood to be violated, since their very being asked for it! Perversely enough, the chaste were those who could potentially be raped, since they stood to 'lose' worth; whereas those who were constitutively 'non-chaste' cannot be said to suffer rape. In either instance though, women were expected to police themselves, even as they submitted to the dictates of the social order.

Stridharma is no mere normative ideal, anchored in the distant past—as is evident from the anxiety that flourishes in the modern period with respect to women's sexual 'nature' and sexuality, especially in deciding whether their violated bodies invited sexual assault or if they were indeed imposed upon. The 'purity' of the victim that is so avidly sought conceals a fear of the taint of sex; for such taint is a mark of unredeemed female vice or of her always already low status. A chaste woman thus cannot be raped, something that is repeated ad nauseum, on the argument that a woman cannot be raped against her will. If she is raped, that means she had done or said something unbecoming of her status. Or it could be that she is lying, because she wishes not to be 'discovered' in relationship with an unworthy man, possibly of low social status. As for the rape of others, those who are 'unchaste', that is not to be wondered at. For one, they cannot help it, being 'low-born' or used to a promiscuous existence; secondly, they cannot expect their social fate to be otherwise. Only by insistently differentiating victims of sexual violence who can prove their chastity, from those who are tainted on account of their questionable birth and sexual habits, does society set at rest its anxiety over the taint of sex.

As for the State, all too often it accepts or finds it convenient to fall in with this line of reasoning: it may be that feminists in India fought hard to insist on equality and non-discrimination in the eyes of the law, and they were supported by liberal-minded men in this regard, but this did not automatically render them citizens, and in the eyes of the State they remain marked by their sexual difference. As to how and why this is so, there are a number of reasons, some of which shall be discussed in the pages to come.

***

Property, chattel slaves, transacted objects, unstable beings 'by nature'—while women are objectified in these and other related ways, they do not passively suffer whatever is imposed on them. They negotiate their place and identities, actively perform or resist roles that are expected of them and actualize or destabilize norms of ideal femininity. They do so as dependents, supplicants, members of particular families and clans and castes, as labourers, cultural workers... In all of this, they stay conscious of the opprobrium that attaches to unchaste women and to women of low birth or status. Ideal femininity is produced out of this consciousness that separates women into respectable and dissolute, domestic and mobile, chaste and promiscuous, wives and concubines, mothers and public women. Female complicity with hierarchical and unjust social arrangements, such as it exists, complicates the question of impunity—especially when States accept and valorize the 'ideal feminine', often citing the examples of those who abide by norms.

***

If sexual violence has to do with how societies define and map 'sexual' and social differences on to each other, how may we understand the mapping? Is the consequent violence a means to assert social dominance and authority, through acts of sexual dominance? Or is it that sexual dominance is asserted in and through a coercive assertion of social differences? That social and sexual dominance express each other, in fact constitute each other, is evident from the experiences of queer people.

The fear, hatred and violence that are directed at recalcitrant queer bodies in the family have been spoken of in many narratives in the Indian context. Alarmed and disturbed by boys dressing up as girls, and girls wanting to be like boys, and unwilling to countenance queer sexual expressions, families seek to school these 'erring' bodies into normative behavior. Disciplinary violence, mental abuse, and confinement are all deployed to this purpose. Queer persons thus experience a denial of personhood in the very core of their bodily being and within the so-called safe space of home. In A. Revathi's recounting of her brothers' anger at her feminine attire, long hair and general demeanour (in her autobiographical *The Truth About Me: A Hijra's Life*), we see how rage focuses on her body, on what is understood to be an embodiment of corporeal betrayal.

When she chooses to live with a man, her brothers are horrified and disgusted. They wonder how she and her husband can possibly have sex and one of them responds thus: 'You don't know how they do it? All these No. 9s, like the one here, take a man's cock in their mouths and suck at it! Seems the ooze is a balm for their parched and hairy throats. These No. 9s have hair in their throats and that's what they do, and that's what he probably does too!'(A Revathi, 2010: 184)

They are also shocked that their brother-turned-sister has dared renounced manhood: 'You're a man, after all. We did not mind you traipsing around in a sari. But how dare you want a husband? If we hear that he's come here again, be sure that we tear his guts out and make a garland out of them!' (*ibid*) This anger at her prospective lover is haunted by what it reviles, evident in their eagerness to differentiate their own lives from lives such as these: 'We are men and we have married women and started families. How can you claim to be a woman, you who have gone and chopped your cock and worn a sari? Do you want to dishonour our name, the respect we enjoy?' (*op. cit*, 185)

Such horrified anger is even more intensely present when girls seek masculine identities. A report from Bengaluru, which reviews queer lives and experiences, notes that women who have chosen to be men are subjected to shocking violence in public, should it be known that they had transitioned from one gender to the other. In one instance, a male stranger who picked up a fight with two such men, when told that the two were not 'real men' immediately tore the shirt off one of them. The report notes: 'The immediate response from the male stranger was to tear off the shirt of one of the FTMs (female-to-male persons). For the stranger, tearing off the shirt meant exposing the female body to the public. When the FTM went to the police station to complain, the police and the stranger verbally abused the FTM. They asked him if he had a vagina? Did he have a hole in his vagina? What was the length of the hole in his vagina?' (Mohan, 2013: 44). This expression of abusive horror, betraying, as it does, puerile voyeurism and misogyny, combines two kinds of outrage: that a woman would dare to pass off as a man, and at the seemingly incomplete male body. It is as if masculinity is not to be coveted, imitated or assumed as a possibility for those who are not always already 'complete' men.

The anger and hatred expressed in these exchanges suggests that what is at stake for those who are uneasy with queerness is the social order itself: if men do not wish to reproduce, and worse, if they renounce manhood, a carefully constructed masculinity, the sense of being male as well as the social and political prerogative that comes with that identity, threatens to unravel. The vicious indignation with which Revathi's brothers refer to her 'female-ness' connotes anxiety and fear at being confronted with the possible illegality of one's 'given' authority. Men loving men is also not to be countenanced, for the same reason—for it is held that to be a man is to be able to impregnate a woman, and only those who cannot achieve this, seek out other men.

If women desire to be men, that clearly is an affront, and must be punished. Their bodies cannot possibly be transformed, for is not femininity irredeemable, as the police who abuse the woman who has chosen to be a man make clear? If women insist on loving women and deserting home and hearth, the social order stands in danger of being dissolved, and therefore they must be subject to compulsory heterosexuality. The unravelling of femininity is not the issue at stake as much as the defiance of the feminine; that women actually dare to choose beyond what has been mandated for them.

Sexual authority exercised in impunity is anchored, in an epistemological as well as social sense, in the demarcation of masculine and feminine roles, spheres and labour, and the value accorded these. This demarcation, written into codes of being, behaviour and representation, is an expression of sexual authority that is haunted by its own illegitimacy, but which cannot countenance such haunting. Such authority might resort to ontological reasoning, but the latter cannot be viewed as the cause of the ensuing violence.

The legitimate question to ask in this context is: how and through what means does sexual authority feel impelled to dominate, not merely in a class or race or caste sense, but in an ontological sense as well?

***

To address and respond to this question, the historical approach to understanding sexual violence and impunity is the most useful and this is what this book will do in the pages to come. In effect, it proposes to understand how, and through what means, women are constituted as 'tainted' sexual beings in particular cultures and the role assigned to sexual violence in this process of sexualization; and how women negotiate and articulate, in the public realm, such processes of violent self-making.

As an illustrative example of the historical approach, I would like to discuss American historian Hannah Rosen's *Terror in the Heart of Freedom: Citizenship, sexual violence, and the meaning of race in the Post-emancipation South*. This is a fine and nuanced historical account of the repeated violence carried out by white supremacists in Memphis in the American South in the 1860s, especially of the sexual assault of African-American women. Following the end of the American civil war and the defeat of the Confederate forces, slavery stood abolished in the South, and African-American people in the city of Memphis, and elsewhere, used the historical moment to proclaim their right to citizenship and rights. As a sort of backlash, their homes were destroyed, several killed, and some women raped. Hannah Rosen reads these events through a fine-grained feminist and anti-racist lens.

Rosen points out that the Memphis riots were essentially gendered spectacles of violence, and understood and spoken of as such by conservative white media. During the Civil War and after, African-American men enlisted in the Union Army. This gave them a measure of dignity and, being armed, they felt empowered to defend themselves against acts of humiliation and violence. Additionally African-American Union soldiers were also deployed to ensure that the Proclamation of the Emancipation of 'Negroes' from slavery was honoured—that is, they were to protect and support African-Americans who left plantations and moved to the city of Memphis to look for work and a free and equal life. In some instances they were asked to—and did—arrest white men, who refused to accept emancipation and insisted on racially violent behaviour, or who attempted to keep African-Americans enslaved, or who sought to humiliate them.

Rosen suggests that the presence of African-American men in public spaces, marching, drinking, arguing, making a living was more than what white men in Memphis could stomach: 'The visible and audible presence of black soldiers in public endowed with the trappings of manhood—guns, alcohol, leisure time, and power over others—challenged whites' sense of privilege as the only urban residents who were "citizens" and white men's sense of privilege as the only ones who were "men"' (Rosen, 2009: 49). The local press, especially papers which resented the presence of the Union army and the end of slavery, lost no time portraying 'freedmen' as violent, given to drinking and incapable of moral restraint. Citizenship, according to those who argued against African-Americans being granted citizenship rights, rested on such restraint, on men's ability to control their passions, and this was not possible for African-American men.

Truth was that this was not really about citizenship, as political ideal or in its moral, abstract sense. Southern racism and white prerogative were so thoroughly invested in a politics of white masculinity and political entitlement that anti-racist policies as well as material—black—bodies that challenged white notions of black lowness profoundly destabilized this politics, and by implication disturbed white conservative men, in their bodily being. Therefore, when the opportunity presented itself, this gendered reasoning resulted in white police and local white men, essentially skilled workers, owners of small businesses, many of whom were of Irish origin, and considered low and despicable just generations ago, shooting and killing several African-American soldiers. This reasoning proved even more devastating and consequential when directed against African-American women. Five women, of whom four were associated with African-American military men, were each brutally raped, in some cases by more than one man. Their association with what white perpetrators considered telling symbols of irresponsible and hateful 'black manhood' rendered them deserving targets of white vigilante violence.

But this was not all. Freed African-American women had incited as much if not more resentment than African-American men; their industry, fearlessness, the alacrity with which they laid claim to equal rights and autonomy of their persons proved galling to white conservative opinion. The white conservative press refused to grant their presence validity or dignity, refused to call them women and instead referred to them as 'negresses' who did not deserve the status conferred by womanhood. Their presence was considered unruly, they were termed lewd, and any attempt on their part to report racial misdoings considered insolent.

The five rapes that happened and were reported were not random acts for another reason as well. As Rosen argues, they began as 'casual, even seemingly perfunctory requests for sex, as if the women they [the rapists] confronted were likely to have been

amenable or even indifferent to anonymous sex with white men'
(*op.cit.*: 70). That is, the men who broke into the women's homes
behaved as if they expected the African American women they
encountered to submit choicelessly, and this in spite of the women
insisting they were not the sort of women who would agree to such
soliciting. In other words, the rapists behaved as they did in the
days of slavery—they asserted their right to these women's bodies,
which, in their opinion were theirs to own, exploit and use. African
American women in their understanding could not claim, or ought
not to claim, bodily autonomy or right.

Importantly, each of the raped women reported what had
happened to her, and was not shy of testifying about the event in
public hearings. When questioned if they had not somehow invited
rape, and if they had resisted what was done to them, the women
responded with dignity: they said they were forced to submit and
that the question of consent did not even arise and was irrelevant.
To quote Rosen:

> They made clear that, as much as they had suffered from the
> rapes they experienced, they did not share the assumption
> that rape would damage them in ways worth risking death to
> prevent. Nor did they accept the implications of the rioters, that
> their submission implied that they were marginal and powerless
> women with no virtue and thus no capacity or reason to resist
> illicit sex.... the women ... had recently lived under a system
> of slavery in which many women faced a grim choice between
> submitting to coerced sexual intercourse with white men or
> risking other physical harm to themselves and their loved ones.
> By inserting black women's experiences of and perspectives
> on sexual violence into public discourse, they challenged the
> prevailing discourse of rape and also of honorable womanhood.
> To them, in this context, honor depended more on surviving
> a horrific experience of violence and violation and protesting

its injustice than on privileging and protecting a patriarchal
notion of women's sexual 'virtue.' (*op.cit*: 79)

This is absorbing history for a number of reasons: under slavery
African American women were deemed un-rapeable. That is, they
had no worth or honour that could be robbed from them and white
manhood relished its prowess to own and dispose their bodies at
will. Such reduction of African American female personhood was
elaborated through other means: African Americans could not
legally marry, and therefore unions between men and women were
constitutively promiscuous and 'proof' of their non-person status.
Nor could mothers expect to raise children, and were thus denied
the honour bestowed on motherhood.

Following Emancipation, African African women lost no time
in rejecting what had been imposed on them, and laid claims to a
radical new subjectivity. In this instance, the presence of the Union
Army in Memphis, the fact that radical American legislators were
willing to push the limits of Emancipation and the economic and
political exigencies that made the north want to exert authority
over the south of the United States played a role in creating the
conditions for them to do so. In the event, the women spoke of
what is seldom spoken: they spoke as female persons who had
experienced bodily violation, time and again, and who were now in
a historical moment that enabled them to name that violation, not
as a 'dishonouring' but a refusal of personhood. Such dishonouring
as existed under slavery, Cornel West the African American
philosopher notes, was nothing short of an 'ontological wounding'.
Therefore, to reclaim bodily being, it was important for the women
in Memphis that they wrest it from non-existence and negativity,
and locate it within normative and ethical contexts on the one hand,
and a new sensibility to do with the body's very existence on the
other. Freed persons experienced not only the virtues of political

freedom and equality but equally the phenomenological autonomy
that comes with the actual and physical freeing of the body from its
former enslaved existence. Women, as much as men, relished this
autonomy and this was what made them speak of sexual assault as
they did, calling attention to its constitutive role in the making and
sustaining of plantation slavery.

Though radical republicanism was very soon tamed in the
American South, history did turn for a brief moment in Memphis
in the 1860s. Such turns help us bracket impunity and view it
as something that is not given, but whose life and authority are
intermittently, if not constantly, interrupted—in ways that force
the State to remake the terms of its existence. In these moments of
interruption and provisional remaking of State authority, sexual
violence stands illumined in its sheer materiality: we are able to
mark its role in the making and unmaking of social relationships
and individual personhood. Such moments also call attention
to how power and authority in a civic context are constitutively
gendered. Thus, it is not that when wielded against women, class or
racial domination takes the form of sexual violence, rather that it
is sexual violence that shapes and lends race and class domination
its fearful and destructive aspect. So much so that when its victim-
survivors discover a context and language to articulate the damage
wrought by sexual violence, class and race power stand indicted in
no uncertain terms.

***

Hannah Rosen's text is apposite to my purpose for a number
of reasons. As I have noted in the prologue, I am interested in
delineating the line of hope that emerges time and again in history
and which enables women to resist sexual violence and speak the
unspeakable, since it is this which shows up impunity for what it is,
as unaccountable authority that feeds on its own ethical and political
pretensions. The history Rosen recounts demonstrates what makes

hope speak to power—both the precise historical circumstances that make this possible, as well as the practice of radical republican politics. This is a theme that this book hopes to pursue.

Secondly, as I have attempted to demonstrate, speech about sexual violence is essentially fraught, and often limited by what it seeks to interrogate and understand, and in this context, it is important to consider such violence, not merely as exceptional, but as something that inheres in the everyday and has to do with the sexual cultures we inhabit and realize on a routine basis. The African American experience recounted in Rosen's book is marked by sexual violence, which has as much to do with slavery and racism as it has to do with sexual domination. This is not an exceptional state of affairs, and is the very stuff of life as it unfolds in a slave-holding society. In the South Asian context, particularly in India, caste as a system of both production and social relationships relies on sexual humiliation and violence to shore up the authority of those who are dominant in this system. The historical forms of American racism are therefore interesting in this regard—for our own analysis of the many lives of caste.

Thirdly, defiant speech, I have pointed out, may not always make for a sustained politics that challenges sexual violence in every instance—as was evident in the Ila Mitra story. In Memphis, African American women spoke with dignity and hope, and their suffering stood out for what it was. However, as subsequent events made clear, such a moment could not be sustained. The possibilities as well as limits to the historical moment that makes recognition of suffering possible stand illumined in this historical account. Impunity appears tractable, but yet it does not go away, and this is a sobering lesson for those of us invested in struggles against it. More important it insists we wager such struggles, even as we remain critical and wary of what they might actually achieve, by way of justice.

REFERENCES

Chakravarti, Uma. 1993. 'Conceptualising Brahmanical Patriarchy in Early India: Gender, Caste, Class and State', *Economic and Political Weekly*, 28 (14): 579–585

Mohan, Sunil. 2013. *Towards Gender Inclusivity: A Study on Contemporary Concerns Around Gender*, Bengaluru: Alternative Law Forum.

Charrad, M. Mounira. 2001. *States and Women's Rights: The Making of Postcolonial Tunisia, Algeria, and Morocco*, Berkeley: University of California Press.

Revathi, A. 2010. *The Truth About Me: A Hijra Life Story*, New Delhi: Penguin India.

Rosen, Hannah. 2009. *Terror in the Heart of Freedom: Citizenship, Sexual Violence, and the Meaning of Race in the Post-emancipation South*, Chapel Hill: University of North Carolina Press.

Saigol, Rubina. 2016. 'Multiple Legal Systems: The Construction of Impunity in the Case of Mukhtar Mai' in Neelam Hussain (ed.), *Disputed Legacies: The Pakistan Papers (Zubaan Series on Sexual Violence and Impunity in South Asia)*, New Delhi: Zubaan.

3

Speaking of Rape in
Late Colonial India

In the South Asian context, sexual violence has occupied public
attention since the advent of the modern historical period. This
is not to say that it was not present in public discourse at other
moments in history. What is clear is that from about the mid– to
late nineteenth century onwards, various historical developments
to do with female identity, status and civic existence clustered
around instances of what we today would call sexual violence.
The crucial historical moments in this regard are those which
marked the emergence of social reform, nationalism, and nation-
building and subsequently, post-independence crises to do with
class, ethnicity, gender, religious identities and caste. During each
of these moments, the complex relationship that exists in our
contexts, between sexual coercion and cruelty and intimate and
social relationships was foregrounded; and this foregrounding
elicited and provoked responses, which made for critical public
'speech' about sexual violence.

Such speech was various, and expressed in diverse registers, of
law, fiction, State policy, parliamentary debates... Depending on
who was speaking—that is, the caste-class location that people spoke
from—and who was being addressed, speech in the wake of sexual
violence proved disquieting, careful, tense. Often the conditions that

enabled speech also restricted the range of meanings that could be expressed, as we shall see. The converse too happened: conditions that threatened to inhibit speech made for startling disclosures!

In the chapters grouped under Part II of this book, I look at crucial moments in the history of late colonial and independent India— from the 1920s-2000s—and mark the contexts and conditions that incited debate about sexual violence. In each instance, I point to what was indeed speakable, and by whom and to what purpose, and what such speech sought to achieve, and actually did. For some chapters, I have adopted a comparative approach, drawing on studies done by scholars and fellow feminists—from Pakistan, Bangladesh and Sri Lanka—for reasons that I make evident.

***

In this chapter, I am concerned with a set of events that unfolded in late colonial India and which rendered sexual violence a matter of public concern. The violence in question had to do with forced sex in marriage, imposed on very young brides by their considerably older husbands.

In what follows, I examine the death of the child bride Phulmoni, which happened in 1890 in the Bengal province, and which resulted in extended public and legal speech about sexual violence. In British Indian criminal law, rape was an acknowledged crime, and as such, did not elicit public discussion. But when it appeared that child brides were routinely raped in their conjugal contexts, that became a cause of contention and argument. I discuss in this context the Age of Consent Bill of 1891, and the amendments proposed in 1927 to existing legislation on rape; these legal measures elicited widespread and often acrimonious public debate. My objective in revisiting these well-known and documented controversies is to point to the different public registers in which rape within marriage came to be discussed, and call attention to women's speech in this regard. I focus on how marital rape was understood, defined and accounted for, in a legal as well as ethical sense, and how the colonial State's approach to the problem shaped and was shaped by what transpired in the sphere of civil action.

Phulmoni's husband, 29 years her senior, had sexually imposed himself on her, though she was yet to attain puberty. This resulted in great pain for the child, and continuous bleeding, resulting in a vector of wounds in the vaginal and pelvic area, and ultimately her death. Tanika Sarkar has written in detail about the historical contexts and conditions that rendered her death significant, linking it to the emergence of nationalism. Early nationalist thought and expression distinguished themselves from social reform ideas on the question of the Hindu woman. Whereas social reformers constructed the latter as the archetypal victim, subject to terror and violence in the form of ritual widowhood, child marriage and wife-burning, nationalists viewed her as a repository of cultural grace, whose body, to paraphrase Sarkar, was unmarked and pure, and subject only to 'our' shastras. In her capacity for sacrifice and forbearance, particularly her ability to bear pain, the Hindu woman stood out. But, points out Sarkar, another strand of nationalist thought wished to also reimagine Hindu womanhood from the point of view of affective sentiment—not only was the Hindu woman capable of patient suffering, she was also the embodiment of, indeed an incitement to great love. Conjugal love, the argument went, was actually a marriage of souls, as far as Hindus were concerned.

Ironically, this sentimental celebration of conjugality happened precisely at a time when public discontent over polygamy was being expressed, and male prerogative in this respect disdained by women (Sarkar refers to the arch aside of a Brahmin widow who points to how Hindu custom binds women and lets men go scot free). This was also when women writing in the vernacular press in Bengal painted somewhat grim and sombre portraits of conjugal life. The ideal Hindu marriage then had to be salvaged, and one way of doing this was to 'uproot' bad practice: Phulmoni's death appeared a fit instance of one, and though her husband was not indicted in court for the crime of rape and murder—though the post-mortem report noted the extent of grave injury—but sentenced to merely a year's imprisonment, his behaviour and its result drew public and legislative attention. They constituted crucial evidence when a Bill was proposed in 1891 in the Central Legislature (a product of colonial constitutional reforms) to raise the age of consent within and outside marriage—for girls—from 10 to 12. The object of the Bill was to 'to protect female children from immature prostitution (sic) and from premature cohabitation'.

The Bill had been drafted in the wake of the Rukhmabai controversy that erupted—a few years prior to Phulmoni's death—in Bombay province. Married when very young, Rukhmabai refused to cohabit with her husband on attaining puberty, citing his insensitive and faulty character, and also that she had been married choicelessly and could not be expected to honour such a union. While reform opinion was on her side, an emergent nationalist elite, prominent amongst whom was Bal Gangadhar Tilak, took against her pronouncements: they held that colonial law had no business interfering with native custom. When her husband approached the courts seeking restitution of conjugal rights, Rukhmabai stood her ground, was prepared to go to jail and did. Eventually the matter was settled outside of court, but Rukhmabai's courageous stance did not go unnoticed and led to the passing of the Age of Consent Act, 1891, which amended Section 375 of the Indian Penal Code that dealt with rape. The Act raised the age of consent for sexual intercourse for all girls, married or unmarried, from ten to twelve years in all jurisdictions, and violations within marriage too were to be treated as rape, and subject to criminal prosecution.

Truth was that the cruelties that girls suffered and often died of, on account of being imposed upon by sexually active and older husbands, were not unknown in British India. That is, it was not merely a matter of recognition in criminal law, and instead was known in civil contexts as well. Instances of child rape within marriage had been reported from as early as 1856 and known to British doctors investigating these matters. Further, in 1860, the Indian Penal Code had prescribed dire punishment for the husband who consummated his marriage with his bride before she was ten years of age—which could include transportation for life. In 1861, the first Age of Consent Bill was passed and the colonial government differentiated the age of marriage from the age of consent; the former was a matter that government did not feel charged to interfere with, since it was backed by religious texts. The latter, the age at which a marriage was consummated, it was felt, could be legislated upon, since it had to do with the physical hurt that a child bride was likely to endure, should she be forced to do her conjugal duties. However it soon became evident that fixing the age of consent did not always deter older men from forcing themselves on their young brides—the law could be bent in any number of ways, and as happened with Phulmoni, it was possible to argue that she had completed ten years of age.

In any case, given the rise of early nationalism, Phulmoni's tragic death became a charged symbol around which supporters and opponents of the 1891 Age of Consent bill gathered and exchanged views. Significantly, opposition to early marriage included the views of several women of Calcutta, who made it known that they looked to government to protect the rights of their sex. Yet supporters of early marriage were loud and vociferous, and the din they created was immense. A good part of their discussions had to do with the onset of puberty in India, whether it happened before or after the age of 12 and if custom had not taken care of possible instances of sexual hurt. In the event, neither Phulmoni's pain nor the evidence of mothers in court on behalf of sexually hurt girl brides mattered as much as what the shastras said about puberty and the need to impregnate the child bride as early as possible (the argument being that a delay in consummating marriages might render the bride's womb [garba] open to 'pollution' thereby injuring her prospects for bearing healthy children that would fulfill Hindu ritual obligations).

Even reformist opinion that supported the passage of the Bill was drawn into this mode of argument. While they wanted the colonial government to legislate, they hastened to add that such legislation was not against shastraic injunctions. They argued that enlightened Hindus (in Bengal, at least) rarely performed the garbadhan ceremony (literally, gifting the womb, in this case, signaling the bride's readiness for consummation) anymore and besides, the shastras did not insist that it had to be done on the onset of the first menstruation, or prescribe a fine for delaying it.

Part of the reason for the rather shrill anxiety which fueled both support and opposition to the Bill had to do with the spectre of assertive and modern women that haunted educated middle class circles around this period. Historian Padma Anagol points out that even in earlier decades, several women had sought legal resolutions to bad marriages through the strategic use of the clause that provided both husband and wife 'restitution of conjugal rights'. Throughout the period of social reform, argues Anagol, women's sense of their dilemmas was profoundly different from what men made of them. Male reformers, she notes, justified their stance by pointing to the deleterious effect early marriages had on the 'race' and how they led to economic ruin. Malabari, the reformer whose name is most closely associated with the Bill, noted that early marriages led to the 'breaking down of constitutions and the ushering in of disease … the giving up of studies on the part of the boy-husband … the birth of sickly children … poverty … dependence' (Anagol, 2008: 295).

On the other hand, women supporting the Bill, observes Anagol, were not concerned with what the shastras said, and nor were they anxious about the possible pollution of their wombs. They understood early marriage in terms of dowry transactions, the burden this placed on the parents of girls and the general understanding that girls were somehow inferior. They were aware too of the authority that inhered in the figure of the mother-in-law and saw that as a reason for women wanting to not only bear male children, but also to marry them off early. Women speaking and writing thus no doubt further enraged sections of male public opinion, which, in any case, was opposed to reform, concludes Anagol. One only has to read Tarabai Shinde's *Stri-Purush Tulana* to get a sense of what perhaps annoyed men: this text, written by a woman whose family was closely associated with Mahatma Phule's Satyashodak Samaj, takes apart male hypocrisy and sanctimoniousness, with respect to the women's question, but more importantly, presents a varied picture of womanhood in late nineteenth century western India, which is at odds with the limited portrayal of women as victims of custom and orthodoxy in reformist literature. The text is also a satiric indictment of male sexual authority, especially its pathetic pretensions, which, Tarabai Shinde makes clear, are upheld only through the power that men command, and not because of their intrinsic worth.

In any case, the manner in which men arguing for and against reform could actually bypass the evidence embodied in a hurt body (in Phulmoni's case, a dead body) and literally 'textualise' that body, speaks volumes for their inability to recognize and name bodily pain for what it was. In contrast, women chose to speak in an experiential register that alluded to the suffering body, even as they drew on an evolving political vocabulary of rights and entitlements that addressed the State. The violence they endured in marriage, particularly the violence of loveless conjugality, was thus translated into a language of self-worth and rights. This enabled them to refuse, albeit indirectly, the stigma of sex, both the so-called taint of birth and character (rather, being or *svabava*). Further, their speech unsettled the alacrity with which sections of the male population affirmed custom and tradition, and challenged social practice that took refuge in impunity, sanctified by custom and doctrine.

***

The Age of Consent instance was raked up again in the 1920s. This time, the issue was forefronted by reformers from the Arya Samaj. The organization was in its assertive phase at this point in time: on the one hand, it sought to uphold Hindu claims to virile nationalism in the face of what it understood to be Muslim political assertion; on the other hand, it addressed issues of social reform to do with gender and caste, convinced that only a reformed Hinduism could serve nationalism. In the 1890s, the question of marriage reform was viewed largely in terms of the right of an alien State to legislate on matters to do with Hindu custom and faith. In the 1920s, the desirability of reform or for that matter legislation was not as hotly contested as before: it was evident that Hindu marriages had to be reformed. The question was to what extent, and to what purpose. As we shall see, reformers were anxious to 'update' practice rather than interrogate its terms; women reformers, while equally intent on changing marriage norms and laws, were additionally concerned with the bodily and material consequences of unsuitable marriages and conjugality. In the event, both had recourse to a register of expression that was decidedly modern, being founded on considerations of female health and well-being on the one hand, and social good and progress on the other. Yet, even within discourses that rendered marriage and its ills 'speakable', women's voices did sound a distinctive refrain, even if a subtle one. In what follows, I analyse the progress of arguments to do with the age of consent reform as these emerged in the 1920s.

In 1924, Arya Samajist Hari Singh Gour proposed an amendment to Section 375, which would raise the age of consent to 14, with respect to married *and* unmarried women. The bill was referred to a Select Committee, which reduced the age from 14 to 13 years in the case of the former. Though taken up for consideration in the Central Legislature, the Bill was not passed. Questions were raised as to the right of the child-wife to prosecute her husband should he force his sexual attentions on her, and there were discussions on who the appropriate authority to speak on her behalf was. Her 'natural guardian' alone could be such a spokesperson, it was claimed. Counter arguments pointed to the provisions in the 1891 amendment that took care of this matter. But it was clear that it was not legal clarity that was being sought; rather those who raised the question of prosecution wondered if the husband could be prosecuted at all! What was not discussed was the notion of consent—and if those considered children in every other instance, were capable of discretion in the matter of conjugality.

In 1925, an amendment to Section 375, building on the Select Committee's suggestion, fixed the age of consent within marriage at 13 rather than 14. This measure did not capture the imagination of the public, whether reformers or the orthodox. Raising the age by a year did not appear a great improvement over what existed, and neither did it appear particularly radical. Gour proposed another amendment two years later, asking for the age of consent to be raised to 14 for married girls and 16 for unmarried young women. This was relegated to discussion, presided over by a specially appointed Age of Consent Committee. Meanwhile another Arya Samajist, Har Bilas Sarda, introduced a bill to restrain child marriages, by seeking an Act that raised the age of marriage to 18 for men and 14 for women. This of course resulted in the passing of the famous Sarda Act, fixing the age of marriage for girls at 14.

In this context, I would like to call attention to the report of the Age of Consent Committee that heard opinions from across the country. It reviewed existing legislation on the age of consent in terms of its use and efficacy, sought, received and summarized public opinion on the proposed changes, discussed the nature of the offence, the words that best captured its inappropriateness—in short

the report produced by the Committee created a map of ideas based
on what it elicited from the public, rearranging views and arguments
within a normative framework that favoured reform; and in terms
that actually strengthened the case to raise the age or marriage,
and not merely the age of consent, paving the way for the passage
of the Sarda Act. From the point of view of our enquiry, there is
rich material here, which points to the impasses that attend public
discussion of a crime that cannot be always named for what it is.
Also, given our continued inability to legislate against marital rape,
we may want to construct for ourselves a genealogy of arguments
and objections that, historically, framed discussions of it.

***

The Committee's report makes it clear that legislation in the past
had not always proved efficacious; in spite of the 1891 Act, and
the slew of amendments thereafter, men continued to consummate
their marriages with very young brides. For one, many were
ignorant of the law. Secondly, given the nature of the offence, being
an act that is carried out in privacy, it was not possible to know if
indeed it had been committed. Thirdly, girl brides, however hurt
and afraid, rarely reported what they endured; even if their families
empathized with their plight, they did not dare prefer a complaint,
for fear of how that would affect their daughters' married lives. For,
not only would reporting the offence disgrace the man, his bride
and their marriage, but if he was convicted, make for lasting stigma.
Further, the girl could not expect to get remarried. The larger caste
community too refrained from intervening, given their jealous
guarding of caste honour. Fourthly, there were legal limitations: the
crime being non-cognizable, police on their own could not prefer
a complaint; then there was the problem of ascertaining the age
of the child-bride, given improper or non-existent documentation
of her birth. Lastly, given the very low rate of conviction as far
this crime was concerned, society at large had not felt the pain

and burden of punitive action, and hence the law did not deter the commission of the crime.

Significantly, even as the report pointed sorrowfully to the continued commission of sexual violence by husbands on their very young wives in spite of a law that restrained them, it refrained from speaking of the ill-effects of such violence except in medical terms. It unequivocally condemned early consummation on the grounds that it compromised the young bride's health, interfered with her ability to bear healthy children, and rendered her person sickly. This is noteworthy, because the 'speakability' of rape is at stake here—the register of medicine and health is enabling in a way that the language of affect and recognition is not. Unsurprisingly, in the sections devoted to examining evidence for and against raising the age of consent across British India, the register of health and medicine frames much of the argument. While the evidence itself is contested, with some witnesses linking early consummation to sickly children, and others finding no cause for such presumption, the narrative makes it clear that howsoever one interprets the evidence, the fact remained that early consummation caused the sapping of vitality in the young mother. It is this devitalized body that is foregrounded as a sort of cautionary warning; whereas the other body, hurt and mutilated, appears only sporadically and in and through the examples furnished by witnesses to bolster their argument for raising the age of consent.

In contrast, rape outside of marriage, rather coercive sex in non-marital contexts, was spoken of in a different and rather robust register. In fact the report was quite frank on the subject, and pointed to the wide prevalence of child prostitution, and the abduction and seduction of young girls, particularly in the North-Western parts of the country, where women were scarce in numbers and therefore 'coveted' and lured to be lovers, prostitutes and wives. It noted that some witnesses that spoke on the subject had reasoned that parents married their daughters early in these parts precisely for this reason. These witnesses had insisted on raising the age of consent outside marriage, to both deter as well as punish abductors. The report made it clear that not everyone agreed with this reasoning: some feared that if the age was raised, it would encourage women to go 'astray'; others noted that if the age of consent for sex outside marriage was raised beyond 16, this would cause difficulties for the prostitute class!

Significantly, arguments about non-marital sexual violence did not prove as combative or defensive as the case may be. It was as if the issues at stake did not merit serious contention, since neither sexual morality nor social ethics was at stake. Further, public concern in this regard had less to do with the young woman's health or well-being and more to do with deterrence of a practice that was grudgingly accepted.

The report's extended note on the nature of the offence—marital rape—is revealing: it examined the history of early marriage and the prevalence of early consummation across communities. It sought to understand the reasons for such practices, and through its choice of example and argument, suggested that the impulse to consummate a marriage when a bride was not ready for it, physiologically, that is, owed more to custom than religious stricture, and this was true for Muslims as well as Hindus. The report reviewed what Hindu and Muslim religious texts had to say on the subject, and declared that neither supported the practice. It also refuted objections to the proposed legislation. I would like to call attention to one of these objections: that the proposed Act takes away from the 'natural rights of a husband'.

The report made it clear that such a right had never existed, that is, it was always tempered and bracketed by custom, scriptural arguments and the law. Both Hindu and Islamic scripture laid conditions that had to attend the consummation of marriage. While agreeing that 'the cohabitation by a husband with his wife was not considered a crime, whatever the age of the girl, before the Indian

Penal Code of 1861', the report nevertheless insisted that if such cohabitation resulted in injury to the wife, 'the husband was liable to be punished for such injury and the marital rights of a husband could not be advanced as a bar to such prosecution.' It went on to quote from the judgment delivered in the Phulmoni case: 'Under no system of law with which courts have to do in this country, whether Hindu or Muslim, or under any law framed under British rule, has it ever been the law that a husband has the absolute right to enjoy the person of his wife without regard to the question of safety to her, as for instance, if the circumstances be such, that it is certain death to her, or that it is probably dangerous to her life—the law, it is true, is exceedingly jealous of any interference in matters marital, and very unwilling to trespass inside the chamber where husband and wife live together, and never does so except in cases of absolute necessity' (Report of the Age of Consent Committee, 1928–29: 117).

Tragically, it is the dead wife who became the measure of justice deliverable by law, and it is the dead wife who drew public attention to the harm caused by a husband exercising his 'natural' right over his wife. The young wife who survived hurt, though injured and mutilated, was not as evocative a figure; and by the same token, her situation was not 'speakable' except in terms that lamented her impaired motherhood. Living or dead, the young bride was not considered a sentient being. Unsurprisingly, the notion of consent escaped interrogation. Yet this is the crux of the problem. For what could consent possibly mean, even in circumstances where the girl in question had reached discretionary age: could she at all refuse cohabitation or repel her husband's sexual demands, on her account, on the ground that she did not want, or desire it? These are not matters that were yet 'speakable', even by women witnesses, who too had recourse to a medical register for the most part. The question of female choice became relevant only in subsequent decades—in discussions to do with the right to divorce. Even then, choice seldom translated into the right to say no to unwanted sex. Sex within marriage would remain an expression of conjugal duty; only the conscious abjuration of duty through divorce would enable, albeit indirectly, freedom from marital rape.

The impasse that marked discussion of sexual hurt on account of early consummation was most evident in the report's note on punishment, should the offence be proved to have taken place. If consummation happened before the age of 12, it was to constitute a higher order of offence, than if it took place thereafter and would therefore invite transportation for life or imprisonment for up to ten years. If consummation took place with brides between the age of 12 and 15, the punishment would be lighter, involving a reduced sentence of one to two years imprisonment and a fine. The reasoning for this distinction in punishment was as follows: 'We are clearly of opinion that the age of the girl in most instances has a real bearing on the extent of her injuries. The later the age, the less serious are the consequences likely to be' (*op.cit.*,125). The report refused to distinguish between injuries resulting in death and other injuries, as also the difference between rape and other forms of violence. It claimed that it was not possible to 'measure' the extent of injury thus, considering that even less grievous injuries could result in lasting trauma—the relevant factor must be age, the report noted.

The impossibility of ascertaining injuries, given the nature of the offence, was also something that bothered the Age of Consent Committee: how may one elicit information? Medical examinations would provoke resistance, and the nature of hurt being what it was, injuries may not always be physically marked or visible. Further, it was not possible to prepare a catalogue of injuries, since there were no reliable tools available to grade injuries.

The aligning of the offence to age, rather than the nature of hurt, the linguistic and semantic impossibility of naming sexual hurt, unless it resulted in death, and the inability of all concerned to name the perpetrator, the husband, as an agent of crime: these impasses make it clear that it was simply not possible to countenance rape in marriage without calling into question the social and sexual authority of the husband. This is also why the Age of Consent Committee refused to name the proposed law as a law against rape. It preferred the euphemism 'marital misbehaviour', a term that left the institution of marriage outside the realm of law and legal liability. Significantly, the Committee rejected Gour's name for the offence: 'illicit married intercourse'. Gour had sought to mark the illegality of an act where consent was not to be had, and force was almost always used. But the Committee was of the opinion that while it did not wish to take away from the gravity of the offence, the word illicit, it reasoned, was 'open to an obvious objection'. Significantly, this 'obvious'ness was neither stated nor discussed.

In all this, one wonders if women witnesses sounded a different note with respect to sexual hurt. The Age of Consent Committee does not register such differences; perhaps it did not consider them acute enough. Most women who were deposed did seek to fix the age of consent as high as they could, both within and outside marriage, and perhaps one may identify in this demand the residue of experience of what women endured. For instance, the report notes with regard to a deposition from Madras: 'Srirangamma and a group of five other Brahmin ladies in giving a pathetic account of the condition of girl-wives advocate 18 as the minimum age in both cases' (*op.cit.*, 58). It is possible that such 'pathetic' accounts were more the norm than the exception in women's depositions. To be sure, they were accommodated within a narrative that used their evidence to illustrate the medical and pathological effects of early marriage and consummation, rather than to call attention to violence and hurt. Yet it is possible that in the depositions there lingered recognition of suffering that was uniquely female.

It is another matter that neither early marriage nor raising the age of consent to 14 and 16 (for married and unmarried girls respectively) addressed the realities of life as experienced by girls from vulnerable communities, especially amongst dalit and other so-called Shudra castes. Their labouring and caste status meant that they could be and were sexually preyed upon by men from the dominant castes—it did not matter that they were married or not, or that they were very young. Neither did the proposed legislation address the burden placed on women from these castes by what has been called ritual prostitution, or mandated sexual labour.

The Devadasi Abolition Bill, which was proposed around the same time (1927), did address the question of 'dedication' of girls to temples, and here again, it was age that took precedence over all else, at least in terms of the public rhetoric against abolition. Yet, even in this instance, it would be productive to identify women's arguments from those put forth by male reformers. Dr Muthulakshmi, for example, drew both on her knowledge of medicine, as well as on the stories of dedicated girls and their plight that were brought to her attention. While she filtered these stories through a moral lens, her deep empathy for these children was evident. It is this 'closeness' to experience that she would foreground to demand justice for women.

***

The question of rape within marriage was understood differently by those active in emergent anti-caste movements in Madras and Bombay provinces. In *Castes in India*, read as a paper at a seminar in Colombia University in 1916, the young Dr Ambedkar had observed that women's conjugal and social status were defined in and through coercive and violent customs that restricted their choices in this respect: sati, early marriage and ritual widowhood, practised initially by the so-called upper castes to retain the parity of women and men within their caste limits, soon came to be emulated by others, and led to the rigid separation of castes along the axis of endogamy. (He would return to the question of violence and the making of gender identities in the years to come, with his writings on *Manusmriti*, the status of women in ancient India and on the shudra castes.)

Radical critics of custom—such as the members of the Self-Respect Movement in the Madras Presidency—pointed out that women were rendered submissive wives, hapless girls and stigmatized public women on account of ideas and practices that sanctioned violence, especially sexual violence against them. These critics located sexual stigma, the taint of sex that rendered women worthy of control not in their femaleness, but in socially sanctioned discrimination against particular castes. Those who supported Gour's amendment and later Sarda's Bill pointed out that early marriage was a norm only for the upper castes, whereas girls from other castes married much later, and well after the onset of puberty: they noted that the upper castes desired to 'guard' and sexually police upper caste women, and ensure they were brought within the ambit of male sexual authority from their earliest years. It was also argued that such policing had its origin in early historical practices that sought to regulate productive labour, through the imposition of untouchability and reproductive labour through strictures to do with appropriate marriage. Sexual coercion, to do with marriage and sacred prostitution, it was made clear, was part of a continuum of social violence that both produced and sustained an unequal social order. These views were argued with verve and vigour through the decades of the 1930s and 1940s, with several women speaking their minds out—Neelavathi, Kunjitham, Ramamrithammal and Annapoorani were particularly forceful in their arguments.

Dalit women from Maharashtra, active in Dr Ambedkar's various political movements, too expressed views that were somewhat similar and were as radical in their criticisms of caste, especially on how it sanctioned discrimination and violence against dalit women—this was evident in their views on mandated prostitution, as was imposed on women dedicated to temple entertainment.

Through the 1930s and 1940s, they came to these concerns, as they addressed issues to do with labour, including sexual labour, and education, and what was available and denied to dalit women on both counts. They—for instance, Sulochanabai Dongre and Radhabai Kamble—pointed to how the routine life of caste compromised dalit dignity, especially dalit's women's personhood, and affirmed Ambedkar's critique of Hinduism and the caste order.

Such arguments however remained marginal. The issues at stake for reformists had to do with rendering conjugality adequate to these modern times and while they were interested in critical appraisals of the past, of shastraic and other sacred texts, and the salutary uses of legislation, their goals were more modest. They were willing to admit that times were changing and that women's lives were being transformed. They had recourse to a secular discourse, however limited, of what women deserved by way of equality and self-respect, and what the state ought to do in these matters. But they were not willing to push these secular arguments to cover domestic and intimate realms. Nor did they think it important to recognize the deleterious effects of male sexual authority. The limits as well as possibilities of such a discourse would be all too evident in the decade that followed.

***

Before I end this chapter, I would like to review briefly the colonial State's responses to the debates around reform and rape in marriage. At all times, the State was sensitive to the question of government 'interference' with custom and faith, and the political consequences of such interference. However, its rule required an assertion of its 'difference', of what rendered it superior. Rationally defined legislation and orderly governance were key constituents of this difference, apart from other racial and civilizational factors that the State's key personnel invoked from time to time. To secure a balance between what needed to be critically addressed and what must be left alone, and meanwhile not lose sight of its strategic interests, the State had developed subtle and not-so-subtle protocols to engage with these matters. In the 1890s, the State's approach was less cautious than what it would be in the 1920s, a decade which witnessed the growth of mass struggles against colonial rule. In the event, law reform was 'left' to the national conscience, so to speak, and the State preferred to watch and wait, and intervene only to ensure that is authority was not challenged.

As far as sexual violence was concerned, the State had recourse to criminal law, as would be expected of it; as we have seen it was not averse to reforming the law, but it erred on the side of caution. Partly, this had to do with its relationship to native society and its beliefs and customs and partly, it was on account of the situation in England, where even at the time of passing the Age of Consent Act of 1891, there existed no legislation to penalize marital rape. This meant that sexual violence remained, in its view, as much a moral issue as a legal one. In turn, this morality drew on unexamined prejudices to do with sexuality and was shaped by the false and repressive decorum that haunted all considerations of it.

REFERENCES

Ambedkar, Babasaheb Dr. 1979. 'Castes in India' in *Writings and Speeches* 1. New Delhi: Dr. Ambedkar Foundation.

Anagol, Padma. 2008. 'Rebellious Wives and Dysfunctional Marriages: Indian Women's Discourses and Participation in Discourses over Restitution of Conjugal Rights and the Child Marriage Controversy in the 1880s and 1890s', in Sumit Sarkar and Tanika Sarkar (eds.), *Women and Social Reform in India*, pp. 282–312. Bloomington: Indiana University Press.

Geetha, V. and S. V. Rajadurai (eds.) (n.d.) *Revolt!—A Radical Weekly in Colonial Madras*, Chennai: Periyar Dravidar Kazhagam

Pande, Ishita. 2012. 'Phulmoni's body: the autopsy, the inquest and the humanitarian narrative on child rape in India', *South Asian History and Culture,* DOI:10.1080/19472498.2012.750453.

Pawar, Urmila and Meenakshi Moon (eds.). 2008. *We Also Made History: Women in the Ambedkarite Movement,* New Delhi: Zubaan.

Government of India. 1929. *Report of the Age of Consent Committee, 1928–29;* http://arrow.latrobe.edu.au/store/3/4/2/9/2/public/B11713409pp1-184.pdf (accessed 15 November 2015).

Sarkar, Tanika. 2001. *Hindu Wife, Hindu Nation: Community, Religion and Cultural Nationalism,* New Delhi: Permanent Black.

Sinha, Mrinalini. 1995. *Colonial Masculinity: The 'manly Englishman' and The' Effeminate Bengali' in the Late Nineteenth Century,* Manchester: Manchester University Press.

4

'Speakable' Justice and 'Unspeakable' Violence in the Nation-to-be

Conjugal and familial health, including concern over the child bride's frailty and imminent death in the event of early marriage and consummation, were the reasons, made publically known, for soliciting changes in raising the age of marriage as well as the age of consent. In the 1930s and after, the vulnerable body of the child bride disappeared from view as a more expansive discourse to do with social and legal reform emerged. It was as if, with the passing of the Sarda Act (which raised the age of marriage to 14), the matter of female sexual vulnerability in marriage had been 'settled', so to speak, and that reformers were now free to engage with broader issues to do with Hindu law—with matters pertaining to not only marriage, but also divorce, inheritance and adoption.

In the 1920s, nationalist claims on the modern world, and on progress in particular, were not as resolute and confident as they would be in the following years; they remained defensive in that crucial decade, which saw Mahatma Gandhi assume leadership of the Indian National Congress. In the 1930s, given the adroit manner in which Gandhi negotiated the claims of culture and progress, the past and present, in short, of what he termed 'Hind Swaraj', nationalism assumed a confident edge. This was also on account of the relentless wave of actual struggles, some spectacular, others substantial, that swept British India during this period. Women participated in these struggles in large numbers, and were articulate and visible in public life more than before. Besides, through the late 1920s and early 1930s, the nationalist women's organization, the All India Women's Conference (AIWC), worked hard in the fields of female education and communication, and these efforts rendered it a formidable body of opinion. The AIWC backed the Age of Consent Committee's findings, supported Har Bilas Sarda's Bill, and endorsed the abolition of the Devadasi system. In the late 1930s and 1940s, as nationalist men debated the need to reform Hindu law in totality, AIWC members too took up the cause of law reform with respect to all existing legal arrangements for Hindu women, and demanded a rational and uniform system of law.

Among other things, women in the AIWC demanded property rights for women, abolition of polygamy and insisted on their right to divorce—in their opinion these were measures that would challenge women's low status in the family and the inegalitarianism of Hindu marriage, particularly the suffering it imposed on Hindu brides. It was in this guise that the fraught female body was returned to the stage of history—as a rights-bearing yet scarred body, on whose behalf articulate women spoke and argued. Significantly, reformist women not only asserted their right to freedom from marital cruelty: rather they redefined cruelty itself, such that it signified deprivation, of the right to property, to secure marriages of one's choice and the right to divorce. Meanwhile, unwanted sex in marriage and the possibility of rape in a conjugal situation remained as 'unspeakable' as before—except that in the late 1940s, in the wake of Partition-related violence, sexual assault had to be addressed, and indeed it was, but not always in ways that bore the imprint of women's experiences.

In this chapter, I examine the legal debates around marriage reform, inasmuch as they both gesture towards, as well as occlude, issues of sexual violence; I also look at the parallel discourse on sexual violence that emerged when horrific stories of abduction and rape came to light, as huge numbers of people crossed the borders of what would eventually become Pakistan and India. Once again, we see how, in the context of legal reform, sexual violence stands challenged in the face of speech that allows its indictment; whereas in the context of civil exchanges on the subject, it remains a shameful secret that may not be spoken of, except in terms of honour and dishonour. Women's voices emerged with particular force in both registers and yet, as will become evident, they remained inhibited as well.

***

Through the 1930s and early 1940s, public opinion was sought on the subject of law reform—opponents and qualified supporters, radicals who wanted more than less reform, and both men and women testified in front of the Hindu Law Committee set up for soliciting ideas and views on the subject. The report of the Committee encapsulated these divergent viewpoints and presented a case for reform (1947). Significantly, the will to reform emerged in the context of arguments to do with marriage and divorce in sections of the Muslim community. The passing of the Muslim Marriages Dissolution Act, 1939, proved germane to developments within the Hindu law reform camp.

This Act expanded grounds for divorce for Muslim women, while noting that apostasy—or the renunciation of faith by Muslim wives—cannot be made a cause for divorce. This particular ground, in fact, had been the only one available to Muslim women trapped in unhappy marriages, given the manner in which Islamic strictures with respect to the divorce claims for women were interpreted in British India. In the 1930s, apostasy provoked anxiety, especially in the context of the 'numerical' war that Hindus and Muslims indulged in, as they sought political representation and linked their claims to their being relative majorities and minorities in different parts of British India. Renunciation of one's faith, as well as the possibility of conversion were matters that both communities deemed important—for even as some Muslim women choicelessly turned apostate to exit from unbearable conjugality, lower caste Hindu men and women turned their back on Hinduism, as they looked to anchor their humanity in either Christianity or Islam. The revocation of apostasy as a ground for divorce must be sought in this complex history. On the other hand, this was not the only reason for the passing of the Act.

Given that debates within Muslim communities about the future of the faith and community hinged on how they understood and interpreted their Islamic identity, a law for Muslim women seeking divorce that would apply across regions and communities and supersede customary laws, and which was in consonance with the principles of the Shari'a, appeared important. Equally importantly, reformers as well as the ulema within Muslim communities recognized that if women had to turn apostates to leave cruel and unhappy marriages, that left women believers who did not do so in an existential bind: they had to endure cruelty or play truant to their conscience. The Act sought to allay this anxiety and to ensure justice for women.

In terms of what it promised, by way of relief from cruelty, the Act was radical: as Lucy Caroll has pointed out, it defined marital cruelty, even when it did not amount to physical hurt, as sufficient ground for divorce, thus placing women's experience of matrimony at the heart of its provisions. In view of the making of this piece of legislation, both marital cruelty as well as the need for legislation to allay it emerged as speakable subjects in ways that proved enabling for Hindu law reform. Given the competitive edge to both Hindu and Muslim nationalist claims, this was only to be expected.

In any case, the Hindu Law Committee's recommendations moved out of the dusty history of legal argument and entered the public domain in the course of the Hindu Code Bill debates (1947–51). This is not the place to go into the making of the Hindu Code, and I do not intend to do so, but I would like to point out that these debates as they unfolded in the Constituent Assembly brought to a head decades of wisdom on, as well as opposition to, Hindu law reform. More to our purpose, they furnished a context and occasion to think through the meaning of female freedom, equality and citizenship.

All the women members of the Constituent Assembly endorsed the need for a reformed Hindu Code, and argued their case for women's rights to property, marriages of their choice, and most importantly to divorce. I am concerned here with arguments to do with divorce, since they take us to the heart of the discourse around marriage and women's rights within that institution. Women arguing for an expansive divorce law drew on their own experiences, of listening to women's testimonies to do with unhappy and cruel marriages and witnessing many a woman go to psychological ruin. Thus, even as they spoke of the virtues of a recognizably modern ideal of marriage—monogamous, companionable, and protected by women's right to property—they could not but help suggest that these were not always sufficient conditions for happy conjugality, and that the latter could well prove to be a bitter experience. Women's right to divorce, they insisted, had to be seen in this light—as a remedy that a woman needed to protect herself from wilful cruelty and violence. As with earlier debates, the husband as perpetrator of violence remained a shadowy figure; meanwhile female suffering was granted a premium and rights claims upheld on the basis of recognition of that suffering.

Proponents of divorce, including Dr Ambedkar who moved the motion for the adoption of a Hindu Code and defended its content, pointed out that a vast majority of castes in the country had long-standing separation and divorce provisions in place, and that the law was merely seeking to affirm what was actually practised by a majority of the population. In effect, Dr Ambedkar and others made it clear that society at large did not countenance female suffering or for that matter unhappy marriages. It was only the orthodox and defenders of custom who appeared impervious to suffering, it was argued.

Significantly, articulate women supporting women's rights to divorce had to be on their moral guard. At all times they had to distinguish the freedom that they upheld from the recklessness that conservative opinion associated with it. Rather than heed women's reasoning with respect to divorce rights, opponents of law reform took to accusing women of frivolity and wanting to destroy the family. In the event, women's attempts to bring the question of cruelty and violence within the ambit of rational argument had to necessarily proclaim their moral intent.

Women members in the Constituent Assembly responded to this pressure to be moral at all costs in three ways. For one, they argued that neither culture nor tradition was against justice being done to them, an argument that had been made by social reformers for over decades now. But they did not go on to argue, as male reformers were wont to, about what was allowed or not allowed by tradition and culture. Rather, they insisted they desired to remake Hindu society, that is, they counterposed their interest in rendering the Hindu world and by implication the family, adequate to the times, rather than seeking a mandate from the past. Thus, it was said that 'Hindu society was full of defects' and that they merely wished to make it 'healthy and wholesome' (Babasaheb Dr Ambedkar, *Writings and Speeches*, Volume 14: 312). Secondly they noted that they were staking claims to equality and justice that had already been accepted as valid (in the context of conservatives arguing society was not ready to accept such claims and women's claims would lead to moral disarray). Sucheta Kriplani for instance referred to the Indian National Congress' Karachi resolutions of 1931, promising equality to all, irrespective of birth and sex and pointed out that these embodied a pledge that was being honoured now. Given that conservative members questioned the authority the Constituent Assembly had given itself to reform Hindu law, she felt that history had to be invoked in the cause of women. Such gesturing towards history also made it clear that women's rights were indivisible, that political freedom must necessarily go hand in hand with social equality and justice.

Finally, women also sought to redefine conjugality, drawing on the experiential mode of reasoning—rendering female experience the ground for defining their rights claims as moral ones. They made it clear that conjugal inequality, and the power that flowed from it and was vested in the husband, rendered marriage a disharmonious state of affairs for many women, and often a violent experience. Renuka Ray declared that scores of people had come to her, with their daughters, who had suffered gravely in marriages that were not happy; and that women suffer such hardship that they need to find relief, which is why, she noted, she and others were in favour of liberal divorce provisions. Kamala Chaudhari went so far as to say that marriage need not appear an institution carved in stone, rather had to be seen for what it was, a 'compromise for the lifetime' and that people tried and made the most of it, just so to raise children. To claim, as some were wont to, that divorce would mitigate marriage as such, she noted, was untenable. For, if that had been the case, given the generous divorce provisions allowed to vast sections of the population, neither culture nor religion would have evolved. Yet, she noted with acuity, 'if under any circumstances the separation be deemed essential, then I think the legal right must lie with the woman...' (*op.cit.*, 660).

In contrast to those who spoke thus, we find conservative men refusing to acknowledge that the issues at stake had to do with the destructive effects of the familial and sexual authority they habitually exercised. We also find them blaming individual morality or the lack of it, and the effects of colonial rule for all that was wrong with the Hindus: the ill-effects of alien colonial rule, and individual men being immoral and women being unchaste, they argued, had produced a dissolute public morality, and it was up to the Hindus to retain and nurture moral worth in their homes. They set themselves up as 'natural' custodians of family and community, culture and tradition.

It was this notion of custodianship that was time and again put forth in the opposition that conservative men mounted against law reform, particularly reform of laws that would affirm choice in matters of marriage, and freedom with respect to divorce. When finally the Hindu Code Bill debates were abandoned and Jawaharlal Nehru withdrew support to the measure, these custodians were triumphant. Eventually of course, aspects of the Hindu Code were extracted and passed as individual pieces of legislation in the 1950s, but the normative framework that, along with Dr Ambedkar, liberal men and women in the Constituent Assembly helped put together came unstuck: familial and social justice ceased to be central to the practice of democracy, as Dr Ambedkar desired it to be, and women's rights came to be defined by piecemeal laws which did not enable a questioning of either unequal family and community structures or hegemonic masculine authority. As far as women's challenging of this authority was concerned, particularly its violent aspects, that would have to wait on other developments. All that valiant speech women had mustered in this regard remained, meanwhile, a forgotten legacy.

In this context, I foreground another development—the experience of Partition—which brought to the fore sexual crimes of an appalling nature. How was this received in the Constituent Assembly at the time the Hindu Code was being debated? How did women, who had worked hard to render marital discontent and cruelty 'speakable', engage with these acts of violation and hurt? How did they square their responses to these latter, such as they were, with their resonant affirmation of democracy and rights?

What framed their expressions, and equally their evasions and silences, and how may we understand their speech in this context?

***

I would like to begin with this familiar detail to do with the violence of Partition: of Hindu and Sikh women 'choosing' suicide over dishonour, as they fled marauding mobs of violent Muslim men. This was clearly no simple choice, and we have enough evidence to indicate that as families and homes were ripped apart and men saw their paternal authority challenged in unexpectedly cruel ways, they sought to retain whatever sense of honour they could by calling on their women to kill themselves—in effect choose real death to the symbolic death that ensues when a woman is raped and her honour, and by implication familial honour, is lost. That women agreed to this or did so on their own does not take away from the fact that questions of honour in this instance were adjudicated by male family heads, or in deference to them. Those were extraordinary times, no doubt, and men and women did things that cannot be imagined in retrospect without a shudder. Yet the fact remains that intense anxiety about sexual dishonouring translated into self-destructive violence: for, as Urvashi Butalia has pointed out, fathers and brothers who sent their women to death, to save their honour, suffered on that account, and a part of them died as well. In the event, even as family and community honour were sought to be affirmed, deeply cherished conjugal, familial and community ties were sundered.

Less dramatic, but no less horrific, were instances of women being abducted and forcibly married to their tormentors; or brutally raped and abandoned. From 1947 onward, bereaved families entreated their respective governments—in India and Pakistan—to help recover abducted and abandoned women. In 1947, both governments entered into a pact—the Inter-Dominion Treaty of December 6, 1947—to carry out a series of 'recovery' operations:

their objective was to find women who had thus been forcibly possessed and bring them back to their respective countries. Both Nation-States deemed this task to be of 'national' importance, involving questions of national sovereignty and honour. It was as if, given the fact of impaired custodianship, that is, the fact that male heads of families could not play effective protectors, the State had to step in and play this role.

Interestingly, the men who were most insistent on their role as moral custodians of the Hindu home were also the ones who were vociferous about the need to restore national honour. Thakur Das Bhargava and Rohini Kumar Chaudhary, who spent the longest hours opposing the Hindu Code Bill, were also most concerned with the so-called recovery operations and with upholding 'national honour', in the face of partition-related abduction and rape. A collapsed patriarchy thus sought to reinvent itself in and through the protocols of State action.

As for the women who debated rights and remedies in the course of Hindu Code Bill debates and their response to abduction, sexual violence and recovery, they were acquainted with the cruel fate visited on thousands of women, including details of hurt, displacement and so on. Some of them were involved in the recovery operations, directly and indirectly, and in rehabilitation efforts undertaken by the government of India: the setting up of makeshift camps to feed those who had nowhere to go, technical schools for those who cared to learn, and care homes where the most affected and unwanted could sojourn. Unsurprisingly, the plight of female refugees, as these women were termed, was invoked in the Hindu Code Bill debates: in the course of arguments about women's right to property and livelihood. On the other hand, neither the sexual fate imposed on refugee women, nor their experiences of abandonment, incited as much discussion.

Part of the reason for this had to do with the fact that the question of sexual violence had got entangled with the question of national wrong—as I have noted earlier, conservative nationalists made sure of that. From the early months of 1947, the fate of women during such riots as had already taken place—Calcutta killings, Naokhali—was public knowledge. Women had been abducted, assaulted and forced into conjugal unions on both sides of the border. Families were filing complaints of abducted girls, children, wives... and the magnitude of what had transpired was not lost on any one. However the problem acquired a particular edge when both India and Pakistan conferred and insisted that 'their' women be recovered and returned to them. It appeared entirely in order that both countries demanded 'their' women be recovered and returned to them. It was as if women's status as citizens of the new nations rested neither on their self-sovereignty nor the rights that were theirs in the new republics that had come into being; rather it was made clear that they were citizens by virtue of belonging to, and affirming affinity to family, kin, community, and by implication the nation. Thus, the arrangements which, earlier, had been outlined in the Inter-Dominion Treaty were coded into law: the Abducted Persons Recovery and Restoration Bill was passed in December 1949.

Why did both states agree to carry out a joint recovery operation at this moment in time? As far as the Indian instance was concerned, 1949 heralded a phase in nation-building that was contingent on the State asserting its independent authority over its constituents. The events that transpired during whatever was left of this momentous decade, especially in 1948—the banning of the Communist party, police action in Hyderabad state, which forced the Nizam to accede to the Union of India, war with Pakistan over the status of Kashmir, and persistent opposition to being part of India in what would eventually become the state of Nagaland—led the Indian State to assert its sovereignty in rather bellicose and gendered terms.

If we are to evaluate the Abducted Persons Bill in this context, its draconian provisions appear entirely in order with how the State had come to view itself. These provisions granted insuperable power and authority to the recovering authorities, and in one fell swoop deprived the women to be recovered of their fundamental rights. In spite of loud protests and innumerable amendments that were suggested, the Bill was passed in its original form. The government's aggressive eagerness, as Ritu Menon has pointed out, has to be seen as a defiant flexing of national muscles: at the purportedly slower rate of recovery of 'our' women; at the news that a considerable number of 'our' women were being held hostage in Kashmir in the wake of the trouble over accession to the Union of India; and in the context of assertions that held that Indian women cannot possibly be expected to live their lives out in a 'theocratic' state, when their own was avowedly 'secular'.

The gendered logic of nationalism appeared entirely natural to the votaries of State-sponsored recovery operations, and besides, as Menon observes, cast the Indian state as a 'parent-protector' who wished to keep women safe from the marauding intentions of the state of Pakistan, which was seen as unwilling to abide by the agreement it had earlier signed and which appeared set in impunity. Even as recovery operations were pursued with intense intent, it became evident that not all abducted women desired to be 'recovered': some had found their 'peace' in whatsoever a fashion, and did not want to be displaced again; others were angry with their families for abandoning them in the first place, or trading them sexually in return for safety of other family members; yet others were concerned about the children born to them in their new homes; many could not countenance meeting with kin that might disparage them, and several were not willing to re-live the past, which they must, if they agreed to go back to their so-called homes.

Though aware of these issues, women members of the Constituent Assembly did not find it easy to refer to these incidents: the embarrassment of it all, the fact that sexual violence was 'endured' in a certain fashion, 'accepted' both by perpetrators and victims and others, as an experience that marked their sense of who they were, and the victim-survivors' manner of negotiating a fragile peace for themselves were matters that could not be spoken of with the words at one's command. For one, these matters mocked at the earnest attempts afoot in the Constituent Assembly to ensure fair and just terms for women in matrimonial arrangements; and for another, they raised questions about female citizenship. What rights could women assert in such contexts as had defined their national identity, especially when their States expected them to bear the burden of that identity in explicitly gendered and sexualized ways?

Women's speech in this regard was impeded on another account as well. As we have seen, from the time of the reform debates of the past, law-making and reform had recourse to a speech register that acknowledged sexual violence and the denial of bodily integrity, only to recast that understanding in terms of a protectionist discourse: women had to be shielded from bad custom just so that good custom may triumph; they had to be restored to health so that they could be good mothers. The Hindu Code Bill debates had reworked protectionism and turned it around such that women demanded protection from the State, in their capacity as free and equal citizens. So, when the State had set itself to do precisely that, 'protect' women from marauding others, the shame that attended such violence proved overwhelming as well as curiously 'enabling' in that it fuelled State action; and questions of honour and pride determined understanding of the sexual anomie of the times.

Members of the Constituent Assembly did bring up issues to do with the rights of recovered women, and asked hard questions about the insuperable power granted to police and other state machinery to make decisions in the course of a recovery operation. But this did not mean that one could therefore speak of sexual violence in relation to the Nation-State or of male sexual authority in relation to nationalist politics in a post-colonial context. To speak of these relationships was, in effect, to compromise nationhood itself.

***

Yet, the horror of sexual violence and hurt in the context of Partition and all else that followed was registered by women in rather distinctive ways, outside the precincts of the Constituent Assembly. While women engaged with the recovery process were mostly convinced of what their government had enjoined them to do, as they came in touch with affected and hurt women they grew increasingly uneasy with the logic that informed recovery operations. For instance, Kamlabehn Patel, who assisted Mridula Sarabhai in coordinating recovery efforts, was completely unconvinced of bringing away mothers from their alien homes without their children; Rameshwari Nehru did not think it was right or feasible to separate women from homes where they had found a measure of peace. Even Mridula Sarabhai was not as insistently sanguine about what her government had counselled her to do: she was aware of the immense emotional and political difficulties the project entailed and shrewdly knowledgeable of the very many contingent reasons that shaped the desire, on the part of women, to be recovered or not recovered.

Yet, these reflective and complex views did not, could not, challenge what the two Nation-States had set themselves to undertake in the face of righteous national ire and indignation that informed recovery processes. In private conversation, in fiction, even in memoirs written later, much could be and was said, but as I have noted above, what public and political register was available at that time—particularly for women—to speak of sexual violence that had been foundational to the emergence of Nation-States?

***

One of the most prescient voices to sound a note of caution in this respect had been that of Dr Ambedkar's. In his complex 1940 text, *Thoughts on Pakistan* (reissued in 1945 as *Pakistan or the Partition of India*) Dr Ambedkar had warned against nationalisms invested in marking and claiming, or hurting and discarding women's bodies, as the case may be. In a section devoted to chronicling the details of Hindu-Muslim riots during the 1920s-1940s, he suggested rather provocatively that for decades Hindus and Muslims had been in a state that may only be described as 'civil war'. Central to this war was the fate that befell women. Arguing that '...the attitude towards women-folk is a good index of the friendly or unfriendly attitude between the two communities' he observed, '...acts of barbarism against women, committed without remorse, without shame and without condemnation by their fellow brethren show the depth of the antagonism which divided the two communities. The tempers on each side were the tempers of two warring nations.... What is astonishing is that these cold and deliberate acts of rank cruelty were not regarded as atrocities to be condemned but were treated as legitimate acts of warfare for which no apology was necessary' (Babasaheb Dr Ambedkar, *Writings and Speeches*, Volume 8, 1990: 186). (Dr Ambedkar is particularly harsh on the violence meted to Hindus in this context, yet he also makes clear his argument is of general import.)

Elsewhere in the same book, discussing divorce provisions as contained in the Dissolution of Muslim Marriages Act, 1939, particularly the clause that was devoted to de-legitimising apostasy as a ground for divorce, he noted that both communities were mindful of the consequences of their women converting to the other's faith: 'The conversion of Muslim woman to Hinduism and of Hindu woman to Islam, looked at from a social and political point of view, cannot but be fraught with tremendous consequences. It means a disturbance in the numerical balance between the two communities. As the disturbance was being brought about by the abduction of women, it could not be overlooked. For woman is at once the seed-bed of, and the hothouse for, nationalism in a degree that man can never be …' (*op. cit.*, 243).

Dr Ambedkar's point was that nationalism required blood sacrifice, and to avoid such an eventuality it was best to agree to a demarcation of boundaries, before nationalist sentiments of Hindus and Muslims got the better of their reason. The blood sacrifice he considered repugnant included and was underwritten by the sexual coercion directed at women. (He added in a footnote, 'The part played by woman in sustaining nationalism has not been sufficiently noticed. See the observations of Renan on this point in his Essay on Nationality' [*ibid*]).

Significantly, Dr Ambedkar's vision of the nation was fundamentally republican and he did not imagine that nationalism as ideology was necessary to sustain a Nation-State. While he was convinced of and prepared to defend national interest, he associated that less with the State's perception of its own needs, and more with democratic aspirations and the needs of the poorest sectors of the population and importantly with women's emancipation.

Tragically, South Asian states have remained more nationalist than republican, and at one time or another, in the name of safeguarding national sovereignty, each of our states has turned violent against its own citizens, who appear to them to be 'anti-national'; this violence has remained fundamentally gendered, targeting as it does women belonging to so-called insurgent and anti-national groups in ways that are calculated to stigmatise group identity and punish it. Punitive sexual violence has thus come to be routinely deployed in the course of various counter-insurgency operations.

REFERENCES

Ambedkar, Babasaheb, Dr. 1995. *Writings and Speeches, Volume 14, Dr Ambedkar and the Hindu Code Bill, Part I and Part II.* New Delhi: Dr. Ambedkar Foundation.

Ambedkar, Babasaheb, Dr. 1990. *Writings and Speeches, Volume 8, Reprint of Pakistan or the The Partition of India.* New Delhi: Dr. Ambedkar Foundation.

Butalia, Urvashi. 1998. *The Other Side of Silence: Voices from the Partition of India.* New Delhi: Viking Penguin India.

Caroll, Lucy. 1987. 'The Muslim Woman's Right to Divorce', *Manushi* (38). http://www.manushi-india.org/pdfs_issues/PDF%20files%20 38/the_muslim_woman's_right_to_divorce.pdf (accessed 15 Novomber 2015)

Kidwai, Ayesha. *The Abducted Woman in the House: Newspaper and Parliamentary Discussions, 1947–56*; https://www.academia. edu/5143344/The_Abducted_Woman_in_the_House_Newspaper_ and_Parliamentary_Discussions_1947-1956 (accessed 15 November 2015).

Menon, Ritu. 2004. 'Do Women Have a Country?' in Rada Ivekovic and Julie Mostov (eds.), *Gender and Nation.* New Delhi: Zubaan.

Menon, Ritu. (with Kamla Bhasin). 1998. *Borders And Boundaries: Women in India's Partition,* New Delhi: Kali for Women.

Newbigin, Eleanor. 2013. *The Hindu Family and the Emergence of Modern India: Law, Citizenship and Community,* Cambridge: Cambridge University Press.

Patel, Kamla. Uma Randera (transl.). 2006. *Torn from the Roots: A Partition Memoir,* New Delhi: Women Unlimited.

Sinha, Chitra. 2012. *Debating Patriarchy: The Hindu Code Bill Controversy in India (1941–1956),* New Delhi: Oxford University Press.

Part 11

Part II.

5

Sexual Violence and the New Nation
The Limits to Speech

The discussion so far has focused on historical moments—in the Indian context—that enabled public speech about sexual violence during the first half of the twentieth century. During this entire time, what was not addressed was the following: the sexual violence experienced by women who belonged to underprivileged and disenfranchised communities, whose daily experience of sexual humiliation and discrimination had as much to do with the social order that considered them low and beholden to those above them in the hierarchy, as it had to do with the uneven conditions of matrimony and property-lessness. To be sure, the criminal law on rape addressed violence that awaited the socially powerless, but only as an individuated crime, and not as one that was constitutive of the social structure that placed socially and economically vulnerable women at the sexual service of dominant caste men, whether landed or otherwise.

Dr Ambedkar's understanding in this context is instructive. He held that social reform initiatives in the past had addressed the caste Hindu family, concerned as they were with the wrongs suffered by upper caste Hindu women. In his view, social reform had to do more. It had to, necessarily, interrogate and transform the caste system. As he argued time and again, the graded inequality that characterized caste divisions was kept alive by keeping castes apart. The imposition of the law of endogamy, which ensured that marriages across castes did not happen, secured this apart-ness. To remedy this state of affairs, enabling legal norms and provisions were required. The Constitution, with its Bill of Rights, and the Hindu Code Bill, which enabled new norms of marriage into existence, where caste ceased to be relevant, and which endowed women with the freedom to exit unhappy marriages, thought Dr Ambedkar, would assist in challenging the hierarchy of caste.

Yet, Dr Ambedkar was also deeply aware that the law was only one instrument of change, and a rather limited one at that. At best, law can create appropriate contexts for socially oppressed groups to assert their justice claims. As he had argued decades earlier, it cannot persuade people to cultivate feeling, respect or social affection for others, all of which are lacking in caste society. It was the business of human beings, acting together, to achieve these particular ends. Dr Ambedkar understood action that sought to instill social affection and comradeship, in short, fraternity as central to democratic practice. To him democracy was not only a political idea, but a socially powerful one as well—it stood for social fellowship, and to serve the ends of democracy, both political as well as social, freedom and equality had to be realized. Legal protocols could facilitate the former, but the latter, which he considered a necessary condition for the realization of democracy in all its fulsomeness, could only be done through active social persuasion, argument, protest and movement, and a radical new vision of human subjectivity, relationships and action.

If we are to address the question of sexual violence in the light of Dr Ambedkar's reasoning, it ought to be clear that sexual hurt was recognized as a problem only in the context of women's status in the family, and often this was the caste Hindu or upper class family—raising the age of consent was a measure that was meant to elevate her role as wife and mother. As we saw in an earlier chapter, the experiences of women in lower caste and so-called untouchable families were not germane to the discussion about women's rights. Further, the rights of women outside marriage, even when addressed, did not possess the same resonance—and were often invoked to ensure social health and well-being, and not on their own account. When more expansive legal measures were sought—and they were outlined in the course of the Hindu Code Bill debates—the subject of reform was the individual woman, unmarked by caste and class. The right to property, a marriage of one's choice, divorce and adoption assumed that the rights-bearing female citizen was one who could assert her claims to equality in the context of her relationship to men in the propertied family, but chiefly in the precincts of the State. That is, the State was to be her addressee, which meant that the family as a context for debate and discussion to do with her status was left to its own devices, until and unless it came into conflict with the law. Further, women's rights in the context of their relationship to community, to the caste of their birth, and the consequent demarcation of rights that they experienced were not addressed.

In independent India, this conundrum to do with family, caste, class, gender and rights acquired a particular edge. With the piecemeal enactment of laws to do with marriage, property and divorce in the 1950s, both civil society and the State appeared confident that they had, indeed, 'settled' the women's question. All that remained was that the State act in a just manner when it came to the justice claims of its marginal citizens. The manner in which family, caste and class arranged sexual fates and identities remained a matter of address for and in law, and was not debated as vigorously in the public domain. What did this mean for violent sexual crimes committed against poor, lower caste, dalit and adivasi women, or for that matter sexual crimes that debased women in marked ways on account of their caste status?

In this chapter I address this question by looking at two contexts that enabled speech about sexual violence: the first has to do with the law and courts, but my concern here is not with legal detail; rather I am interested in asking questions about what the law and State make of sexual violence and the manner in which their responses are mirrored—or not—by social prejudice and common sense. In the second half of this chapter, I look at radical political practice of social and political movements of the underclass and subordinate castes. Did these contexts enable speech about sexual violence in ways that the law and State do not and could not?

As a postscript to this chapter, I would like to look briefly at the decade of the 1940s-60s in Pakistan and Sri Lanka—to point to the manner in which, as in India, women's concerns during this period were mediated through an appeal to the Nation-State and all that it purportedly stood for. It was as if the possibilities of civil speech that addressed violent realities were guaranteed by the very existence of a newly constituted Nation-State, and one that had been wrested from colonial rule.

***

The independent Indian State was not a 'new' entity. It was a product of colonial history and had come into existence over a period of time, and on account of various Acts of rule that constituted it. The Constitution that marked it as a republic was one important moment in that genealogy. Secondly, the independent Indian State was not merely a normative entity. It had an institutional life and history of its own, shaped not merely by ideas but by the mess of practice and the caprice of individuals, whether legislators, jurists and advocates, bureaucrats or policemen; as well as by the play of class and caste interests. As far as matters to do with women's rights and entitlements were concerned, the State's personnel were not just men who 'read' the law and principles of justice and equality into all that they said and did. They were flesh and blood individuals, many of whom were socially privileged, being mostly from the upper and dominant castes. To be sure there were reformers amongst them, even radical men, but it would be naïve to imagine that as a class, government employees heeded the call of the republic. On the other hand, when the opportunity afforded it, some amongst this class of men did not aver from drawing on the reserve of impunity that social privilege and State power brought with it.

It is this everyday life of the republic, the quotidian functioning of the State, both in terms of how its institutions worked and how its personnel conducted themselves in the course of carrying out their duties, and otherwise, that merit attention. For, when not challenged by social demands and debates, the State in its everyday guise could and did mirror the violence and inequality that structured society.

I would like to draw attention in this context to a rather notorious instance of sexual violence that went to the courts in 1957. This happened in the first decade of independence, and one of the judgments associated with the case went on to make judicial history. My interest in it, though, is not on account of this. Rather, I wish to use the case to draw attention to the everyday life of the independent State—whose officers could and did take refuge in the social 'protection' afforded by their caste and professional status to escape accountability for even grievous crimes such as rape and murder.

Known as Rao Harnarain Singh vs. the State, 1957, the case at hand had to do with the alleged commission of a crime of gang rape by three men, two of whom were government employees. Harnarain Singh was an advocate and Additional Public Prosecutor at Gurgaon, and Ch. Mauji Ram was Deputy Superintendent Jail, Gurgaon. The third accused was Balbir Singh. All three had got together one evening in Harnarain Singh's house for a celebration, since one of them was going away on a transfer. Kalu Ram, who lodged with Harnarain Singh and was a servant in his house, was recently married to a 19-year-old. In the course of the evening, he was cajoled and coerced into bringing his young bride to the three men, who wished to be 'entertained' by her—and this resulted in them raping her. She had protested vehemently when told what was expected of her, but neither her reluctance nor her husband's pleading proved to be of any avail. She died in the course of the night and her body was cremated with undue haste. Amidst rumours of what had transpired at Harnarain Singh's house, all three men were arrested on charges of rape and murder.

Even as the case was pending trial, the accused applied for bail, and when refused, petitioned the Supreme Court, with their lawyer arguing their case on the following grounds. There was no body to be examined to establish a case for murder. The charge of rape cannot be substantiated, and in any case in the absence of a body, evidence of violence cannot be established. Further, the accused are respectable men and deserving of bail. The presiding judge summarised the defense lawyer's argument thus: 'The girl was produced for the satisfaction of the carnal desires of Rao Harnarain Singh and his guests, with the consent of the girl's husband Kalu Ram.... The girl was also a consenting party and she surrendered her body to the three persons willingly and with the approval and at the bidding of her husband.... She was a grown up girl of 19 years, and a married woman, and death could not result in consequence of sexual intercourse with her by three persons. Her death ... was fortuitous and probably due to sudden failure of the heart.... Rao Harnarain Singh and his guests were having "a good time" and had gathered there for a little bit of "gaiety and enjoyment"'(AIR 1958 P H 123, 1958 CriLJ 563).

The judge—Justice Tek Chand—refused to accept such grounds as valid. 'I cannot accept the suggestion of S. Bhagat Singh Chawla [defense lawyer] that Kalu Ram, the husband of the girl, was a pander who had willingly agreed to minister to the baser passions of his clients. I cannot even persuade myself to the view that his wife was a dissolute young woman who willingly lent her body to her ravishers to gratify her own lustful propensities' (*ibid*). He further said: 'The orgy of lust and debauchery to which the accused are said to have abandoned themselves was an act of unmitigated reprobates rather than of the so called "respectable persons"' (*ibid*). He then went on to note that to claim that the victim 'consented' to being thus assaulted was a misnomer. Ultimately he denied bail to the accused.

This judgment has since become well known for the judge's elaboration of the meaning of consent in matters of sexual violence, and his laying down of principles that help differentiate the conditions of passive submission from active consent. Having specified these principles in unequivocal terms, the judge nevertheless made it clear that his refusal of bail must not be construed to mean an opinion on the guilt or otherwise of the accused. The balance Justice Chand sought to establish between the gravity of the offence and the rights of the accused to a fair trial was a delicate one. For one, even as he conceded that it is the trial court that must decide on complicity, he did not desist from characterizing the offence itself as morally reprehensible ('an orgy of lust and debauchery'; interestingly the defense lawyer also agreed that his client had committed immoral acts, but argued that he ought not to be denied bail on that account). The judge also expressed a perceptible moral shudder at the circumstances of the crime ('I cannot bring myself... etc.'). Clearly the hideous nature of the crime, as well as the humble and powerless state of the victim underlay his moral reasoning; and it is this that lends his arguments about consent a powerful ethical resonance.

This ethical register stands illumined across time for what it tells us about the ways of governmental power and its victims, in this instance, a couple from a lower class, if not caste, who appeared to have been coerced into a state of stupefaction. Further, we also are brought face to face with the nature of violence, which even if linked to debauchery is not therefore framed exclusively in terms of 'sex', but is instead located within the ambit of power—the argument the judgment offers to distinguish consent from submission proceeds from such a context. Kalu Ram's low and dependant status, his powerlessness, his wife's indignant protest at what was expected from her, her being overcome by her husband 'agreeing' to lend his wife and her unnatural death, preceded by loud cries and finally Kalu Ram retracting his testimony that indicted the accused, under pressure: all these are taken note of in the judgment. Speech about sexual violence—in a judicial context—that places it in the context of an exercise of power with impunity is made possible by the nature of the crime itself. In turn, such speech helped frame a routinely abusive practice as a 'crime' that needed to be interrogated.

Interestingly, the judgment does not comment on the offices held by the accused or their social and caste status, except to note that they were men who could influence the investigation. This appears to have been a factor in public discussions of the case, as is evident from contemporary newspaper reports. In fact the latter were annoying enough for Harnarain Singh to file contempt proceedings against the editor of an Urdu paper for 'tarnishing' his name while reporting the alleged rape and murder. Singh accused the editor of deliberately mobilizing public opinion against him, while building sympathy for the accused. This case too came to the notice of Justice Chand, who then passed strictures against the newspaper and slapped a fine on it.

In a sense, the two judgments taken together are evidence of the possibilities as well as limits of excellent and ethical judicial reasoning that yet stops this side of social commentary and observation. In his judgment on the contempt petition, Justice Chand insisted that freedom of expression cannot be absolute and that speculative news reports cannot be expected to have a bearing on the workings of the law. Courts, he observed, ought to carefully exclude from consideration 'facts and circumstances, other than those which are presented in a formal manner, according to the rules of procedure and evidence. The decision rests on the material on the record, and extraneous matters, howsoever palpable, or seemingly important, are kept severely outside the judicial purview' (AIR 1958 P H 273, 1958 CriLJ 952).

Fair and right as this seems, it also mitigates considerations of entrenched and systemic power structures and how these impede and organize justice transactions. In this case, the accused were upper caste or dominant caste men, with two of them being State employees. Their soliciting of the girl appeared to them entirely 'natural' and the manner they dealt with her death was not only callous but expressed routine disdain and contempt for one lower than themselves in the class and caste hierarchy. As far as sexual violence against poor, working class or lower caste women is concerned, it remains a truism that in all instances, the crime is entwined with class dominance and caste-empowered masculine authority. Except in rare cases, where the larger context in which the crime is committed is hard to ignore, the law systematically reads sexual violence as an individuated act. Social meanings invested in female sexuality and the uses of sexual violence, the caste and class authority and hegemony it expresses and affirms, remain outside the purview of the law. It is useful to remind ourselves in this context that sexual humiliation and violence in caste society, to paraphrase Anupama Rao, serves a 'pedagogic' function: it demonstrates 'normative' behaviour and helps perpetuate upper caste authority and hegemony.

This brings me to my second example: the Sirsagaon case. In 1963, dalit women from Sirsagaon village in the Aurangabad district of Maharashtra were dragged out of their homes, stripped, beaten and paraded naked all the way to the village square. Their crime, ostensibly, was drawing water from a common well. The accused were identified, arrested and the District Court convicted them of illegal trespass, violence and molestation. It is not clear if the case went on appeal. The District Court judge was horrified by what the women had endured, and refused to accept the alibis provided by the defense. He also railed against untouchability and the inhumanity it sanctioned. Yet he could not bring himself to refer to the actual act of the women being paraded naked or dwell on the larger circumstances that had resulted in them being shamed thus.

For in truth they were punished not for accessing water, but because one of them had refused the sexual advances of a dominant caste man and then complained to the man's wife about it. The wife had counselled discretion, but her husband continued to harass not merely the woman he had propositioned but her family; whereupon one of her male kin visited his home and again spoke to the wife, only this time he asked her to imagine how it would be, if it was she who was thus being solicited. She appeared to have been taken aback at his reasoning and complained to her husband about it. In turn he went with a group of people to 'teach' a lesson to the dalit family that dared be insouciant. It is said that when the dalit women were paraded naked, the wife was witness and appeared to have relished the humiliation. Clearly, she did not perceive her sexual vulnerability as something that bound her to other woman. Rather, even the mention of her vulnerability seemed a challenge to her sexual and caste identity.

The constitutive violence of the caste-gender order, and the fact that sexual humiliation was intended and used to affirm caste relationships of dominance and control, escaped the good judge's reasoning, for these were matters that the law could not take hold of or address. In this sense, sexual violence was not spoken of and when Anupama Rao interviewed one of the women thirty years later, beyond a point, she was unable to speak about what transpired that day. The burden of shame and stigma heaped on her and others, both because they were dalits and women and the implicit shaming of their families and caste were matters that were at once intimate and public. Their intimate selves were publicly dishonoured, yet if they were to call attention to it as a crime, as an act of violation, they would have to perforce say what is never said on these occasions, and thereby compromise their sense of self. Freeing and liberatory speech that puts by stigma was not possible because of the wilful nature of the crime itself, which worked its effects by shaming its victims. Since the perpetrators of this shame did not stand revealed as such, and were arrested on other counts, the crime they commissioned could not be spoken of.

In both the cases discussed in this section, the accused are recognized as wrong-doers. But in either instance, the everyday life and contexts of sexual violence eluded critique and expression in law and in the discourses of the State. However, the presence of a national government, a State that was avowedly republican, did render certain sorts of speech about sexual violence possible—and this is important to acknowledge as well.

I turn now to the practice of social and political movements that have sought to forefront sexual violence as something that is central to the exercise of economic and social power. Such movements, in essence, are republican in intent and in them, the people are sovereign in an immediate sort of way. Much as they have looked to the State for redressal, with respect to sexual violence, people have also looked to these movements for succor.

***

I consider here two movements, one that emerged before the attainment of independence and continued to be salient thereafter, and another that had its origin in late colonial India. I examine briefly their engagement with sexual violence—to demonstrate what republican practice affords, and what it inhibits.

In the campaigns initiated by Dr Ambedkar's movements (from the late 1920s onwards), sexual humiliation and oppression imposed on dalit women were challenged: the dedication of lower caste women to ritual prostitution, and the assignment of dalit women as entertainers for the upper castes were perceived as sources of imposed stigma which marked dalit women as sexually available. As we have seen, to be sexually available as a caste or race compromises one's personhood: a slave woman or a dalit woman cannot claim humanity or demand that she be treated with dignity and respect. Even if violently dealt with, that act need not be consequential. To refuse this identity, one had to literally exit from it, refuse practices that construct a person as promiscuous yet untouchable. Dr Ambedkar was clear that dalit women must leave behind such vocations, and seek to be like other—caste Hindu—women, whose respectability was beyond reproach. In other words, he and others in his movement argued that like other women, dalit women must have a right to respectability, that is, a right to matrimony and the—admittedly limited—personhood that comes with it.

In a context where to be 'respectable' depends on consistently marking oneself off from the 'disreputable', the right to respectability becomes in essence a public right, an affirmation of equality for those deemed disreputable, not dissimilar from the right to enter temples. One might or might not want to enter temples to offer worship, but nevertheless the right to do so must be available. Similarly those who left behind stigmatized lives may or may not enter chaste matrimony, yet they must possess the right that is refused them.

Dr Ambedkar, it must be kept in mind, did not set great store either by respectable conjugality or the right to enter temples as necessary conditions for active dalit citizenship. These were important rights, but more important was an affirmation of one's right to civic personhood, to fraternity, to be counted as equally and coevally human in every sense. Sadly, such a discourse of personhood has not always been central to struggles to do with dalit women's sexual hurt. Often a discourse of 'honour' which has as much to do with community perceptions of being stigmatised as it has to do with women's sense of their oppressed sexuality, takes over and this inevitably rewrites the particularity of women's experiences into a more generalized description of community hurt. Thus, dalit women's speech becomes fundamental to countering impunity; the challenge in this instance is to speak in ways that call attention to sexual as well as caste hurt, while refusing to be bound by notions of community honour and dishonor.

Such speech would emerge in and through the resonant voices of dalit feminists, particularly in Maharashtra in the 1970s and after. Yet there were precedents. As early as 1908, Shivubai Vallad Lakshman Jadhav-Sonkamble, a murali, or one mandated to be a performer—a status that morphed often into being sexually available—wrote a letter to *Somavanshiya Mitra*, a Marathi dalit newspaper, responding to a dalit man who castigated muralis as social evils whose sexual promiscuity was ruining the community. Shivubai pointed out that girls were dedicated into being muralis by their fathers, and that dalit men must acknowledge their role in the making of this institution. She also noted that to escape such an eventuality, many dalit girls and women had converted to Islam and Christianity.

In the years to come, dalit women would argue their case even more emphatically. They would point to the structures of caste coercion that rendered them economically, socially and sexually vulnerable as well as to familial authority and customs which rendered them vulnerable within their own communities. Such speech intersected as well as contended with concerns articulated by non-dalit feminists, most of whom were from dominant if not privileged castes, and whose voices were resonant from the late 1960s and early 1970s.

I now turn to my second example: the Telengana armed struggle of the 1940s. Radical peasant and agricultural workers' movements that emerged across the Indian sub-continent in the 1930s and were very active through the 1940s, had to reckon with sexual violence as a feature of relations of production—for sexual servitude was what was expected from lower caste and particularly dalit women who were viewed as not merely labourers, but chattel slaves, available to landlords at all times. Further, in these struggles, where radicalized lower caste peasants and dalit agricultural labourers clashed with landlords and their henchmen, counter-violence was inevitably gendered: women were sexually attacked, humiliated, brutally dealt with... Importantly, it was women who insisted on such crimes being addressed, as is evident from women's testimonies to do with the great Telangana struggle (1946–51), which unfolded under the leadership of the Communist Party of India.

But this does not mean that speech about sexual violence, in the wake of political struggles that understood it to be a systemic crime, was easy; rather it was fraught. While sexual violence was understood as an expression of unequal and exploitative social relations, or individual moral turpitude, it was seldom viewed as having to do with a man's easy assumption of sexual authority. On the one hand, when party cadres imposed themselves on working class women who granted them shelter and fed them, they were taken to task and punished. Some were even put to death for having crossed the line as far as sexual violence was concerned. The Communist Party also outlined a moral code which forbade promiscuous behaviour, either by men or women. However, there persisted a measure of unease, with respect to thinking through the category of the 'sexual' as such, and of the manner in which sexual relations are consistently shaped by unexamined notions of male sexual prerogative even within progressive political organizations.

Thus, when women activists had to negotiate sexual or emotional demands from fellow fighters or comrades, they were not sure about the limits to comradeship and commitment or about situations and relationships that straddled intimate and political spaces and relationships. If one had to remain moral, as the party expected cadres to be, what does one do with persistent sexual attention that men impose on women, or with women's own needs? As a Telangana activist noted, for women, it seemed that the only option available in such circumstances was marriage—which defined and regulated sexual decorum.

Once again we see, as we did with the reform debates, that permissible speech about sexual violence is possible only within bounds, even if the context is one of radical political transformation. Sexual violence viewed as part of a system of economic and social exploitation could be spoken of and this was important, answering as it did to the experience of thousands of peasant and labouring women. On the other hand, the domain of the 'sexual', as such, was not seen as one that is as structured by power and authority, as economic and social domains. Sexual violence remained something that happened 'out there', in unregenerate feudal worlds, and it did not seem that it could have anything to do with 'everyday' social and sexual lives, as they exist all around us, including in spaces deemed progressive and transformative. In post-1960s India, as elsewhere, this would emerge as a pertinent issue, as Indian women associated with the Left joined the worldwide debate to decide the future of what, ironically, has been referred to as the 'unhappy marriage between Marxism and feminism'.

***

As in India, the women's question in Pakistan was framed by what may be achieved in a nascent Nation-State, and through the 1940s and 1950s we find women working towards and lobbying for women's place in the legislature, for an expansion of opportunities for education and for more equitable laws. Women's groups that had been active from the Partition days, and which were involved in rehabilitation measures following the violence of the 1940s, particularly the All-Pakistan Women's Association, were active in pushing the cause of legal reform and as a result of their sustained work, during the Presidency of Ayub Khan, the Family Law Ordinance was passed in 1961. This made the registration of marriages compulsory, protected women from arbitrarily contracted polygamous marriages, and guaranteed their right to divorce. The women's wing of the Communist party was also present in public life, and had its own women's organization that worked on issues to do with labour and wages.

Generally speaking, during the first decades of Pakistan's existence, women's sense of their entitlements and rights were framed by a broader impulse towards democracy, which, tragically, was continuously suspended in the years after independence. This has proved consequential for how issues to do with gender injustice got framed in Pakistan. The 1960s were important in this respect: this decade witnessed women being active in labour circles and present in the various movements for a repeal of military rule—instituted by Ayub Khan in 1958—and for a restoration of democracy. In all these contexts, where women's status was discussed in terms of what they were entitled to, by way of education, marriage and conjugal rights and remedies, the inequitable conditions of their lives, and the violence that underwrote it, were undoubtedly spoken of.

However, the manner in which kinship, community identity and class interests intersected to stifle women's choices, with respect to marriage, property, mobility and education, was not perhaps as avidly debated. Mediated through the trope of honour, which had to be heeded even in the face of death, women's place in the kin and clan structure of communities in different parts of Pakistan remained outside the purview of legal debates to do with equality and equity. For one, the trope of honour was not simply that and was rendered sacrosanct by its association with religious duty. Secondly, as Shahnaz Rouse notes, women who were active in public spaces in the 1940s-50s decade and in fact until the mid-1960s did not dwell on the iniquitous nature of marriage as such, or on the fact that women's bodies were transacted in ways that had to do with sexual belonging, clan cohesion, property and the settling of scores between different groups.

These issues would emerge as central to the women's movements that emerged in the 1970s and make for compelling debates around issues to do with women's place, sexuality, violence and ethnic or national identity. Interestingly, as in India, for the first two decades after independence and the making of nations, the Nation-State was viewed as a neutral arbiter, at worst, of matters to do with the common, including women's good, and, at best, as a context for bringing about reform and change in the lives of women. Whatever its practices, this image of the State remained in place until the 1970s, when it was challenged in ever so many ways.

In Sri Lanka, the national and sovereign State that took over from the British was constituted on the basis of what it sought to keep out of its borders. In this instance, it was the so-called Indian or Estates Tamils—brought from the former Madras Province to labour on colonial plantations—who were deemed unworthy of citizenship, and several thousands were forcibly repatriated to India. Subsequently, the State embarked on a policy of 'Sinhalasation': in 1956, Sinhala was declared the official language, which led to permanent disaffection on the part of Tamils and other minorities. I will return to this later, but I would like to note here that as in Pakistan, the immediate years after independence in Sri Lanka proved consequential for women: while labouring plantation Tamils continued to suffer the ignominy of low pay, sexual exploitation and the denial of civil rights, middle class Tamil women from the north of the island and Sinhala women found themselves benefitting from their government's stance on women's education and employment. Women in factories were unionized, those in State service were active in debating public issues, and by the 1970s, a modicum of feminist awareness, if not political presence, was present on the island.

***

In India, Pakistan and Sri Lanka, the onset of independence was marked by violence and exclusion, but the years that followed, which might be characterized as the 'nation building' years, appeared hopeful, even if troubled. The post-colonial Nation-State seemed an ally of democracy, though it was not free of the hold of class and caste interests and prejudices. Its sovereign character still appeared to rest in a newly freed people, even though personnel of the State attempted to define its interests in less than republican terms. For women, concerned about their rights as citizens and determined to address the ills, deprivation and cruelty they endured, the State did appear an important arbiter of their well-being, even though it allowed and enabled only certain sorts of speech about violence, justice and equality.

REFERENCES

Jayawardene, Kumari, 1985. *Feminism in Sri Lanka, 1975-1985*, Colombo: Women's International Resource Exchange.

Lalitha. K, et. al. 1989. *'We Were Making History…': Life Stories of Women in the Telengana People's Struggle*, New Delhi: Kali for Women.

Rao, Anupama. 2009. *The Caste Question: Dalits and the Politics of Modern India*, New Delhi: Permanent Black.

Government of India. *Rao Harnarain Singh, Sheoji Singh … vs The State*.1957. AIR 1958 P H 123, 1958 CriLJ 563.

Government of India. *Rao Harnarain Singh Sheoji Singh vs Gumani Ram Arya*. 1958. AIR 1958 P H 273, 1958 CriLJ 952.

Rouse, Shahnaz. 1984. *Women's Movements in Contemporary Pakistan: Results and Prospects*, University of Wisconsin, Working Papers 74,

December. http://pdf.usaid.gov/pdf_docs/PNAAY061.pdf (accessed 15 November 2015).

Rouse, Shahnaz. 1988. *Women's movements in Pakistan: State, Class, Gender.* Women Living Under Muslim Law. http://www.wluml. org/sites/wluml.org/files/import/english/pubs/pdf/dossier3/D3-06-Pakistan.pdf (accessed 15 November 2015).

6

Challenging Class and State

The Sexual Politics of Armed Resistance

The 1960s were a troubled decade in the Indian subcontinent. War, famine, class war, and challenges to the unitary identity of Nation-States: the promises of republicanism and independence appeared to have come undone, especially in India. But these were also important years of policy-making and nation-building: the Five Year Plans got under way in India, the Green Revolution was not only a possibility but was actively implemented in parts of the country, and various infrastructural projects to do with power, road-building and expansion of heavy industry were also put in place. Clearly, these developments were related: changes in the economy challenged and caused deep fissures in rural ways of life. Migration, displacement, and Left organizing in different parts of the country brought forth unexpected crises in the republic.

This was also a time when national sovereignty across the sub-continent was called into question by a slew of developments: successive military governments in Pakistan, rumbles of Bangla nationalism in East Pakistan, trouble in Kashmir which brought India and Pakistan into a disastrous short-term war and the slow consolidation of anti-State opinion amongst both Sinhala-speaking Leftists and Tamil nationalists in Sri Lanka. In this chapter and the next I dwell on developments in India and the rest of South Asia that revealed the dark underside of the post-colonial State. Yet State terror was not the only context in which sexual violence emerged as a cause for concern: matters to do with sexuality and violence found expression in radical movements that challenged caste and class arrangements and State authority that endorsed the latter. In what follows, I examine the emergence of a militant Left movement in eastern India, the Naxalbari movement, for what it enabled and encouraged by way of speech about sexual violence; and by the same token, what it rendered 'unspeakable'. My purpose in doing so is two-fold: to underscore the manner in which justice movements which nurture millenarian ideals understood matters to do with sexuality and sexual violence; and to focus on State terror that seeks to upend revolutionary terror and how that made for extreme—and sexualized—violence.

***

In terms of advancing the question of women's dignity and bodily integrity in the 1960s, militant Left movements in India proved catalytic: agricultural servitude of which sexual control of working class dalit women's bodies formed an important element, was challenged as in the Srikakulam struggle (1968) in Andhra Pradesh, in which hill adivasi labourers—girijans—set themselves against entrenched land and state interests in the region. The violence that women endured at the hands of men on whose fields they laboured, as well as at the hands of labour contractors and state officials, was addressed, with women coming forward to join the movement on this account. Similar campaigns gained momentum in West Bengal and Bihar, from the late 1960s onward and extended into the following decade.

I would like to discuss in this context the Naxalbari uprising of 1967 and its aftermath. This was a militant peasant struggle that began in a region of West Bengal that resonated with the memory of the great Tebhaga agrarian struggle of the 1940s, and which gave birth to Left-wing militancy of a distinctive kind. Known since then as Naxalism, after the region where the armed struggle broke out, it has come to define the contours of radical Left resistance in India. Naxalism provoked the Indian State to indulge in brutality that was unprecedented, relentless, and which was directed as much at female political persons as it was at male activists. In the sheer viciousness with which State violence targeted the body of the Naxalite, it posed challenges to the very meaning of bodily integrity. As far as women were concerned, sexual violence and bodily violence stood confounded, and as for violence against men, it led to acts of grotesque and gendered bodily humiliation and suffering. It seems to me that torture of this kind, which makes it impossible to separate sexual from other forms of abuse, created new problems for public speech about impunity (as the last section of this chapter argues). I am concerned here as much with how sexual violence was understood in the movement, as I am with the question of State torture: in effect both could be spoken of in some ways, and not others.

***

I start with a brief account of the Naxalbari struggle, and women's presence in it, so that we get a sense of the gendered boundaries that women—and their male comrades—crossed when they turned militants, as well as what limited them. It seems to me that knowledge of the 'everyday life of gender' in movements helps us identify better those impasses that mark public expression to do with extreme violence; it also throws into relief the violence of the State.

The Naxalites, as those who took part in the armed peasant struggle came to be called, gradually came to be directed by an urban middle class leadership. In the Bengal countryside the movement was taken forward by lower-caste peasants and adivasis, invested in gaining control over crop they had helped cultivate, in wresting land away from hated landlords and challenging entrenched practices of social control and humiliation. Elsewhere, it attracted young, middle and lower middle class, intellectually and politically inclined youth, including young women from Calcutta and also smaller moffusil towns. Eventually the movement shifted focus—and moved away from mobilizing peasants, labourers and their class supporters to concentrate on the practice of 'individual annihilation', or the killing of those identified as class enemies. This led to the making—and glorifying—of a culture of extreme political violence that ultimately destroyed its votaries even as it had to reckon with unprecedented police brutality.

Peasant and adivasi women were active in the struggle from its earliest days: they braved police violence, were part of land and grain appropriation campaigns, played couriers and offered shelter to urban activists. Several wielded guns as well, and in some instances killed individual men who were known tyrants in the region. Many of them drew on local traditions of female political valour, honed in the course of earlier struggles, especially memories of Tebhaga. This was particularly so amongst the Santhals and the Munda people. An intergenerational history structured their sense of political worth and identity.

However, in what has come to be official memory and history of the movement, the nature, content and conditions of rural women's activism have not been sufficiently acknowledged; in fact several urban male leaders from that time assert that women's participation was meagre, yet in the same breath agree that women were very useful: they provided food and shelter, they were effective couriers... Very few leaders remember women's peasant activism and on the rare occasion that they do, they see peasant women activists as being aware of practical concerns to do with advancing the movement, but not necessarily possessed of political consciousness. As for urban middle class women activists, they feature in the memory of most male leaders as romantic, immature and given to hero-worship of young men that they admired and on whose account they joined the movement.

It is evident, as Mallarika Sinha Roy has argued, howsoever Naxalite men engaged politically with their female comrades during the course of the struggle, their expressive sense of what women did hinged on unexamined notions of women's place and role, in political movements and in society at large. Even in the face of contrary evidence, for instance, when confronted with women's ability to fight back or to actually kill an enemy, male leaders explained such actions as instances of personal vendetta for sexual hurt that the women had endured. This meant that they could not, in fact, did not possess the linguistic means and political sensitivity to view women as conscious political actors, with their own political investment in the struggle and who were as determined as men to render the grain and land question their own.

Of course not all male leaders were partial: peasant leaders such as Kanu Sanyal were very aware of the roles played by women, as were other lesser known figures active in the districts, but as Mallarika Sinha Roy notes, it is the urban, specifically 'Calcutta'-centred memory of the movement that has informed its history, and this memory is less mindful of female presence and participation and more inclined to accommodate women's presence within a narrative that privileges the impassioned male intellectual-activist. On the other hand, women's sense of their roles in the movement has turned out to be startlingly different. Sinha Roy notes that there were both young and older women who were active in the peasant ranks, and the latter mentored the former, drawing on their experience in older struggles. They thus inserted what was clearly an unprecedented moment of resistance, on account of its scale and the repression it invited, into a continuity of struggles, to do with wage increments, better working conditions, rights over cultivable land, for better roads, homes, and against the everyday humiliations and violence inflicted on women in the name of caste and gender. This bringing together of the everyday and the exceptional was unique, notes Sinha Roy, and points to the specific nature of women's activism.

In cities, middle and lower middle class women, eager to be part of what was clearly understood to be a total movement against oppression, had less defined roles to play compared to their peasant counterparts. They were welcome as message-bearers, could be useful propagandists, and in some instances were supported in their attempts to mobilise people into joining the movement. Some of them enthusiastically decided to give up their own caste and class privilege and took residence in slums, went to work in factories, or moved to the countryside. The party that emerged out of the movement—the Communist Party of India (Marxist-Leninist)—was not prepared either in an organizational or ideological sense to consistently support such work, but nevertheless, some women at least went ahead with what they had chosen to do. Their sense of vulnerability notwithstanding, they made the best of situations—but as an activist Sinha Roy spoke to years later noted, they had to leave their chosen arenas of struggle when it became clear that their comrade hosts realized they could not be responsible for the sexual safety of urban women activists.

Significantly, this sense of feeling imperiled was something that was not easy for women activists to either accept or speak of, even when interviewed years later: a middle class woman who went to live amongst peasants was hesitant in explaining her unease, and her expressions were inhibited. Admitting that not all male comrades were supportive, she noted that 'You know when a young woman is alone and when she is travelling and living alone … there will be problems… actually then for a woman human beings are far more dangerous than wild beasts… whether it is a Santhal village or any other village…' (Sinha Roy, 2011: 99).

In recounting an instance of sexual harassment, Srila Roy (in her study of the Naxalite question with respect to gender) observes that the woman in question rebuked her assailant for his behavior and counseled the right political line. The man in question being a leading organizer and from a 'subaltern' background meant that the party was less likely to view his behaviour for what it was, and more likely to condemn hers. In yet another instance the party blamed the woman, claiming that because she was upper class she found it easy to complain of a dark-skinned worker. Eventually when the woman was raped, the man had to be taken to account, but while he was reprimanded, his action was put down to unregenerate consciousness. It was as if the Naxalite male subject could be effectively disembodied and reduced to a category, in this instance of class.

On the other hand, if a complaint was strong enough to cast aspersions on the Naxalites' public identity, then action had to be taken, and often punitive action was preferred. Sinha Roy reminds us that such an approach was part of the problem: 'Their ... condemnation of sexual oppressors to death and their readiness to give life to secure women's honour reveal an undeniable core of violence in the benevolent, protective ideals of masculinity' (Sinha Roy: 123).

For many women in the movement a sense of sexual vulnerability was offset by the discovery of comradeship between men and women, and also with other women. The 'magic' of the movement did make it possible for urban women to forge deep ties with rural and adivasi women, or with working class women (amongst prisoners and in shelters). This did not mean that class and caste boundaries were not salient anymore. In a context where gender norms were not uniform and instead angled and shaped by social location, differences amongst women, in terms of responding to events or understanding certain situations remained, and mattered, just as comradeship did. An upper class and upper caste woman who went to work in a leather factory, to both declass herself and mobilise her fellow workers, discovered that her fellow workers' response to sexual advances made by male supervisors was not quite what she imagined. They appeared to view it as something that was part of their conditions of labour, and some of them clearly viewed the granting of sexual favours as a way of improving one's material prospects.

There were other issues that women had to contend with, chiefly to do with marriage and care of children. The party arranged marriages and presided over separations and divorces. It upheld the claims of revolutionary coexistence—people chose their partners and agreed to either live together, or announce that they were married. Sometimes they exchanged vows, using Mao's little red book. Marriage was not only about conjugality, it was made clear, and was meant to be a testament to revolutionary comradeship. Conjugal happiness, to do with romantic love and children was now seen as limited and revolutionary sacrifice defined the meaning of matrimony. That is, for the larger cause, all was to be put away: desire, children, family and kin obligations. Krishna Bandhopadhyay, a prominent woman activist, notes that it seemed to her then that men appeared capable of noble asceticism whereas she did not think she was quite as self-sacrificing and felt mortified on that account.

Yet even where marriage appeared transformed, it was not quite clear how it would be sustained over a period of time, as another activist notes. There were no given or formal modes of affirming marriage within the movement, and yet young people were expected to heed tacit moral codes. Living together was possible, yet there was the shadow of 'loose' behaviour that women had to be wary of. Further, marriages did not prove resilient, and many couples were estranged. In the opinion of at least one activist from the Naxalbari period, the more serious instances of estrangement had to do with urban men 'marrying' peasant women and leaving them. Then again, though marriage ties were loosely defined, when the husband or comrade with whom a woman lived, died in action or in police custody, she acquired the status of a martyr, and was marked as the keeper of a revolutionary's memory. Often, this meant that her choices, political or emotional, had to be subjugated to the symbol that she had become.

Child care was equally problematic. As Srila Roy points out with reference to Calcutta-based urban Naxalite women activists, young mothers, who could not count on family or kin networks to help with childcare, had to shoulder the burden of motherhood on their own or make do with minimal care arrangements. Further, if a mother were to display 'undue' concern that all was not well with her child, she could be censured for being bourgeois and individualistic.

Some of the Naxalite men who were interviewed years later on the question of women's presence in the movement were reflective on this count: they confessed that it did not occur to them that they ought to consciously address women, or consider them political beings like themselves: '([t]hough we had already read Engels' book and had a pretty clear idea about the way women became part of the male patriarch's property within the family, we never felt that we should make an extra effort to involve the women separately. Yes [...] you can say that we also treated the women as the property of our peasant male comrades. Now it seems strange that it never occurred to us' (Sinha Roy: 60).

Yet, it was not as if the gendered dimensions to political struggle were entirely absent in the Naxalite male political imagination. As we have seen, with respect to their attitude towards marriage, convention was upturned whereas sexual difference itself was not. Likewise, motherhood remained routinely sacrosanct. Gender proved germane to the Naxalite men's understanding of desire, and lust and violence as well. Thus for many of the ardent young male activists of that time, one of the more eloquent symbols of feudal oppression was the sexually exploited peasant or adivasi woman. Mallarika Sinha Roy quotes Charu Mazumdar to this effect: 'I have seen the barbaric sexual torture of the class enemy on the newly-wed Muslim peasant-bride. I have heard the pleading of her unarmed, unfortunate husband, 'Can you avenge this, Comrade?' (Sinha Roy: 77).

Mazumdar's sense of the peasant's plight, of one male comrade speaking to another about feudal violence, was not quite how women understood sexual violence. For one, they did not view themselves as wives that had to be protected. A Santhal woman recalled her role in the movement thus: 'I organized not only the Santhal women in our village but also the Bauri (a lower caste) women. We, women organized a procession to Surf (the district Head Quarter) when one of our comrades, Naba Bauri was captured by the police. You know, that procession of angry women actually engaged in a hand-to-hand skirmish with the police and forcibly released Naba!' (Sinha Roy: 109).

Secondly, peasant women's sense of sexual victimhood was not what urban male activists imagined it to be. As a leading male activist, ruminating over past events put it: '[o]ften peasant women were ruthlessly sexually exploited in those villages. It was very surprising to us that neither they themselves, nor their husbands ever urged us to take any revenge for that. They were far more occupied with the issue of capturing land. Sexual honour was important to us, but it was not a priority to them' (Sinha Roy 2003: 1-2).

The point is that unlike urban male activists who were horrified by sexual violence and saw themselves as fighting on behalf of women who had suffered it, labouring peasant and adivasi women experienced sexual exploitation along a continuum of other sorts of violence (as we saw with respect to the violence that women endured at the hands of the Khmer Rouge in Cambodia). In the male political imagination, sexual violence provided a trope as well as context to underscore their own heroism and sense of justice, whereas for women, especially peasant women, it was a condition of existence that had to be addressed and challenged and was; both as part of a system of agricultural servitude and as an objectionable act in itself. Peasant and adivasi women were determined to take on domestic violence as well, and to set terms and conditions to their men. But neither their actions, nor their sense of their own political worth were expressed in so many words, and even when they were, they did not recast the nature of public discussion about revolution that was in the air at that moment in history. So, in spite of women's presence, the gender of liberation remained male, and that is how it was encased in dominant public memory as well.

***

In this context, I wish to return to and address the question of women's political subjectivity: that in spite of women's roles, work, perceptions and political understanding, this subjectivity was defined either in terms of their dependent and supplementary status or their sexual victimhood. Since women were not viewed as political beings, but in terms of their 'feminine' character and roles, their work in the movement was marked as something that one could expect women to do, because they were women; the flipside of such reasoning was they were seldom trusted with political tasks that men did habitually. Mallarika Sinha Roy suggests that it is not that the Naxal men were particularly insensitive to gender or dismissive in their attitudes to women. But they did not imagine that sexual difference had to be interrogated, nor did they think this was an important political question. Then again, the turn taken by the struggle—from being a mass movement to one that annihilated individuals—foreclosed women's active participation in certain ways. Women were not seen and perhaps did not see themselves as carrying out acts of killing, for the most part. Besides, there were women—Krishna Bandhopadhyay and Shanti Munda, amongst them—who actively disagreed with the killing of class enemies and yet they had no space or presence to voice their dissent.

Within the normative world view of Naxalism, 'femininity', which was taken for granted, was central to the everyday life of Naxalism as women experienced it, and the restrictive norms that constituted it remained within the grey area of habit, norm and custom, and were not quite seen as diminishing personhood.

However, something changed when some women were picked up by the police, severely tortured and humiliated. The woman prisoner became a charged political subject, an embodied creature whose brutalized body was an indictment of the State, particularly its 'rapist' character. The spectacular violence of the State, it would appear, had become the measure of all violence against women. This viewpoint is present in other armed Left groups as well—witness the roll call of female martyrs from the rank of the Maoists in Andhra Pradesh and Chattisgarh, which that party seeks to maintain. While a poignant record of what women in the movement endured and had to endure at the hands of the State, this archive also makes us wonder at the everyday lives of women in militant Left movements, including those who were involved in the Naxalbari uprising; and if these movements, or for that matter women who were part of them, considered those experiences politically significant. Writing of Maoist adivasi women activists, Anuradha Ghandy had noted how they challenged discriminatory tribal customs once they were politicized—calling attention to the remaking of the everyday. Did this translate into a critical understanding of sexual politics as such? It is not clear.

By sexual politics, I mean the politics of sexual difference and sexuality, as it shapes and structures everyday life; where sexual difference is sewn into gesture and tone, defines intimacy and affection and renders female sexuality to the care and protection of men. Within Maoism, indeed within all revolutionary movements, what was questioned in this instance, and what was accepted as given? In practice, women refused to be bound by the logic of difference as we have seen, but we also saw that in Bengal, they had to negotiate the everyday on their own, with very little help or understanding from their male comrades, or for that matter, the party. Where they took to radical action, this remained unmarked or was accepted as an instance of revolutionary heroism, including by women revolutionaries, and not necessarily as something that unsettled gender roles or boundaries. In the event, the eloquent silences that mark female political expression and the evasions that mark male political understanding tell their own story.

***

Significantly, another sort of speech-making was made possible in the context of Bangla Naxalism: and one that would connect with effective speech against sexual violence in the years to come. Such speech emerged in the context of prosecuting against State terror and torture. In a sense, this was republican practice in the most fundamental sense of the word, and which pitted the citizen's sense of her rights and entitlements against the authority that the State exercised with impunity. But republican truth-telling, as we shall see, was shadowed by repressed trauma, sorrow and pain.

Of the many instances of torture and violence that remain in public memory from the heyday of police terror in the Bengal of the 1970s, the Archana Guha case is the best-known. She, her sister-in-law Latika and a friend Gauri were arrested in their homes. Later on, Latika's husband and Archana's brother Saumen was also arrested. All were accused of being Naxalites and subjected to continuous torture and incarceration. The State that thus destroyed their bodily integrity acted in ways that made it difficult to separate pain on account of torture and a sense of anomie that had to do with sexual humiliation. Archana Guha was the worst affected and lost the use of her lower limbs. Subsequently, Amnesty International took note of the case and launched a rights campaign on her behalf.

Saumen and Latika meanwhile prosecuted the case in local courts for the next two decades, when the officer who had presided over their torture was indicted and sentenced to a year's imprisonment.

For Saumen and Latika, notes Srila Roy in her essay on torture, memory and healing, the Archana Guha case became almost a lifetime project, or to quote Saumen, 'the most beloved baby in the bosom of the then childless couple, my wife Latika Guha and me' (Srila Roy, 2015: 159). Latika, observes Roy, bore the role of witness and crusader in equal measure, and in her memory of that time, the wrong inflicted on Archana, indeed on all of them, came to stand in for a collective wrong which she felt pledged to fight. Roy argues that Latika's recall of torture—as evident in her writing— veered between a juridical recitation of what happened, with almost mechanical precision, and an ethical sense of the value of suffering. Both modes of framing speech, she says, helped steer memory away from the achingly personal dimension it would otherwise, have to engage with. Further, such framing also rendered Latika's testimony 'representative', of a time, place and a cause. Such representation, concludes Roy, is a function of traumatic memory, for what it achieves is a repetition of the past, in all its density. Further, the witness is compelled to silence her own pain and hurt, and this in turn renders her situation precarious.

Clearly, such speech, which functions as if it were a political and ethical imperative, cannot be always personally healing—and here is where one needs to pause and review the work of those who work with affidavits and testimonies that bear witness to extreme and shaming violence inflicted by the State. How much can the pursuit of justice achieve by way of healing? This is a question that continues to haunt feminist movements across South Asia, as they grapple with the tragedies wrought by war and conflict, sustained by the violence of both State and non-State actors. I will return to examining this question in a subsequent chapter.

REFERENCES

Bandhopadhyay, Krishna. 2008. 'Naxalbari: A Feminist Narrative', *Economic and Political Weekly*, XLIII.

Roy, Srila. 2006. 'Revolutionary Marriage: On the Politics of Sexual Stories in Naxalbari', *Feminist Review* 83: 99-118.

Roy, Srila. 2007. *The Everyday Life of the Revolution: Gender, Violence and Memory* https://core.ac.uk/download/pdf/381243.pdf (accessed 19 November 2015).

Roy, Srila. 2008. *The Grey Zone: The 'Ordinary' Violence of Extraordinary Times*, https://www.academia.edu/424899/The_Grey_Zone_ theOrdinaryViolence_of_Extraordinary_Times (accessed 19 November 2015).

Sinha Roy, Mallarika. 2003. 'Metropolis and its Others: Women's Speech and Silence in the Naxalbari Movement, India', Asian Studies Journal, University of Philippines, 39: 1-2.

Sinha Roy, Mallarika. 2011. *Gender and Radical Politics in India: Magic Moments of Naxalbari (1967-1975)*, London and New York: Routledge.

Sinha Roy, Mallarika. 2012. 'Rethinking Female Militancy in Postcolonial Bengal', *Feminist Review*, 101: 121-131.

7

Resurgent Nationalism, State Violence and Sexual Assault

If the early years of independence witnessed the consolidation of the Nation-State, rather than the republic of India, with the security and sovereignty of the nation defining the limits to republican ardour and assertion, the 1960s threw that effort into sharp relief. In the manner in which Naxalism was contained, the State stood defined in its impunity and its commitment to sustaining the interests of the ruling classes and castes. In any case, as we have seen, the everyday life of the State was enmeshed with local and regional structures of class and caste domination and oppression. In the 1970s, leading to the 1980s, States in the sub-continent turned particularly vicious towards their citizens—and sexual violence was a crucial axis along which such viciousness found expression.

In this chapter, I examine the conditions in which, across South Asia, nationalism, defined in terms of national security, asserted its claims and came to deploy coercion and violence, particularly sexual violence to secure the Nation-State.

***

The 1960s in Pakistan saw the consolidation of military rule and the unleashing of terror against political dissidents, particularly in East Pakistan. The stirrings of Bangla nationalism already evident and visible in preceding years led to a full-fledged civil war, in which India threw its weight behind Bangla nationalists. Pakistan had to concede to its increasing unpopularity in the east; meanwhile, it sought to inscribe its territorial control literally on the bodies of Bangla women, who were raped in the thousands by its army. In turn women from Bihar, resident in East Pakistan, were raped by those who were opposed to Pakistan. Unlike Partition-related violence, the numbers did not tally and rape by the army, systematic and clearly an instrument of war and terror, remained exceptional. The civil war ended with the establishment of Bangladesh in 1971.

During this period, Pakistan's dictator Yahya Khan was not without his critics and opponents—there had been protests against his rule, with students, labour leaders and professionals of various sorts joining hands. The repression in the East that preceded the creation of the new nation was criticized by a small but vociferous minority, many of whom identified with Left politics. Tahira Mazhar Ali and others came out onto the streets, braving ultra-nationalist opposition to protest their country's actions in Bangladesh. Following Pakistan's defeat in the civil war, and the birth of Bangladesh, Yahya Khan's tenure as President came to an end. The democratically elected government of Zulfikar Ali Bhutto (1972–77) brought to end the long decades of military rule. Bhutto's time as Pakistan's Prime Minister brought into focus a liberal populism that opened up spaces for women's presence in public and political life and enabled them speak and discuss matters of import to feminists. Zia-ul-Haq toppled Bhutto's government and replaced it with harsh authoritarian rule.

President Zia, whose regime enjoyed the financial and military backing of the United States of America, embarked on what he considered a programme of Islamisation of the country. He declared that women were best off when they heeded their 'given' and domestic place and position—and remained veiled and within the four walls of the house. His government issued proclamations banning women from participating in international sport, attempted to repeal the Family Law Ordinance of 1961, and announced its intention of doing away with co-education and setting up separate universities for women. Writing in the wake of these developments and at a time when women had rallied together to offer a concerted opposition to these policies, Shahnaz Rouse noted that subsequent to these highly objectionable announcements, new laws passed in Zia's regime (the controversial Hudood laws) 'reduced the status of woman to that of half a man in terms of her ability to bear witness in court. In cases of rape, a woman's testimony is to be considered inadmissible, and the murder of a woman should not warrant the same penalty as a similar crime against a man' (Rouse, 1984).

Rouse notes that Zia drew on the rhetoric of Islamisation to forge new political and class alliances; the new laws which were created during his time, and which targeted women, helped him forge an ideological consensus with regressive sections of the clergy (they were agreed on this matter, though divided on other issues, to do with capital, labour etc.), landlords and the military. Such consensus revolved around the question of Pakistan's Islamic identity and the role assigned to women in sustaining it, through an observance of chastity, piety and subservience. This also meant that the curbing of women's rights to equal citizenship was central to the constitution of resurgent nationalism in Pakistan.

I would like to examine the Hudood laws in this context: put simply, they sought to secure maximum punitive action against practices considered un-Islamic, including alcoholism, fornication, adultery and apostasy. The zina ordinance and changes in the law of evidence were the most important in this context. Zina or illicit sexual relations, broadly defined, included non-marital sex as such—the latter was deemed a crime punishable by whipping and whipping unto death. As far as women were concerned, to escape the charge of having indulged in illicit sex, they had to prove that they had been coerced into the act. Where such evidence was not forthcoming, it was deemed that they had 'consented' and therefore were guilty. In some instances, they could even be considered as initiating the act and therefore guilty of rape. The question of evidence, complicated in all instances to do with rape and across cultures, became particularly fraught in Pakistan under the new laws: for one, a victim of assault could not testify on her own behalf, and secondly women were not deemed reliable witnesses.

What this meant in practice was that women who suffered assault as well as women who had indulged in consensual non-marital sex were both deemed guilty. This conflation of the act of sex and the act of rape ended up criminalizing women's sexuality as such. Such criminalization was not only nightmarish, but banal and evil in an everyday sense. For one, it placed enormous power in the hands of even minor state officials, allowing them to incarcerate women with impunity. Given the moral hysteria that the zina ordinance created, it was easy enough to pounce on women that were vulnerable. Many of those arrested were deemed guilty by association—that is, the charge against them was that they had been 'go-betweens' for those who eloped, committed fornication etc. Further, a substantial number of women charged with zina were poor, working class women: their ignorance of the law, the suspicion that they were prostitutes, their inability to pay a bribe and to take their cases to court meant they were easy targets. Not only did they suffer on this account, but they were also sexually assaulted in custody. This terrorizing of women proved an object lesson of sorts, not unlike the 'pedagogy of rape' that Anupama Rao speaks about in the context of caste Hindu society. It was clearly meant to school women into being 'chaste' as the regime defined the term: their 'chastity' was to serve as the embodied proof of the nation's putative Islamic identity.

Feminists were outraged by the Hudood ordinances and their collective indignation led to the forming of groups and alliances amongst various activist women who came to oppose these laws—

these laws diminished not only women's personhood, but also their claims to citizenship. The restoration of democratic rights and the repeal of the Hudood ordinances emerged as intertwined demands in feminist responses to the State's transgressions. Beginning in the late 1970s, the battle for rights on all counts raged on into the next decade and gave rise to a forceful feminist politics, which brought to the fore the State's complicity in both legitimizing as well as actually endorsing sexual violence against women.

I will return to examining the nature of feminist speech that was possible at this juncture in a subsequent chapter. Here I wish to note the following: the acute gendering of authoritarian rule in the Pakistani context made for a sustained critique of the State from a feminist perspective, which is amongst the most valuable in the South Asian context. In the Indian context, such a critique would not be forthcoming for another decade at least, and even then only in contexts where the women's question and the question of sustaining civil liberties were brought together. While feminists were on surer ground when it came to aligning women's rights with the campaign for human rights as such, they did not always pick up the gauntlet with respect to the challenge thrown by the Indian State's brazen disregard for civil liberties, so evident in its policies with respect to the Kashmir valley and the North-Eastern states of the Union. This, in spite of the fact that an entire generation of women was politicized into its feminist politics by the struggles they waged against the Indian Emergency of 1975 and have since been active in the civil and democratic rights movements.

As Uma Chakravarti has pointed out, it is as if a tacit division of labour exists with respect to doing civil rights: the men work at calling the State's anti-democratic practices to account, while the women interrogate its patriarchal violence. Seldom do these critiques merge; by and large, male civil rights activists do not integrate feminist approaches to dealing with sexual violence and civil rights in a substantive conceptual sense; by the same token, except for the rich writing on Partition, feminists have not worked at bringing their experience of working with women and on sexual violence to advance a powerful critique of the State. To be sure there exists a corpus of writings on particular instances of State violence, but feminist strategies have not drawn on the work of the civil liberties tradition, for the most part—a lacuna that is most evident in feminist engagement with caste violence, as we shall see.

***

Even as Pakistani feminists mobilized against Zia-ul-Haq's policies and regime in the late 1970s and early 1980s, feminists in the newly-born nation of Bangladesh had to reckon with the horror and scale of mass rape. Yet, speech about what Bangla women had experienced, indeed of all that women had endured during the nine months of civil war, remained inhibited. It is not that the fact of mass rape went unnoticed. Rather, it was publicly acknowledged by those who wielded authority in the new nation—raped women were declared 'biranganas', brave martyrs who had sacrificed what was most precious to them, for the cause of the nation. They were to be 'rehabilitated' and viewed with sympathy. The State also announced that it would arrange for abortions for those who had been forcibly impregnated. Several thousands of abortions were carried out; apart from these, women on their own too had attempted to get abortions, usually with the help of local quacks. Where abortion was not possible, officials were told to put out the babies for adoption. Amena Mohsin notes that Mujib-ur-Rahman, Bangladesh's first premier and the man who led the national liberation movement, declared that he did not want the seed of the enemy nurtured in independent Bangladesh: 'I do not want to keep that polluted blood in this country' (Mohsin, 2016).

Dina Siddiqi however points out that 'Mujib's gesture of embracing biranganas as daughters and sisters—irretrievably patriarchal and steeped in the language of war as it was—could be read as a 'progressive' move for the times, not appreciated fully, perhaps because of the ensuing burdens of the birangana designation.' For, 'under cultural conditions that stigmatized rather than heroised women willing to go public with their experience of wartime rape ... the designation of birangana could not but embody stigma.' This was unavoidable, observes Siddiqi, especially in the absence of 'a corresponding effort by the State to bring the perpetrators to justice' (Siddiqui, 2016).

The so-called heroines of the liberation war were thus returned to shame and silence and in many cases to a state of neglect and forgetfulness. To quote Siddiqi: 'Once the abortion and adoption programs had been completed, the identity of biranganas was literally erased from the nationalist record, ostensibly as protection from future stigma. State functionaries determined at some point that it would be in everyone's best interest to destroy all bureaucratic traces of the government's "rehabilitation" efforts. The destruction of these records—names, addresses, ages, locations where the women and girls had been held—permanently "disappeared" rape survivors from official historical archives' (*op. cit.*).

In public and common memory, the biranganas suffered other fates. For one, they were not referred to as such and instead they were described in routinely negative terms—soiled, tainted, harassed, disgraced, ruined, fallen, tortured... The call for patriotic men to marry them had some currency in the years immediately after independence, but not thereafter, and women suffered ignominy when it was known that they had been raped. Many women kept quiet, or as Yasmin Saikia points out, rape was literally 'unspeakable' for them, given local convention and the national context in which they were hailed as heroines. The strategic silence of the State, its failure to bring perpetrators to book, the return of former collaborators into mainstream politics, the military dictatorships that followed the killing of Mujib-ur-Rahman and the manner in which wartime rape figured in popular discourse:

through the 1970s and 1980s there was literally very little discursive or political space available for even feminists active in other spheres of public life to speak of 1971 and sexual violence.

As in Pakistan and India, while sexual violence and more generally the routine humiliation, degradation and violence that informed women's lives were not 'speakable' except as specific crimes that were taken note of by the criminal justice system, in Bangladesh too, silence reigned. Again, as with these other countries, women in public life, especially those concerned with the women's question, were active in other contexts: demanding rights and representation for women in education, politics, ensuring welfare in contexts where women deserved it, being part of debates about policies of development, growth and well-being... It was not until the early 1990s, in the wake of the international outcry against the mass rape of women in Bosnia and Rwanda that feminists from Bangladesh returned to that nightmarish past.

***

The Sri Lankan Nation-State had to reckon with Tamil political militancy in the 1970s. This followed on a decade and more of political discontent which may be traced to the decision by the government in 1956 to declare Sinhala the national language. Tamil political groups protested the measure, following which the original decision was rescinded and allowance made for the use of Tamil in the Tamil-majority provinces. This was resented by chauvinist groups within the Sinhala community, including disaffected small traders, peasants, vociferous Buddhist monks and students. Rioting and violence against Tamils followed, resulting in the death of over 150 people. Ghastly incidents including the burning alive of people were reported. It is possible that women too suffered their share of violence during those dark days, but in the available literature, there are no particular references to their experiences. While Left parties and movements were rightly aghast at this expression of Sinhala chauvinism, tragically, they too began to draw on its rhetoric in the 1960s. The compulsions of electoral democracy made for strange partnerships during this period and Left parties found themselves having to accommodate their concerns and objectives within the terms of a greater Sinhala chauvinism.

This culture of heady political populism has been interpreted as a response to the economic crisis that beset Sri Lanka in the late 1950s and after, with a crisis in the balance of payments and growing unemployment. This is not an unfamiliar scenario given that a similar situation of economic discontent existed in India in the 1960s and after—which saw Indira Gandhi's Congress government respond with a dose of 'socialist' populism, including the nationalization of banks. In the Sri Lankan context populism, even if self-declaredly 'socialist', assumed a virulent anti-minority character, leading to widespread and sustained violence against Tamils through the 1970s. The growth of Tamil militancy during this period helped sustain this admixture of populism and violence, with disastrous consequences for the Tamils and eventually for the poor sections of the Sinahala-speaking population, who were drawn into a protracted war only to become its cannon fodder.

Meanwhile, as with populist States elsewhere, even as they waged war against dissenting citizens and armed militants, successive governments in Sri Lanka embarked on development and welfare policies as well; some of these devolved on securing women's education, employment, representation in government. The daily business of State-making appears to have included a slew of measures that (ostensibly) addressed grim unequal realities, which helped build a broad horizon of expectations amongst educated and socially privileged women, who then came to position themselves as spokespersons for their sex. While working class women and peasants, as in India and Pakistan, continued to be part of various protests for a betterment of their lives and economic prospects, the language of feminism came to be expressed, as in the rest of

South Asia, in and through a register that emerged from Sri Lanka's educated middle and upper classes. The 1970s proved crucial in this respect—on account of the growing politics of ethnic chauvinism and violence and their impact on women, and the visibility granted to women's issue in the wake of the United Nations Declaration of the Women's Decade in 1975.

Nimanthi Perera has argued that the question of violence against women, including sexual violence, emerged as pertinent only in the 1980s—that is, it assumed analytical and political significance for feminists only in that decade. Earlier feminist work addressed issues to do with class, labour and development, and even when acts of sexual violence were noted by feminists, these were not marked as having to do with sexual inequality and male sexual authority. She notes that in 1971, the infamous rape and murder of Premawathie Manamperi, suspected to be a Janata Vimukti Perumana (or JVP—an armed Left group that was formed in 1971 and was largely Sinhala) accomplice by the Sri Lankan army, was not notated as 'sexual violence', rather it appeared at that time as part of the general State violence against the Maoist JVP (Manamperi was not only brutally assaulted, but stripped and paraded naked through the town where she lived; she was later shot and dumped into a makeshift grave.) Perera points out that during this period rape was not absent from public discourse, and indeed was a staple feature of Sinhala cinema—as it was of Tamil, Hindi and other cinemas in India—but it was represented in somewhat 'generic' fashion: sensational music, unusual camera angles and at the centre of it all, the poor, duped, innocent victim who is to be violated or experience the threat of violation, just so that the good-hearted hero can 'save' her honour and establish his moral legitimacy and secure his role as her protector.

All this changed in the 1980s, given the transnational discourse on violence that travelled to Sri Lanka as well in the UN decade of women. For one, these years witnessed the decline of the

Sri Lankan Left, and feminists whose politics had been nurtured under its auspices by then had come to reckon with sexual politics as well, and come to look beyond a class and development agenda, which, in any case, was in retreat. Secondly, the anti-Tamil violence that came to be an established feature of Sri Lankan political life in the 1970s made it impossible to not take note of sexual violence—which came to be routinely deployed against Tamil women, suspected to be militants. Significantly, Manamperi was 'remembered' in a poem by a Sri Lankan Tamil woman who recalled her fate, while recounting the tragic tale of a Tamil girl, Krishanthi, also assaulted and killed by the Sri Lankan armed forces.

While feminist responses to sexual violence acquired form and coherence in the 1980s, the Sri Lankan State's populism as well as the resurgent nationalism it encouraged were constitutively gendered. This was evident not only in the manner in which the 'terrorist' other, as Manamperi was identified, was sought to be sexually humiliated, but also in the very conception of the nation and women's relationship to it. While Sinhala-Buddhist women were expected to be devoted mothers of the putative Sinhala-Buddhist homeland and play their part in resurrecting its former glory (the notion that Lanka was the famed Dhammadvipa of the Buddhist imagination), Tamils were viewed as both inglorious and profligate. In a book addressed to young Sinhala learners, Junius Jayawardene, President of Sri Lanka under whose regime Sinhala nationalism reached a sort of apotheosis, noted how Tamil invaders from India not only spread ruin in the countryside, but also bred in vast numbers: 'In the first quarter of the thirteenth century from South India came Magha—the Tiger. The wasteland he created became the kingdom of malaria, the domain of the anopheles, breeding prodigiously in the dark stagnant waters of the great irrigation works' (Sankaran Krishna, 1996: 310).

In the years to come, Tamil nationalism would have recourse to its own gendered strategies: enlisting women in its ranks (the

Liberation Tigers of Tamil Eelam did this most systematically),
both to utilize their fighting qualities, and to provide them with
a space of 'safety' against army depredations; creating a politics of
revenge around sexual violence, in this instance of Tamil women
by members of the Indian Peace-keeping Forces (IPKF), which
was then used to 'explain' and 'justify' the use of a 'human bomb'
to kill former Indian Prime Minister Rajiv Gandhi. Through the
period of the conflict, the sexual hurt suffered by Tamil women
would be mobilized, as trope and argument, to call attention to the
suffering of the Tamil people as a whole. This, coupled with the
LTTE's strictures against sexual expression of any kind, between
cadre, or cadre and civilians, rendered their invocation of wounded
honour suitably credible and affective.

***

In the Indian context, Naxalism, as we have seen, was brutally
crushed. Well into the 1970s, the violence of the State was all too
evident in the manner it hunted down activists and sympathisers.
Yet in nearby Bihar, the air was resonant with the cry of revolution
and militancy. In Andhra, as we have noted previously, girijans
or hill tribal communities fought to keep land. Agrarian unrest
soon spread from the hills to the plains, leading to prolonged and
sustained struggles through the 1970s and well into the 1980s,
under the leadership of the armed Left, whose politics was inspired
by Naxalism. In Tamil Nadu, peasants and agricultural labourers
organized into unions, demanded higher wages and held out against
a socially repressive and cruel system of landlordism. In Uttar
Pradesh, home to several peasant struggles in the past, widening
social and economic disparities brought about peasant unrest. In
Maharashtra, the onset of drought in 1971 provided the occasion
for several Left organizations to emerge with region-specific claims
on distributive justice, including of land. These organizations also
took to undertaking radical trade union work. Meanwhile, as the

1960s gave way to the 1970s, a rash of industrial strikes took place across the country, the most well-known being the railway strike of 1974.

These protests were not merely 'economic' in content, rather they were defiant of social oppression and affirmative of the peasant and labourer's right to protest and demand what was hers by right. Whether a particular campaign was for land, the possession of grain, for higher wages, or against feudal servitude, it was always and everywhere waged in the name of wounded personhood and dignity.

In addition to these challenges posed to the authority of State and class, there were other signs, generated from within the State apparatus, that indicated that all was not well with the Indian nation. As early as 1960 the Dhebar Committee, appointed to enquire into the status of India's tribal population, had reported on the vast injustice that commanded those lives, including trouble at the hand of corrupt forest officials, massive displacement and the alienation of forest rights. While this was read as a consequence of forest and other policies that had their origin in the colonial period, the record of independent India was clearly none too great. In 1965, the government of India had appointed a committee under L Elayaperumal, Member of Parliament from Tamil Nadu, to enquire into the working of the Untouchability Offences Act, 1949 and to produce a comprehensive report on the status of untouchables in the country. The report was released in 1969 and revealed a very sorry state of affairs. Regional reports that were produced thereafter—for instance, in Tamil Nadu and Madhya Pradesh—revealed in all its grime and detail the continuing subjugation, everyday humiliation and violence that the so-called untouchables endured. In 1974, the Committee on the Status of Women tabled its report in Parliament and that proved to be as dismal, and raised fundamental questions about the meaning of equality in the Indian context, as far as its female citizens were concerned.

Further, the state of the Union was itself challenged. As early as 1971, Naga nationalists in the North-east of India, who had not accepted what they saw as their forced integration into the Indian Union addressed a letter to Prime Minister Indira Gandhi, drawing attention to the conduct of the Indian Armed Forces in the north-east of India, particularly the rape of several Naga girls and women. A similar letter was forwarded from Manipur.

Unwilling to address structural economic concerns or socially urgent issues to do with civic justice, the Congress government headed by Indira Gandhi declared a national Emergency in 1975. The Emergency, as it came to be called, was marked by economic populism—addressing, ostensibly, poverty, corruption, private capital—and political fascism. Through the period of the Emergency (1975–1977) the Indian State relied on a host of coercive and extra-judicial tactics to combat dissent and challenges to its authority. Sexual violence was an important weapon deployed by the State.

Sadly, the lifting of the Emergency did not improve matters, as far as the State's attitude to protesting workers or peasants or democrats—as is evident in the horrific instances of rape and violence that accompanied State attempts to quell economic and political militancy in the city as well as the countryside. Sudesh Vaid, Monica Juneja and Amiya Rao, who wrote a report titled, *Rape, Society and State* in 1979 listed some of the more shocking incidents of sexual violence: in 1978, police fired at agitating mine workers in Bailadilla and raped a number of women; in 1979, in Singbaum, Chaibasa and Santhal Parganas, a number of adivasi women were assaulted brutally when they sought to reclaim land appropriated by landlords and moneylenders, by the henchmen of the former and by the Central Reserve Police. Apart from these shocking and deliberate acts there was the everyday and routine violence that haunted the local police thana and beat. Vaid and others listed such acts as well, drawing on newspaper reports: amongst those accused of molestation and assault were a gram sewak, a Sub-Inspector of Police, a magistrate, a forest official, military men...

In this context, the routine violence of the State, including sexual violence, bears looking at in some details. An Emergency-related story—of Nagamma—is instructive in this context. Nagamma was picked up and tortured for days on end in the last months of the Emergency. She had married outside her caste and moved into what was seen as a 'lower' caste neighbourhood, inhabited by dalits. She had also raised questions about the manner in which locally powerful men from caste Hindu families cornered government auctions of public resources. When the Emergency was imposed, locally powerful caste Hindu men deliberately filed a case of theft against her. Nagamma was arrested, taken to the local station and assaulted, sexually humiliated and hurt. Her husband and her daughter, who had delivered a child only six months earlier, were also brought to the station and beaten—with the latter being repeatedly gang-raped. When the Emergency was lifted, Nagamma was released on bail—and thereafter walked a long and twisted path to a justice whose frontiers appeared ever in retreat.

While she did manage to secure a hearing before the one-man Emergency crimes redressal commission appointed for the purpose, and also a measure of compensation, this did not come about easily. For, prior to that, she took her complaint from one police officer to the next, until she was assured of an enquiry. Ironically enough, she discovered that the man assigned to enquire into torture directed at her was one who presided over her ignominy. Sure enough, he declared her insane and untrustworthy. This is not unusual—women who make so bold as to speak about sexual assault are not viewed as 'normal'. In Nagamma's case, the police officer was implicated in the violence and that was reason enough for him to declare her mad. It was only during the hearing of the one-man Emergency Commission that was appointed for the purpose that she was subjected to another psychiatric inspection and her testimony heeded.

However the justice she secured was modest, and amounted to a meagre compensation for the violence she endured while in custody. To her chagrin, the original circumstances that had led to her arrest— local caste Hindu authority, caste hatred and misogyny—were left unaddressed; as also the sexual violence inflicted on her daughter. Which is why in writing of Nagamma, Mythily Sivaraman, long-time member of the CPM and AIDWA, pointed out that Nagamma's story unfolded in the context of emergency-related torture, but in essence was representative of the fate of the poor in their everyday engagement with society and the State.

***

The crisis of the nation state in South Asia in the 1960s–1970s—in the wake of economic discontent, social and political inequality, and ethnic discrimination—was 'resolved' in and through violence on the part of the constituent States (the case of Bangladesh though, as we have seen was different; during this period, nation-building was still in process, and the sort of resurgent nationalism that was evident in other parts of South Asia was not evident in Bangladesh). In all instances, this was accompanied by an invocation of national security and honour, integrity and sovereignty—writ large, and literally, on the bodies of women. It was as if resistant women or women who appeared to symbolize possible political threat to, and caused sexual anxiety in a 'nation in crisis', had to be shown their place, their sexuality regulated and put under surveillance, and punitive action undertaken to break their resolve.

REFERENCES

Chakravarti, Uma. *Archiving the Nation-State in Feminist Praxis: A South Asian Perspective.* http://www.cwds.ac.in/OCPaper/uma%20 occasional%20paper.pdf (accessed 16 November 2015).

'A Letter to the Prime Minister', 'A Memorandum from Manipur Women's Association', in A.R. Desai (ed.), 1991 *Expanding Government Lawlessness and Organized Struggles: Violation of the Democratic Rights of the Minorities, Women, Slum-dwellers, Press and some Other Violations*, pp. 81-86. Mumbai: Popular Prakashan.

Jayawardene, Kumari, 1985. *Ethnic and Class Conflicts in Sri Lanka: Some Aspects of Sinhala Buddhist Consciousness for the Past 100 years*, Colombo: Centre for Social Analysis.

Khan, Shahnaz. 2001. *Gender, Religion, Sexuality and the State: Mediating the Hadood Laws in Pakistan*, London: Centre for Research on Violence Against Women and Children.

Krishna, Sankaran. 1996. 'Producing Sri Lanka: J. R. Jayewardene and Postcolonial Identity', *Alternatives: Global, Local, Political*, 21 (3): 303–320; 310.

Mir-Hosseini, Ziba and Vanja Hamzić. 2010. *Control and Sexuality: The Revival of Zina Laws in Muslim Contexts*, London: Women Living Under Muslim Law.

Mohsin, Amena. 2016. 'History of Sexual Violence, Impunity and Conflict: The Bangladesh Context' in H. Hossain and A. Mohsin (eds.), *Of the Nation Born: The Bangladesh Papers (Zubaan Series on Sexual Violence and Impunity in South Asia)* New Delhi: Zubaan.

Mookherjee, Nayanika. 2012. 'The Absent Piece of Skin: gendered, racialized and territorial inscriptions of sexual violence during the Bangladesh war', *Modern Asian Studies*, 46 (6): 1572–1601.

Perera-Rajasingham, Nimanthi, 2004. 'From Murder to Violence: The Beginnings of a Feminist Debate in Sri Lanka', *Nivedini: Journal of Gender Studies*, 11:103-136. Colombo: Women's Education and Research Centre.

Rouse, Shahnaz. 1988. *Women's movements in Pakistan: State, Class, Gender.* http://www.wluml.org/sites/wluml.org/files/import/english/pubs/pdf/dossier3/D3-06-Pakistan.pdf (accessed 15 November 2015).

Saikia, Yasmin. 2011. *Women, War and the Making of Bangladesh: Remembering 1971,* Durham: Duke University Press.

Siddiqui, Dina. 2016. 'Gendered States: A Review of the Literature on Sexual Violence and Impunity' in H. Hossain and A. Mohsin (eds.), *Of the Nation Born: The Bangladesh Papers (Zubaan Series on Sexual Violence and Impunity in South Asia)* New Delhi: Zubaan.

Sivaraman, Mythily. 2013. 'Story of Nagammal' in *Haunted by Fire: Essays on Caste, Class, Exploitation and Emancipation,* pp. 306–314. New Delhi: Leftword.

Vaid, Sudesh, Monica Juneja and Amiya Rao. 1970. *Rape, Society and State,* Delhi: People's Union for Civil Liberties and Democratic Rights.

8

Challenging Sexual Violence

The Making of Resistance Politics

It is evident that in all the various historical contexts I have referred to above, political crisis translated into sexual anxiety which ultimately turned violent. States across South Asia achieved their ferocious intent through the mechanisms of governance, and in concert with ruling elites who were not averse to using sexual violence to intimidate those who demanded better wages, dignity, safety and better working conditions. In an everyday sense, it was those entrenched in class and caste power that were the face of violent authority, and it was the powerful amongst them who proved to be sexually rapacious. Unsurprisingly, those who protested against such authority challenged social and economic class actors as much as they challenged State action that supported the latter. Significantly, through the 1970s such challenges also foregrounded the question of sexual violence, as is evident from these examples from India.

The militant Dalit Panthers of Maharashtra, comprising writers in the main, shocked caste Hindu society by raising questions about how the latter perceived—and devalued—dalit women's personhood. Raja Dhale, one of the founding members, bitterly wondered at a state of affairs where an affront to the national flag was charged with a fine larger than what was imposed on a man who sexually humiliated and assaulted a dalit woman. Jagdish Mahato, a peasant leader from Bihar, who advocated a politics that combined elements of Marxism with Ambedkar's ideas, understood the significance of his movement in terms of how it had come to challenge the impunity with which upper caste landlords sought to possess the bodies of dalit and lower caste women. Disturbed by the rape of Bhil women by caste Hindu landlords in Dhule district of Maharashtra, Ambersingh, a Bhil Gandhian, active in the Sarvodaya movement, abandoned the quiet politics of Gandhism and took to militant organizing against landlords (in 1972). The non-violent activists of the Chatra Yuva Sangharsh Vahini, which also emerged in Bihar but soon spread to other parts of Northern India, desired to wrest land away from a corrupt and large religious institution in the sacred precincts of Bodh Gaya; in the event, they called attention to the sexually predatory attitudes of its religious head and leader. We have already seen how those fighting for national self-determination in Nagaland and Manipur addressed the Indian state—by calling attention to the sexually violent behavior of the Indian army in their contexts.

In what follows, I examine these developments for what they tell us about resistance to sexual violence. I look at specific movements and their responses, and also call attention to an emergent feminist tone that animated discussions in some of these movements. Except for the responses from Manipur and Nagaland, the others that I examine in this chapter address structural inequality and violence, even as some of them point to State complicity in sustaining the latter. In this sense, the resistance that this chapter foregrounds is one honed in the context of class and anti-caste struggles, which nurtured also an incipient feminism.

***

The Dalit Panthers of Maharashtra (the organization was founded in 1972) consciously modelled themselves on the African-American

Black Panthers and in doing so distinguished themselves from existing dalit political parties. Arguing that a dalit was not merely an 'untouchable', 'outside the village walls and scripture' but a 'worker, landless labourer and proletarian', and therefore, quintessentially a member of an incipient revolutionary community, the Panthers observed, of the present dalit political leadership: 'They never united all the dalits and all the oppressed. Above all, they conducted the politics of a revolutionary community like the dalits in a legalistic manner. The party got enmeshed in the web of votes, demands, select places for a handful of the dalits and concessions. So the dalit population scattered over the country, in many villages, remained politically where they were. The leadership of the party went into the hands of the middle class in the community. Intrigue, selfishness and division became rife'(Dalit Panthers' Manifesto, 1973).

Their own politics, they noted, was transformative, and they desired a 'complete and total revolutionary change'; they did not want a place in a 'brahmin alley', rather they wanted to wield power in the most fundamental sense of the term (*ibid*). To this end, they rejected the parliamentary Left parties as well and initially at least linked caste and class concerns, and attempted to yoke together Marxism and Ambedkarism.

If we are to consider Raja Dhale's anguish over the vast indifference that greeted the everyday sexual violence and humiliation that dalit women experienced in the context of these words and sentiments, then we get a sense of the precisely gendered nature of this radical politics: from being a detail of caste Hindu oppression, the dalit woman's existential vulnerability, the denial of her personhood becomes the very mark of the caste order's ethical anomie. It is not so much a question of wounded community honour merely, but of the banal evil of caste itself. In Namdeo Dhasal's magnificently angry *Golpitha* we are presented with a blinding dystopic vision of a world that destroys itself, or rather is called upon to destroy itself. Consumed by its own violence and hatred, this world dies.

Dhasal's vision of what follows thereafter comprised images of what ought not to be done. Included in this list of proscriptions are the following lines: '... one should stop committing the crime of not recognizing one's kin, not recognizing one's mother or sister' (Namdeo Dhasal, 2006: 36). Caste Hindu society's habitual disdain of fraternity, its incipient disregard for women that are not considered quite human—these exist together and in an anticipated utopia, this must not be.

This radically gendered vision of sexual vulnerability and violence did not translate into concrete political claims or demands, as far as dalit women were concerned, as is evident in the fact that the Dalit Panthers' Manifesto did not contain explicit demands to do with the women's question. Yet the fillip that the movement provided to militant dalit politics proved consequential in the struggle that shook Maharasthra in the late 1970s—the Namantar struggle, to do with the renaming of Marathwada University as Dr Ambedkar University. Several dalit women participated in the Namantar movement and came to espouse radical views on women's status and liberation.

I turn now to Jagdish Mahato and the agrarian struggle in Bihar. Mahato was a koeri by caste, a school teacher and supporter of the Communist Party of India (CPI) in the town of Arrah in Bihar. He had read Ambedkar before he read Marx and started a paper which he titled *Harijanistan*. Beaten up by upper caste landlords for supporting the CPI during an election, he was gradually drawn to the Naxalite model of peasant revolt, and began to organize the murder of several landlords and their criminal henchmen. Gail Omvedt points out that the issues which koeris as well as dalits considered pertinent had to do not only with abominably low wages, but also with matters of social honour, 'especially honour defined in terms of the unrestricted and arrogant access of the upper castes to dalit women' (Omvedt, 1991: 59). Mahato was believed to have said to a fellow teacher, before he was killed in 1971: 'Brother, I know that

I am going to die one of these days. But I will die partly satisfied. For one change that our movement has brought about is that landlords now do not dare to touch the women of the poor' (*op.cit.*, 59).

The routine possession of dalit and lower caste women by landlords was widely resented, and it is significant that it came to be seen in terms of the larger 'agrarian problem' as such. Mukherjee and Yadav, narrating the story of a police-peasant encounter in Chauri, an obscure village in Bihar, call attention to the fact that an agrarian problem to do with wages was complicated by the fact that Bhumihar landlords expected lower caste women to sleep with them to 'earn' a better wage. In a particular instance, a visiting grain trader was robbed of the grain in his possession by a group of peasants and in the police firing that followed, several people died. While the robbery attempt was made much of by local government and the police, the larger picture was conveniently obscured. A local lawyer who enquired into the incident however pointed out that the wife of one of the peasants shot by the police noted bitterly how she was solicited by the son of the landlord, while harvesting. Her husband was with her, but he could not respond though he was incensed. He was part of the group that waylaid the trader later. Mukherjee and Yadav note of Chauri in this context: 'One of the reasons for the growing unrest was that the Bhumihar landlords of Chauri were coercing the lower caste female labourers to do harvesting at night for obvious sexual benefits. Added to this was the problem of reduced or inadequate wages paid to the labourers' (Mukherjee and Yadav, 1982: 122).

While the peasant struggles in Bihar during this period did forefront the question of sexual violence, this did not prove catalytic enough to mobilize women into a politics that would enable them to ask questions about the organization of the household, their place within it and the links that held family and caste together. Such a politics emerged in Andhra Pradesh in the heyday of Naxalism in that State—and led to thoughtful thinking on the relationship between everyday life, sexual violence, class and State. I examine this development in a latter section of this chapter—but for now, I want to note that such speech as emerged in Andhra and in some other struggle contexts had, perhaps to do with conscious feminist speech, elicited by the presence of 'feminist outsiders'. This was the case with developments in the Chatra Yuva Sangharsh Vahini and the Shramik Sanghatana.

***

The Chatra Yuva Sangharsh Vahini, an organization founded by Jaya Prakash Narayan, led a non-violent movement demanding land to the tiller in Bihar. They undertook a sustained struggle against the famed Shankara Mutt in Bodh Gaya, which owned an enormous amount of land—during and after the Emergency years, that is, 1975 and after. In the course of the struggle, the organization came to address other issues to do with the Mutt and its relationship to lower caste peasants and labourers. The luring of young women into the Mutt's precincts and the sexual rapacity of a range of religious leaders emerged as matters of concern to Vahini activists.

A mixed group of activists, men and women was present in the Vahini: women agricultural labourers, most of whom were dalits, a few peasants from castes such as yadavs, middle class activists, and erstwhile socialists. This disparate group looked to link issues of the everyday with public wrongs. In the event some of them espoused a politics that linked sexual violence to other forms of inequality, and which demanded that not only sexual vulnerability that women experienced outside their homes, but that in their families too, be addressed.

Reporting on the struggle in the 1980s, Manimala observed that the local leadership was firmly in dalit hands, but when it came to women's issues, particularly within the household, men were less likely to respond with urgency. Even when it came to issues of women being harassed and assaulted by the henchmen attached to the Mahant, women were viewed with suspicion, were stigmatized and seen as contributing to the problems that assailed them. Though men's attitudes altered in the course of the struggle, this did not result in women sharing political roles with men on an equal footing or emerging as leaders in their own right. While issues to do with sexuality and violence in the family were spoken of quite openly, this did not translate into critical perspectives on violence in familial and conjugal contexts that would have a bearing on political practice.

As in Bihar, in Dhule, in the region of Shahada in Maharashtra, a mass organization provided the context for the emergence of what was clearly a 'feminist' perspective on violence. Bhil agricultural labourers were mobilized into the Shramik Sanghatana, which, among other things, took up issues to do with the sexual oppression of women even as it sought to uphold the integrity of Bhil identity and dignity. Bhil women, rather than men, emerged as active participants in the campaign against violence—and significantly, demanded that domestic feuding, including drunken violence was addressed as well. While Ambersingh, the charismatic Bhil leader was moved enough by tales of sexual violence inflicted on Bhil women, to trade his Gandhian politics for one of non-violent peasant militancy, Bhil women entered public life, not only on account of labouring in humiliating conditions and for low wages, but also because they desired to lessen the burden of violence that inevitably was theirs, at home and outside. Their views were affirmed by middle class women activists who had associated with the Sanghatana. Originally part of a Left group called Magowa, they were keen on reviewing and discussing everything, including class struggle and Marxist thought. Some of them came to discussing feminism, which in turn fed into Bhil women's questioning of the violence they endured in their domestic as well as public contexts.

***

The anguish expressed in the letters from Nagaland and Mizoram was of a different order from what we find in the instances to do with sexual violence that I have listed above. Sexual violence against Naga girls and wives (the letters make this distinction) was viewed clearly as State strategy. While the behaviour of the Indian army is described as 'bestial debauchery', an instance of 'animal passion' and 'sexual depravity', its motives are viewed as solely political: 'The sexual depravity of the Indian Army personnel against Naga girls is a tactical move of the Indian army offensive in Nagaland. It has been widely demonstrated in all parts of the country during the sixteen years of Indo-Naga conflict (A. R. Desai, 1991: 82).' The report goes on to describe the 'sacrilege' committed in the premises of a church, where several young Naga women, including a child of 11 years, were confined and raped, and notes that such acts are perversions that only the Indian army can perform. Contending that the slaughter of Naga womanhood and the desecration of Churches are calculated acts of the Government of India, the report places on record its condemnation of all events described in its content (*op. cit.* 82–84).

Significantly, the report notes, earlier complaints to the government of India were delicately worded, given the fact that such things cannot be freely spoken of; and also because 'chivalry springs from the religious and social order in Nagaland and every daughter is offered courtesy and guaranteed safe conduct' (*op. cit.* 82). The report is unequivocal in stating that the Indian Army has continuously transgressed the 'moral code of humankind' through its actions.

The immorality of the assaulter, and of the authority that sanctions assault, are new themes: it is not only power that is challenged and condemned, but the ethics or the absence of ethics that goes with it. While Naga culture is contrasted with Indian culture, the acts of assault are not seen as violations of the former, rather they are viewed as testimony of the latter's fall from moral grace. Naga militants, meanwhile, position themselves as angry yet mindful men, possessed of a refined sense of personhood, in contrast to the barbaric men of the Indian army.

The letter from Manipur is different. For one, it is written and signed by women (the letter from Nagaland is signed by the Deputy Secretary of the Federal government of Nagaland) and is titled as a Memorandum from a women's association in Manipur. After listing the brutal treatment accorded to women who, along with men, were called in to assist officers of the Indian army in their homes, the memorandum strikes a note of anguish: 'Common sense and human nature fail to know how it would be necessary to select women for the punishment of their brothers who are in the underground Naga' (*op. cit.* 85). Pointing out that in spite of and after the brutal assault of two women, their brothers continued to be underground, the memorandum in bewilderment notes: '...no human being would dream of pushing sticks into the private part of women' (*op. cit.* 86).

The tone of the Memorandum is distraught, but not harsh or critical. While making it clear that the behaviour of the security forces meant to protect and safeguard populations is reprehensible, it yet rests its faith in the possibility of redressal—it notes that the army has made a mockery of the Constitution, and demands justice in the name of the latter. The rape of women, it is made clear, cannot be a legitimate act of war or violence, and has to be seen for the vile crime that it is. While the Naga condemnation is directed at the Indian army and government, the Memo from Manipur speaks from a location of bewildered torment and anger. One despairs of justice from the Indian State, whereas the other is convinced that it cannot but hold the latter to account.

***

People in movement, the availability of a new register of protest, and the alarming nature of the violence imposed on women: each

of these provided an anchoring context for women—and men—
to articulate their misgivings over what they endured. This took
the form of speech as well as action, and in every instance was
determined by the speakers' and actors' conviction that protesting
sexual violence was necessary, and central to an assertion of dignity,
of personhood.

During this period, in some parts of the country at least, women
spoke of sexual violence for other reasons: because they had
something to say that had not been said before. To be sure, their
speech was occasioned by the context of struggle that they found
themselves in, but some of them also spoke in a tone that was
decidedly new, and which reflected new influences. I start with an
instance from Andhra Pradesh, which, as I have noted, witnessed
widespread agrarian unrest during this time; so much so that parts
of the state came under the notorious Disturbed Areas Act, which
invested insuperable punitive power in the hands of the police. A
1978 report from Karimnagar district, prepared by the Stree Shakti
Sanghatana, a Left-leaning women's organization that was present
state-wide, noted several instances of violence against women;
as also strategies of resistance on the part of the women. Noting
that a lot of this was possible because labourers in the region were
organized under the auspices of the militant, Left-led Ryotu-Coolie
Sangham, as well as the Mahila Sangam, a women's organization
affiliated to the militant Left, the report went on to observe that rape
was an inseparable aspect of class war in these rural parts. While
women were as yet bound to their husbands' authority, both were
in effect the landlord's property; this meant that the landlord had
the right of possession over wives (and daughters) of the labourers.
A woman forced to submit to a landlord's dictum or violently
possessed by him was however not viewed as 'fallen'—for one, this
was a fact of rural feudal life, the report concluded, and besides,
'virtue' in such a context cannot ever be strongly imposed. However,
the report hastened to add, all this was being challenged at present.

Women were doing this both through their presence in the general organisations of the working class as well as in Mahila Sangams.

Whether they would be able to take on both feudal and domestic oppression remained to be seen, the report admitted, and suggested that for this to happen, Mahila Sangams would have to function with a measure of autonomy and independence. The report was both admiring and anxious: it acknowledged how the extreme violence of the feudal structure, which is directed at women with particular force, was being challenged; but was not quite sure if the everyday forms of violence, wife-beating included, would engage the political imagination of the Ryotu-coolie Sangham.

The relative autonomy of women's oppression was also taken note of by dalit women's groups in Maharashtra, which meant that they too acknowledged the significance of criticizing familial and domestic ideology and practices: the Mahila Samata Sainik Dal formed by Buddhist women students in Aurangabad, notes Gail Omvedt, 'rejected pativrata, condemned as phony the male attack on feminism, of saying that "freedom does not mean free sex", called the Buddha the first to free women from slavery, concluded with a salute to Angela Davis and with a vow that "we are battling for equality with men in the liberation war for human liberation called for by Dr Ambedkar".' A dalit student journal from Nanded, *Janweedana* announced in one of its editions that 'women hold up half the sky' and in an editorial argued that 'it is essential to change today's oppressive marriage system from the roots' (Omvedt: 83).

Further, Radha Kumar and Shoba Sadagopan, writing of State-directed sexual violence in the Santhal Parganas, took note of the resistance offered to such violence by the Jharkhand Mukti Morcha, but added a rather worried caveat that such resistance sought to 'domesticate' adivasi women, in the manner of their peasant counterparts.

This speaking-aloud about family and domestic violence was on account of a new political register that had come to be. Decidedly 'feminist' in the manner it attended to regulation of women's lives, choices and behaviour in intimate and personal realms, such speaking aloud was evident in urban women's groups and in universities-based students' groups, though it might well have been articulated elsewhere as well. Armed with this new and exciting philosophy, young urban women in Bombay, Pune, Hyderabad and Patna took to examining not only their lives, but also the larger, and often Leftist, political contexts they were affiliated to. This was how urban women attached to mass organizations such as such Shramik Sanghatana and Chatra Yuva Sangharsh Vahini came to articulate their understanding of sexual violence, which, to be sure, represented an assertion of class and caste dominance, but they also saw it as arising out of the sexual politics of everyday life.

How and through what means did urban women acquire such an understanding? Let us take the case of the Progressive Organization of Women (POW) from Hyderabad, formed in 1974. K Lalitha, one of the original members of that group, notes that its members were determined to be an independent organization, while retaining their ties to the larger—and Leftist—student body that was active in Osmania University. Their early campaigns centred on dowry and dowry-related violence, 'obscene' representation of women in advertising and films, eve-teasing, as sexual harassment in public spaces was referred to then, and in attempting to forge links with women in the city's bastis. Recalling the making of their feminist consciousness, K Lalitha writes that like many women on the Left across the world, they too could not resist categorization, and therefore deployed terms of analysis such as 'liberal feminism', 'radical feminism' and 'socialist feminism'. POW, she observes, considered itself 'socialist feminist' yet it desired to not entirely merge with Left formations. Around this time, the literature available to them, she adds, comprised the standard texts of the American second wave: Shulamith Firestone's *The Dialectic of Sex*, Betty Friedan's *The Feminine Mystique*, Simone de Beaviour's

The Second Sex and Germaine Greer's *The Female Eunuch*. Armed with these critical tools, urban feminists—in the making—strove to create a politics that linked oppression faced by women in the outside world with the limited and violent nature of their everyday lives.

Gail Omvedt has suggested that urban educated women had to reckon with the possibilities that awaited them as they went to university or to work, as well as the constraints imposed by home and family. This led to many of them speaking of the inequality that lay at the core of marriage and by extension the larger family. This may well be the case, yet such reflections proved valuable. For one, they made available a context and vocabulary of violence to think through women's everyday experiences of discrimination, abuse and hurt, and these elicited interesting and varied responses in the many forums, including mass movements, where feminism found itself. Secondly, the violence of the everyday, of family and marriage, came to be discussed and debated in ways that would prove consequential to critiques of sexual violence that we today identify with the women's movement.

***

The foregrounding of sexual violence as a cause as well as condition for resistance—whether in the context of class war, or in struggles to do with asserting one's right to dignity—connoted the emergence of a politics that understood such violence to be an acute expression of class, caste and State power with impunity, and resistance to such violence as an assertion of dignity and personhood. I have not dwelt on how the various movements referred to above contended with State power, which they did—such contention did not however unfold only along the axis of sexual violence and had to reckon with the overall tactics of terror that the State came to deploy. In this they were supported by the work undertaken by civil rights groups, particularly in the post-Emergency period; these groups

took to meticulously transcribing the many infringements of rights
by the State, including acts of custodial sexual violence.

REFERENCES

Basu, Amrita. 1992. *Two Faces of Protest: Contrasting Modes of Women's Activism in India*, Berkeley: University of California Press. pp. 79–106.

1991. 'A Letter to the Prime Minister', pp. 81–84; 'A Memorandum from Manipur Women's Association', pp. 84-86; Stree Shakti Sanghatana, 'Report from Karimnagar, 95–98; Radha Kumar and Shoba Sadagopan, 'Rape as a Form of Reprisal in Peasant Movements: A Case Study of Santhal Parghanas', 104–107—in A.R. Desai (ed.). *Expanding Government Lawlessness and Organized Struggles: Violation of the Democratic Rights of the Minorities, Women, Slum-dwellers, Press and some Other Violations*, Mumbai: Popular Prakashan.

Dhasal, Namdeo. 2007. 'Golpitha' in Namdeo Dhasal, *Poet of the Underworld, Poems 1972–2006*, Selected, Introduced and Translated by Dilip Chitre (with photographs by Henning Stegmuller), New Delhi: Navayana.

Lalitha, K. 2008. 'Women in Revolt: A Historical Analysis of the Progressive Organisation of Women in Andhra Pradesh' in Mary E. John (ed.), *Women's Studies in India: A Reader*, pp. 32–41. New Delhi: Penguin India.

Manimala. 1984. 'Zameen Kenkar? Jote Onkar!' in Madhu Kishwar and Ruth Vanita (eds.), *In Search of Answers: Indian Women's Voices from Manushi* London: Zed Press

Mukherjee, Kalyan and Rajendra Singh Yadav. 1982. 'For Reasons of State: Oppression and Resistance, A Study of Bhojpur Peasantry', in Arvind Das (ed.), *Agrarian Movements in India: Studies on 20th Century*, pp. 119-147. London: Frank Cass.

Omvedt, Gail. 1993. *Reinventing Revolution: New Social Movements and the Socialist Tradition in India*, London: M. E. Sharpe and Co.

9

Feminist Perspectives on Sexual Violence

By the late 1970s, women's groups with a decidedly feminist perspective had emerged across South Asia. While the circumstances that shaped this perspective were different, and had to do with specific realities, the influences that underwrote an emergent feminist sensibility were somewhat similar: debates to do with sexuality and sexual politics in Anglo-America; the stirring example of women raising questions about their place in society in several parts of the so-called third world, including the Philippines, Vietnam and in many regions of West Asia and Africa; and the contentious questions raised by women in progressive Left movements across the world. In greater or lesser measure feminists in South Asia responded to these influences, made them their own, and came to forge an understanding that answered to their realities. Significantly, their engagement on the ground with matters to do with sexual violence lent their feminism an acute edge. Such an engagement was necessitated in South Asia due to region-specific developments, as well as the hostile manner in which the State, in all regions, responded to the question of sexual violence.

In this chapter, I look at developments in India, Pakistan and Sri Lanka for this period—which extends from the late 1970s to almost the end of the 1980s.

***

In 1978 in Hyderabad, a young Muslim woman Rameeza Bee was returning from a late night cinema. Her husband left her in the rickshaw they were in while he went to 'answer nature's call'. Two policemen who were coming that way dragged Rameeza Bee to a nearby police station. She was accused of being a prostitute, and then repeatedly raped by four men in uniform. She was then brought home by the police, who called her husband out, accused him of being a pimp and then took him and Rameeza back to the station. When they were at the police station she told her husband of how she had been raped, whereupon he lost his temper and started verbally abusing the police. This led to them beating him so badly that he could barely walk. However they were not allowed to leave the station until a bribe had been paid. With the help of her husband's Uncle with whom they were staying, Rameeza took him to a hospital, only to have him pronounced dead. The news of this death sparked a huge wave of protests, first in the city of Hyderabad, where the incident happened, and later across Andhra Pradesh. Police were called in to deal with a restive public, and in the agitations, over 20 persons lost their lives to police bullets.

A commission of enquiry, the Muktadar Commission, appointed to investigate the incident of rape and murder and the deaths due to police firing, placed the blame squarely on the policemen, but the police rejected its findings. Even while deposing before the Commission, the police had tried to exonerate themselves by placing all blame on Rameeza Bee: they brought in witnesses who claimed she was a prostitute; they insisted that they were merely doing their duty by law in taking her to the police station as they did. They argued she was habituated to sex and the charge of rape against them was untrue. They also demanded that the case against them be heard outside of Andhra since public opinion, being against them, could influence the hearings. Subsequently the case was transferred to a Karnataka court, which acquitted the policemen of all charges.

The Progressive Organisation of Women was amongst the many groups in the city of Hyderabad that protested the gruesome rape and murder. A civil liberties organization went on a fact-finding mission in the wake of the police firings which left many people dead, and wrote a report on what transpired that fateful day in March 1978. Writing of the incident and the Justice Muktadar Commission's findings two years later, K Lalitha who was with the Stree Shakti Sanghatana (the POW had been cast into disarray during the Emergency years, but some of the women were now part of this organization), argued that the manner in which the case was viewed and represented—by the State, in the media—pointed to a fundamental fact about how society views sexual violence: 'The society has two types of images for women. One, the virtuous woman who remains confined within the four walls of the home, accepting all the patriarchal norms, and it is this woman whose honour should to be protected. The second is a woman of loose character who breaks all societal norms and comes out of the confinement and it is this woman who could be attacked and raped and she deserves this. This is what happened to Rameeza' (A. R. Desai, 1991: 89).

Lalitha then drew attention to the manner in which the police were determined to prove Rameeza Bee was immoral and a prostitute; how they had tampered with forensic evidence; and how they had arranged for a line of Muslim witnesses to testify to her soliciting. She also noted that while Justice Muktadar had very ably demolished the police story, neither government nor the public were persuaded by his just and rational arguments. A noted 'social worker' refused to have Rameeza Bee stay at her home for women during the time of the trial. Members of the legislative assembly joked about her 'liaison' with Justice Muktadar, a member even alleged she was pregnant, but that he was not responsible for it. Later on a film was made about Rameeza (*Nagansatya—The Naked*

Truth) which showed her to be a prostitute who was made victim of a tragic fate.

Lalitha's note on the Rameeza Bee story was part of a paper she presented at a conference convened in Bombay in 1980—the first of its kind to bring feminists across the country together to debate the content of their evolving politics, from sexual violence to their complicated relationship to Marxism and also mass movements. While women had spoken of sexual violence in the context of the movements they were part of, and in diverse historical circumstances, an acute and new edge to such speech was discernible, especially in contexts where women had taken to discussing such violence and much else in all-female groups. It was as if rape was not only about stigma or shame; nor only an instrument of class, caste and State power. Instead it appeared an act that expressed violent sexual authority and power, deployed against women, to keep them tied to their subordinated status, at home, and in the world at large. There was also wry anger at how civil and State institutions and practices colluded in declaring a woman either virtuous and therefore deserving of justice, or immoral and therefore deserving of whatever ill-fate that has befallen her. Most important, there was also present in the expressions that emerged out of these all-female, and eventually feminist spaces, a sense of calm about what feminists may do in to challenge this state of affairs.

Between 1978, when Rameeza Bee was raped and 1980, when Lalitha wrote this note, two important developments took place which had a bearing on how feminists, as many women active in women's groups across metropolitan (and in some places moffusil) India called themselves, came to define their perspective on rape.

A group of Delhi university teachers, Upendra Baxi, Lotika Sarkar, Vasudha Dhagamwar and Raghunath Kelkar wrote an open letter to the Chief Justice of India in 1979, expressing dismay over the quashing of a high court verdict in what has since come to be known as the Mathura rape case. Mathura, a 15-year-old adivasi girl, was raped in police custody in Maharashtra, and while the Sessions court acquitted the policemen who were held responsible for the vile act, the High Court in Bombay reversed their judgment and sentenced the two men. The Supreme Court however upheld the view of the Sessions judge. The reasoning was that medical examination had proved that Mathura was promiscuous and habituated to sex. It is likely that she had consented to sex with the two policemen; besides there was no evidence of her having resisted sexual violence, nor was the forensic evidence clinching. Upset and shocked by the Supreme Court's verdict, the letter writers observed: 'There is a clear difference in law, and common sense, between 'submission' and 'consent'. Consent involves submission; but the converse is not necessarily true. Nor is absence of resistance necessarily indicative of consent. It appears from the facts as stated by the Court and its holdings that there was submission on the part of Mathura. But where was the finding on the crucial element of consent?' (Upendra Baxi, et. al, 1979).

The letter writers went on to note that the presumption of innocence, no doubt an important consideration, ought not to, however, 'negative all reasonable inference from circumstantial evidence'. Further, 'cold blooded legalism' must not be allowed to overpower other details: 'the Court gives no consideration whatsoever to the socio-economic status, the lack of knowledge of legal rights, the age of victim, lack of access to legal services, and the fear complex which haunts the poor and the exploited in Indian police stations' (*ibid*). The letter also made clear that justice in India continued to be heavily biased by considerations of class, caste and misogyny: 'the Court, under your leadership, has taken great strides for civil liberties in cases involving affluent urban women (e.g. Mrs. Maneka Gandhi and Mrs. Nandini Satpathy). Must illiterate, labouring, politically mute Mathuras of India be continually condemned to their pre-constitutional Indian fate?' (*ibid*)

The letter concluded with a plea to submit the case to a fresh hearing, but not before it called attention to evidence of police maltreatment of women in other instances, such as the Rameeza Bee case. Here again, a new note was expressed: quiet indignant anger at the failure of the republic, at the social and structural caveats that framed and directed the application of the Constitution in an everyday sense.

The other important development that transpired was the publishing—in 1980—of two booklets. One was titled *Rape and the Law* and was published by the Lawyer's Collective, a Bombay-based group; it presented a critique of the existing rape law and counseled reform. The other was *Rape, Society and State*, which I have referred to earlier. These two documents outlined a position and plan of action that suggested a new decisiveness with respect to addressing a crime that appeared all too pervasive.

The 1980 conference, in which Lalitha read her paper on the Rameeza Bee case, took stock of these developments along with several others, including the use of rape as a terror tactic against dissenting political movements (which I have referred to in earlier chapters). In a sense, the conference became the occasion to offer an Indian feminist critique of sexual violence, and this is what Sujatha Gothoskar, of the Bombay-based Forum Against Rape (later Forum Against Oppression of Women) attempted to do. Focusing on debates within the group she was part of, she distinguished between different kinds of rape: those that happen during wartime, communal and caste riots, and class struggles; rape by police and underworld; and rapes that happen in work places. Each of these acts of violence possesses its own distinctive politics, and feminists seeking to battle rape ought to therefore develop different strategies, she noted.

Years later, reviewing the 1980 conference proceedings for her study on Indian women's movements, Geetanjali Gangoli pointed out that while the Indian feminist position was certainly more nuanced and sensitive to social differences than what was available in standard—Western—texts such as Susan Brownmiller's *Against Our Will*, some connections that would become apparent in the years to come were not spelt out. For instance, the rape of civilians by the army was not addressed; neither did the rich debate on custodial rape extend to considering marriage and family as 'custodial' spaces and institutions. Yet discussions amongst feminists at the 1980 conference were rich, and following from those, it was suggested that women ought to learn to put by the stigma of it all and not sink into low self-worth. They were after all victims, and rape was meant to silence them, strike terror in their hearts, and thereby secure their passive consent to the entire system of exploitation that treated them as secondary persons and citizens. In this sense, rape ought to be seen not for the exceptional act that it is, but as existing in a continuum with other acts of violence directed at women.

Importantly, and following from the conference, these ideas and arguments were articulated in the public sphere, and in a language that addressed what was understood as women's direct experiences; that is women lived these realities, and so knew them, but what was required was to grasp them critically, as this leaflet put out by Forum Against Rape in February 1980 suggested:

> 'Isn't it time that we looked rape in the face? Isn't it time we accepted that it occurs all the time, everywhere? Accepted that all women are potential victims—be they young or old, attractive or plain, 'nice' or 'not nice', rich or poor? Only if you're not Mathura—an illiterate farm labourer—the chances are less. The Mathuras of this country are doubly oppressed, they are women, they belong to an already oppressed section in a nation where justice is the privilege of the few. And then women don't face the terror of rape as individuals—but as a category. Mass rape, often used as a weapon to demonstrate power... Have you forgotten what has happened to the wives of railway workers

during the 1974 railway strike? To the wives of the miners of
Baila Diila in 1977? To dalit women at Chandigarh, Bhojpur
and Agra? Or Muslim women at Jamshedpur, Aligarh, and in
almost all communal riots? To Mizo and Nepali women at the
hands of the Indian army?

But you don't have to be raped to realise what you're up
against. Don't you know it already? … Watching a film where
the graphic rape scene and the encouraging whistles and hoots
from the audience turns your stomach? Walking down the
road, travelling in a bus or train, trying to ignore remarks,
taunts, someone's hand feeling you up, brushing against you.
Did you ask for it? Invite it?' (Maria Mies, 1998: 172).

What we have here is a condensation of a decade's history, of
struggle and resistance, and the State's handling of it, as well as
society's collusion with the worst sort of male sexual authority.
Diverse situations and circumstances are unified in this invocation
of a common sexual fate to which all women are subject, in lesser
or greater ways. An appeal is made to what women already know
in their bones, and in a language that is part rhetoric and part
invitation, to participate in a new politics of protest. The stakes
are high, the leaflet goes on to say, and have to do with each one of
us, and the men who are part of our lives, and who certainly don't
want see their sisters or mothers endure what all women could
potentially endure. 'What will you do?' the leaflet demands, and
lists what women have done in different places to challenge sexual
violence and state impunity.

Fittingly enough, the leaflet concludes: 'Yes. There is safety in
numbers. And strength. So let's change the balance. Join us. Let
us look rape in the face…' (*ibid*, 172). While everywhere, from
Shahada to Bhojpur there had been resistant women, they acted
in their immediate context, but here we have a transcendence of
the empirical moment, of the space of a particular city, town and
village and the proclamation of an incipient community that is

everywhere. While particular experiences are cited as examples worthy of emulation, the leaflet also gestures towards new ways of understanding and acting in the world, where women realize the essential injustice of their condition and act on it.

These were themes that would echo through the decade of the 1980s and even after, as women across India came together to challenge sexual and other forms of violence against women. The anti-dowry campaigns of the early 1980s and the move to mobilize law and public opinion against what came to be defined as domestic violence would aid this process.

The anti-rape campaign thus became a founding moment of a feminist politics that saw in sexual violence an experience, a social condition that no woman was exempt from. While granting differences of class, caste and faith, this politics yet resounded over and above these latter in the name of an embattled sisterhood, united by a common experience and knowledge of sexual violence. From being a 'dirty secret' rape was proclaimed a public and pervasive crime that all women endured; by the same token, it was defined as an act that indicted men, in many instances powerful men, even as it positioned women as embattled yet resistant victims.

Meanwhile the social structuring of sexual violence, its use as a tactic of class terror, and as an object lesson to instill compliance with local caste-class relations of power and production, while acknowledged, would remain an argument in this emergent feminism; but would not be 'grasped' as an ineluctable part of social reality that required its own analysis and practical strategies of resistance, including conversations and alliances with subaltern men. Also the complicity of the State in acts of violence against women, even while recognized, would not be forefronted in ways that enabled feminists participate in struggles for civil rights—as happened, for instance, and as we shall see, in Pakistan. To be sure, there were individuals, self-identified feminists, who did so, but women's groups' engagement with the civil liberties tradition remained notional rather than actual, and where present, was sporadic rather than consistent.

***

Sexual violence emerged as pertinent in other South Asian contexts as well. As I have noted in an earlier chapter, the Presidency of Zia-ul-Haq that lasted for more than a decade was a troubled time for Pakistani women. But this period also saw them offer organized resistance at many levels: several women's groups came together to form the Women's Action Forum which then became a context and space to pose and address issues to do with women's right to a life of freedom, dignity and equality. Since many Pakistani feminists during this period located their feminist politics within the larger struggle for democracy, they were necessarily ranged against the State. They opposed the application of Hudood laws, particularly the zina ordinance, and meanwhile attempted to legally and emotionally support women whose sexual and marital choices were considered inherently 'wrong' in the eyes of the law as well as faith.

The question of rape was rather complicated in Pakistan during these years, as I have noted earlier. Women had to prove they had not consented to sex, yet their testimony was not considered legally valid. The new law of evidence did not help matters, since it was so biased against women. Further, women's sexual and conjugal choices could prove fatal, since they stood in danger of being considered immoral acts deserving severe punitive action— and in some circumstances, women actually could be accused of rape. Pakistani feminist activists, lawyers and those articulate in public forums laboured to get the Hudood laws repealed, which was a process that lasted over two decades. In the opinion of some scholars, this experience proved foundational to the making of the women's movement in Pakistan, and in fact defined its trajectory.

Importantly, the challenging of the Hudood laws was also an incipient challenge to military rule and the suspension of democracy.

While the laws were themselves biased against women, the very fact of their existence meant that informal systems of adjudication, which continued to be active in rural and tribal areas and even in urban community contexts (as in India and Bangladesh), received a fillip. Their 'religious' authority was compounded and it became even easier to push ahead with decisions that were clearly misogynistic: in many instances, pronouncing against women meant a strengthening of the system of alliances between groups, or amongst families, which left male kin in charge. In such a context, to struggle against the Hudood laws meant that one was also struggling against social (clan and tribe, in some cases, kin networks in others) and familial authority that set itself above democratic norms, even as it sought legitimacy from its own interpretation of faith and faith-mandated law.

Unsurprisingly, those who worked on individual cases to do with the zina laws were also active in monitoring the human rights situation in Pakistan—Asma Jahangir, for instance—and as it became clear that these laws had resulted in large-scale incarceration of poor women, the enormity of what was at stake in both retaining as well as getting these laws repealed, stood defined. A corrupt state system, so familiar to all citizens across South Asia, local and petty dispute-settling measures, habitual misogyny: all of these intersected in callous fashion to deny the rights of several hundreds of women. A majority of the incarcerated women had been unable to prove the charge of rape, and therefore stood accused of adultery, which was of course a serious offence, deserving of public whipping and in some instances death.

For feminists, the challenging of the Hudood laws meant also that they took on the issue of 'Islamisation' of the republic. For these laws were not passed in isolation, and in fact were part of a policy and worldview that sought to regulate intimate and social life in Pakistan on the basis of what the purveyors of such a policy considered 'Islamic'. To challenge the laws then meant that one could be accused by critics of being 'anti-Islamic', 'agents of the West' and as subverting national interests. The women's movement in Pakistan, particularly the Women's Action Forum rested its opposition on the amended Pakistan Constitution of 1973, which contained an expansive definition of human rights. It also sought to expose the inherent irrationality of these laws—through street demonstrations, discussions in the media and protests against the palpable injustice with which the Hudood Ordinance was sought to be implemented in particular cases. Just as in India, mobilizing around individual cases gave the women's movement force, direction and character—and in fact this is what led to the formation of the Women's Action Forum in the first place.

In the Pakistani context then, public speech about sexual violence was also speech about democracy, the need for reformed laws as well as a carefully articulated position on religion and its role in civic life. One can only imagine how fraught such speech would necessarily have to be, and the courage and intelligence required of those who desired to speak out.

***

In Sri Lanka too the 1980s demanded enormous courage of women activists and feminists. As noted above, it was in this decade that sexual violence emerged as a pertinent political concern, even for feminists. The anti-Tamil violence of 1983 proved a catalyst, and the increasing role assigned to the army in 'settling' the Tamil problem bothered feminists who knew just what a toll this would exact on women's rights to a life of equality, dignity and freedom from violence. As in Pakistan, the question of sexual violence became, in a sense, inseparable from the larger question of democracy and rights—the impossibility of ensuring 'accountability' on the part of the State in the context of an all-out civil war, which actually encouraged impunity, was all too evident. The earliest reports published by the University Teachers for Human Rights in Jaffna testify to this state of affairs. The life and work of Rajani Thiranagama and other women who worked with her in Jaffna in the early phase of the civil war—through the 1980s—bear witness to the sort of speech about sexual violence that was possible or which was most effective.

As in Pakistan, such speech emerged in necessarily fraught conditions. To record and document instances of sexual violence by the Sri Lankan army, and in the late 1980s, by the Indian Peace-keeping Force, to account for undemocratic and anti-civilian violence on the part of various Tamil militant groups, while keeping alive the rights claims and political aspirations of the Tamil people of the north and east—this was no easy task. Further to insist on the importance of countering sexual violence, sometimes by Tamil men, in a context when there was widespread displacement, torture and everyday suffering proved even more difficult. Even a cursory reading of that classic text *The Broken Palmyra* would reveal the acute edginess which characterized such work.

Women activists had to simultaneously engage with the question of sexual torture and individual instances of trauma, as well as with questions of law and legal reparations, which in many cases could not be had or even demanded. Practice proved pertinent, especially as the war years dragged on, with intra-militant violence on the one hand and the worsening relationship between Tamils and Muslims in eastern Sri Lanka, on the other, exacting their toll everywhere, but particularly in the East. In the early 1990s the work of groups such as Suriya Women's Development Centre in Batticaloa would prove pertinent in this context. Working with victims of displacement, rape, war-related trauma, especially to do with those who were 'disappeared', by the State or militant groups, attending to safety as well as livelihood concerns, negotiating with the State as well as with various armed groups in the region: such work, often available only through the monotone of reports or through layered personal narratives, is simply not visible: one can only guess what it meant to pick one's way through a veritable political landmine while remaining open to women's experiences of violence and sexual assault.

On the other hand, women's solidarity networks which brought together Tamil, Sinhala and Muslim women played an important role in ensuring that extreme violence did not paralyse feminist speech entirely. For one, discussions of violence that women suffered anchored a wide-ranging critique of the State as well as its militant opposition (both the JVP and the armed Tamil groups), and of the patriarchal norms that structured it. Secondly, such discussions enabled different feminist registers to coexist: to do with State policy, the need for peace, cultural norms that compounded women's difficulties in those troubled times.

***

The emergence of sexual violence as a foundational issue for feminist organizing and politics in the 1980s was not restricted to South Asia. As has been well documented, this was so in North America and the United Kingdom as well. What is not sufficiently acknowledged in this context is the organizing around equality, violence, sexuality and rights that happened in diverse social and cultural contexts. A brief gesture towards such spaces is useful, for debates that ensued from those contexts did feed into feminist discussions in South Asia, particularly on issues to do with sexuality and violence. I look at one such context here.

In 1984, a motley group of women from eight countries— Pakistan, Bangladesh, Morocco, Algeria, Sudan, Mauritius, Tanzania and Iran—advanced a distinctive feminist politics under the rubric, Women Living Under Muslim Law (WLUML). To quote their reasons for coming together: 'WLUML was formed in 1984 in response to three cases in Muslim countries and communities in which women were being denied rights by reference to laws said to be "Muslim" requiring urgent action.' From the very beginning the organization acknowledged that to live under laws defined as 'Muslim' did not mean that all women who practised Islam were equally and uniformly oppressed: 'Our different realities range from being strictly closeted, isolated and voiceless within four walls, subjected to public floggings and condemned to death for presumed adultery (which is considered a crime against the state) and forcibly given in marriage as a child, to situations where women have a far greater degree of freedom of movement and interaction, the right to work, to participate in public affairs and also exercise a far greater control over their own lives' (WLUML Dossier 3, 1988).

Yet, there was this similarity: '… we recognise that the division between the public and private spheres of life plays a critical role in controlling women. In the specific case of women living under Muslim laws, this emphasis on the private and the personal becomes critical since, unlike the differences that may separate us, similarities often relate to the private and the personal domain.' For this latter was regulated by laws that claimed to be 'Muslim' in content, and women often had no way of knowing what was actually meant or understood, or to distinguish customary from faith-based laws. To remedy this state of affairs, the women of WLUML argued that they intended to make available information and a feminist perspective, based on what women in different countries were doing and saying—'which can all help us realize that women in Muslim countries and communities, far from being spiritually destroyed, are alert, and active in many different ways, and that their analysis and actions can be an inspiration for each other' (*ibid*).

This effort made for concerted speech about sexual violence across cultural and national contexts, and if we are to read such speech in tandem with the more familiar and 'global' arguments that ensued from North America, we see a variegated map of feminist thought emerging. The concerns that animated feminist initiatives in South Asia straddled these several worlds, besides being attentive to their own contexts and histories.

It appears important to remember the founding moment of WLUML, if only to bring the argument back to history: speech in the context of sexual violence, I would like to restate, is always already historical. Discussions of violence in the context of the work that WLUML set out to do are startling, to say the least. For one, they state the problem in terms that are at once historical, political and legal; rather than speak of the 'sexual' contradiction that cuts through all our societies, they point to the structuring of the sexual, to its constitution and thereby push arguments about sexual violence and sexuality beyond the familiar defining line, drawn by Anglo-American feminism of the so-called Second Wave. The problem, it becomes evident, does not only have to do with the 'sexualizing' of women, as feminists from this tradition argued, and their subsequent or simultaneous downgrading, in custom, law and practice; rather it has to do with the particular forms such sexualization takes, as an early article on the Pakistani Hudood laws makes clear. This emphasis on the specificity of sexualization—in WLUML texts—is noteworthy, since it set itself against a discourse that foregrounded the biological-natural inferiority of women. This was done systematically in Iran, but was also a staple of discourses by local leaders in countries as different as Pakistan and Sudan. Secondly, this attention to the specific went hand-in-hand with the comparative approach: for instance in an early discussion of female genital mutilation, there were women from several countries—Sudan, Gambia, Kenya, to name a few—who were party to the debate.

Alongside this historical turn to the 'sexual' we have the programmatic turn to the global in international fora: the UN-inspired debates on 'violence against women' that emerged in the late 1980s and early 1990s, and which aligned women's struggles for equality and justice to international covenants, such as the

Convention on the Elimination of all Forms of Discrimination Against Women (CEDAW). This made for a generic and authoritative discourse about violence rather than a layered one, but by the same token, rendered sexual violence visible in an unprecedented and often dramatic manner. This process acquired momentum in different parts of the world, in keeping with the tempo of local events and circumstances, and was aided by the support extended by the United Nations and various bilateral donor agencies. In the event, 'violence against women' emerged as a rubric which acquired global weight and resonance. In the early 1990s, for instance, during meetings leading up to the Beijing International Women's Conference, public hearings on violence were organized, and in these quasi-tribunal spaces, truth-telling about sexual violence proved cathartic, though there was always the risk that it was also thereby objectified as something that could be understood outside of conjuncture and context.

This coming-together of historical, contingent and global moments framed and set directions for feminist endeavour against sexual violence in the 1990s and after. Meanwhile the work begun in the 1980s, to do with the entangled nature of sexual violence with matters of religion, class and caste had to reckon with new challenges. Before I discuss these changes, I would like to consider, in the following chapter, the nature of feminist engagement with law, one of the more productive expressions that came out of the feminist 'moment' of the 1980s.

REFERENCES

Baxi, Upendra, Lotika Sarkar, Vasudha Dhagamwar and Raghunath Kelkar. 2013. *An Open Letter to the Chief Justice of India*, http://pldindia.org/wp-content/uploads/2013/03/Open-Letter-to-CJI-in-the-Mathura-Rape-Case.pdf (acessed 16 November 2015).

Gangoli, Geetanjali. 2007. *Indian Feminisms, Law, Patriarchies and Violence in India,* Hampshire: Ashgate.

Hoole, Rajan, et al. 1992. *The Broken Palmyrah: The Tamil Crisis in Sri Lanka, An Inside Account.* Colombo: The Sri Lanka Studies Institute.

Lalitha, K. 1991. 'A Report on Rameeza Bee', in A.R. Desai (ed.), *Expanding Government Lawlessness and Organized Struggles: Violation of the Democratic Rights of the Minorities, Women, Slum-dwellers, Press and some Other Violations,* pp. 86-95. Mumbai:Popular Prakashan.

Mies, Maria. 1998. *Patriarchy and Capitalist Accumulation on a World Scale: Women in the International Division of Labour,* pp 171–172. London: Palgrave Macmillan.

Rouse, Shahnaz. 1988. 'Women's Movement in Pakistan: State, Class, Gender. Women Living Under Muslim Laws. http://www.wluml.org/sites/wluml.org/files/import/english/pubs/pdf/dossier3/D3-06-Pakistan.pdf (accessed 15 November 2015).

Rouse, Shahnaz. 1984. 'Women's Movements in Contemporary Pakistan: Results and Prospects', University of Wisconsin, Working Paper 74, December; http://pdf.usaid.gov/pdf_docs/PNAAY061.pdf (accessed 15 November 2015).

1988. Women Living Under Muslim Law, http://www.wluml.org/node/221 (accessed 15 November 2015).

Hélie-Lucas, Marieme. 1997. 'Heart and Soul', Women Living Under Muslim Laws, http://www.wluml.org/sites/wluml.org/files/Heart%20and%20Soul_Marieme%20Helie-Lucas.pdf (accessed 15 November 2015).

10

Redressing Sexual Violence

Feminist Engagements with Public and Legal Spaces

Feminist responses to sexual violence were, as we have seen, somewhat millennial, at least in India. Yet they had to and did address the realities of the criminal justice system. The manner in which sexual violence was not taken heed of, with respect to Mathura as well as Rameeza Bee, even as their cases found their way into courts, disturbed feminists and those engaged with civil rights issues. Following these two infamous instances was a third—an upper caste pregnant woman, Maya Tyagi, was subjected to rape by policemen, stripped naked in public and paraded through the streets. Clearly the criminal justice system as well as the existing law on rape had to be critically interrogated, and if necessary, reformed.

In what follows, I sketch developments in India, as feminists undertook public and legal campaigns against rape through the late 1980s and into the 1990s. Similar narratives may be constructed for other South Asian contexts as well—this section is only an illustrative example of what happened in one instance.

***

Two reports, as I have noted above, set the tone for further discussions: PUCL and PUDR's *Rape, State and the Law* and the Lawyer's Collective's booklet on rape law reform. Eventually, feminist lawyers and activists proposed changes to the law, not only on rape but also the Indian Evidence Act, and called for a re-hauling of criminal investigation procedure as such. Thus began one of the most sustained conversations, even though often one-sided, that feminists have had with the Indian state. In the course of doing this, they came to discuss, amongst themselves, at least, a gamut of other concerns that any instance of sexual assault raised. Such discussions went beyond what the law could do or be made to do and included other concerns: the nature of hurt, the implications of such hurt for a sense of self, for healing and for the victim's relationship with others, including with those she was intimate with. They dwelt too on the absurdity of the legal definition of rape—penile penetration—and listed other ways of destroying bodily integrity, through acts deemed 'unnatural' or 'wrong', through the use of objects, and often simply through the fear that the rapist inculcated in his victim. Not only rape by strangers, but by those a person one trusted, habitually or because he was kin or family she took for granted, was also spoken of.

For many who spoke or listened to those who dared to speak, the experience of actually naming and describing what happened proved deeply burdensome as well as cathartic. For now one had no choice but to acknowledge that such things happened almost routinely; on the other hand, the possibility of speech about it, enabled by the existence of feminist spaces, meant that the experience of rape and the trauma that follows it need not be pushed away or buried deep in the recesses of forbidden memory. This was perhaps what made Sohaila Abdulali write of her experience of being gangraped in an early issue of *Manushi* (1983). Unflinching, honest and yet tremulous, her tone captures both the determination of feminists to fight sexual violence and their worried awareness that rapists, unlike class enemies or caste oppressors are not easily identifiable. Abdulali wrote: 'A rapist could be a brutal madman or the boy next door or the too-friendly uncle. Let us stop treating rape as the problem of other women. Let us acknowledge its universality and come to a better understanding of it' (*Manushi* 16, 1983).

Abdulali's account also communicated the possibility and necessity of recovery, of healing. This was as important as fighting in the court of law, for unless one took hold of oneself, the fight for justice was not likely to happen. It is in this context that women's sharing and consciousness-raising sessions ought to be understood, the rituals that each of us in the women's movement, devised to form that charmed circle of protective sisterhood to enable rape survivors to speak. This was of course not always as cozy as it appears in the telling, nor was it always disentangled from the discussion of practical questions to do with law, relationships, continuing to live in the family, and having to deal with the fact that intimate relationships appeared fearful, and so on.

There were also differences: women's circles that formed in rural neighbourhoods had to reckon with the fact of everyone knowing what happened to the woman or girl in question and the rapist being part of the immediate village environment. If the girl happened to be from a lower caste or if she was a dalit, women's groups had to engage in arbitration, to do with reparations and sometimes even marriage (that is, of the survivor to the man who violated her). While this last proved contentious and was often dismissed as unworthy of discussion, rural activists did not demur from arguing their case: they pointed to the importance of securing accountability, and in the absence of legal pressure or safeguards, how was one to achieve this?

Differences between rural and urban activists, between activists from different regions, conversations, arguments and texts that emerged in particular vernacular contexts: these were pertinent to how one did feminism during this period. Yet the term, as a badge of identity, came to refer to those whose views stood to be widely heard, either because they lived in metropolitan centres or because they could claim 'national' attention, on account of their learning, caste-class privilege or simply because they spoke and wrote in Hindi and English. It is important to keep this in mind, since most of who are described as feminists in what follows are precisely from such contexts, unless marked otherwise.

***

In all this, what appeared most difficult to address and resolve, even in conversation, was the routine rape that happened in the context of caste inequality, and which almost always was directed at dalit and lower caste women. Though described as an instance of feudal power, caste hatred and so on, the legitimization of rape in such contexts, the contention that dalit women and girls had no right to cry rape since they could not but be unchaste, was not easy to unpack. It was evident that society at large chose to disbelieve that the unchaste could be raped, or that lower caste women could be anything but promiscuous. It was equally evident that this smacked of the most awful sort of prejudice and lack of respect for another human person—and yet it proved a difficult conundrum.

This lack of respect was not restricted only to this one instance. As Dr Ambedkar had pointed out time and again, the relegation of dalits beyond the social and the consequent denial of fraternity meant that they need not be considered 'human'. How was one to confront this merging of the political and the ontological? Dalit women perhaps put it best, when they wryly and tersely pointed out that while they were considered untouchable with respect to most things, when it came to sexual violence, the taboo against touch could be easily put aside or overlooked. Without confronting the politics of untouchability and the graded inequality of the caste order that underwrote it, feminists could not hope to understand this vile paradox. However, for the period that I am concerned with, which is the 1980s, feminist understanding and expressions to do with the question of caste and sexual violence, or the 'outrageous everyday', remained largely empirical: feminist forums discussed particular issues of rape and sexual violence, noted the manner in which sexual terrorizing was an expression of class or caste authority, but such observations did not yield a feminist perspective on the caste-gender conundrum or sustained practice against the ugly realities of the caste order. Such understanding emerged only on account of sustained work done by dalit feminists in the following decade, and also by criticisms of feminist perspectives by dalit movements and their leaders. I discuss this in a subsequent section of this book.

Discussions and action to do with rape could prove frustrating in other instances as well: when rape happened in so-called progressive circles, or when rape was not taken seriously by governments that were purportedly progressive. Geetanjali Gangoli notes how the alleged rape of a woman activist of the Kashtakari Sanghatana, an organization that worked in Maharashtra, by men owing allegiance to the CPM's peasant organization in the area raised many questions and eyebrows, especially since the party did not seek to examine the allegation with the critical seriousness it deserved. Likewise, the rape of Bangladeshi women in the streets of Calcutta elicited callous and even mean-spirited responses from the ruling CPM, including female members of the party.

***

Where feminist speech about sexual violence proved decisive was in relation to law, both in how feminists worked to secure legal reform and with respect to their pursuing specific cases of rape to build feminist jurisprudence. Their efforts were affirmed by the recommendations of the Law Commission which delivered its report on a reformed rape law in 1980. Feminist reformulations of the existing rape law addressed two important issues: custodial rape, or rape by persons who held State office, or office held in public trust; and with the question of the victim-survivor's sexual character. Custodial rape, it was argued, was to be considered aggravated assault, and worthy of higher punishment; further in such cases, if a woman claimed she had not consented, her claim ought to be accepted as such. As well, the onus of proving innocence must rest with the accused, and not, as is the case usually, with the victim. The presumption of non-consent, some feminists argued, must be extended to all cases, and not only those that involved custodial violence. Others wanted the category of custodial violence to include rape by employers, landlords and the upper castes. Though earlier judgments, such as the one in the Harnarain Singh case (see Chapter 5), had clarified the meaning of consent, feminist arguments in this regard were novel. They challenged the general understanding of rape as a crime against property and re-defined it as a crime that had to do with power and violence. Likewise, the presumption of innocence—though contested—was new, and had to do with the utter vulnerability of those who had to engage with the Indian State for one reason or another—poor, underclass women, who stood to be coerced and controlled. Critics of this clause argued that this could sometimes work in favour of the State, especially when it sought to implicate those who opposed it, such as trade unionists, political activists and other dissenters.

The second issue had to do with legal reasoning and pertained to sections of the Indian Evidence Act which allowed a woman's past sexual history to be used in adjudicating charges of rape committed on her person—feminists asked for a repeal of this section of the Act. Feminists also challenged the prevailing belief that a married woman cannot be raped, and that sex within marriage cannot be seen in terms of force and consent. They asked for marital rape to be named a crime. In both these instances, feminists argued that a woman's character and status—as wife—cannot be used to deny the commission of sexual crimes on her person. Irrespective of status and morality, sexual violence ought to be treated for the grave crime that it is.

The government of India accepted some of these recommendations, which as I have noted above were also those outlined by the Law Commission. However, the presumption of non-consent and innocence was restricted to instances of custodial rape; amendments to the Indian Evidence Act were rejected, as also was the demand to treat marital rape as an offence. Procedural demands such as the one that asked for rape trials to be conducted on camera were accepted, but the demand to punish policemen who desisted from acting—from filing a report to investigating the complaint—when instances of sexual assault were brought to their notice was not heeded.

These reforms fell short of feminist expectations, but that they were carried out at all indicated that the State had to heed restless and articulate public opinion. For the women's movement, this meant they could pause, take stock and rethink their understanding and strategies. As always, the effectivity of the law lay in its application, in how actual trials were conducted, and in possible shifts in public perception of sexual violence. I discuss both matters below. I start with the matter of public perception.

***

With respect to challenging commonsensical notions of rape, feminist groups undertook the task of debunking the latter through the citation of statistics, case histories and legal verdicts. They also attempted to build a counter-sense, and published pamphlets and booklets that purported to counter 'myths' about rape with 'facts' about rape. There were other interventions as well. In some parts of the country, the vernacular equivalents of 'sexual violence' came to replace earlier usage, which implied loss of honour, or that the act left a stain, a dirty mark and stigma. In Tamil Nadu, for instance, from the late 1980s, the older term for rape, which translated as 'destruction of chastity', came to be replaced by one that simply meant sexual violence—in government references, State-owned media, and very gradually in newspapers and in civil society forums. Yet this sort of change was not easy to sustain: a change of wording did not mean that older ways of thinking about rape had undergone a transformation. Nor did it mean that feminist perceptions of the act were taken seriously. In popular media in Tamil Nadu and sensational news weeklies, rape remained an offence that provoked horror and relish, and for a long time the print media did not desist from featuring photographs of rape survivors, especially if they were from marginal classes and castes. This was the case well into the 1990s.

Another important intervention was to encourage public speech about rape. While this did serve a pedagogic purpose, in contexts where victims were asked to speak it also created unanticipated problems. For instance, a working class or dalit survivor who did not demur from speaking about what she had endured became a subject for voyeuristic attention. Even if those who urged her to speak did so in good faith, the fact that she was in public view, repeating her story for the nth time was not sufficiently interrogated. This happened for instance with Padmini, a dalit woman from Tamil Nadu who survived custodial rape while her husband was killed. Her case was taken up by the All India Democratic Women's Association who ensured that her rapists were awarded the punishment they deserved. But meanwhile, Padmini was endlessly interviewed, and had to recount, to the media and on stage, what she had endured for months after. To be sure, her testimony indicted the State and its officers, but meanwhile she relived her trauma over and over again in front of a public that could not distinguish its ghoulish interest in sexual hurt from sympathy for the victim.

It is not quite clear how one understands this phenomenon. While we have enough evidence of women who have testified to the utter grief and trauma that accompany every re-narration, especially in courts of law, we don't really have a sense of what women experience when they go public and repeat their tale over and over again. Does it make for catharsis of a kind that we have not anticipated? Does it produce numbness that allows the survivor to move on and live in the present? We need a more nuanced understanding of the responses of how working class, lower caste and adivasi women process a crime that is as much of the everyday, as it is exceptional in the hatred and violence that it embodies.

Yet another intervention in the public realm had to do with conducting workshops on the amended law, strategies to be adopted by social workers, lawyers, even the police in working with rape victims, and protocols to do with reporting on rape in the media. These exercises were useful and also helped circulate feminist understanding of sexual violence widely, especially amongst students, journalists and doctors; but they also proved dispiriting to those who conducted them when they had to address strongly-held prejudices against rape, especially on the part of those who were in a position to influence public opinion or held important positions in government.

***

Feminist interventions with the law continued well into the 1990s, since the reformed rape law was still limited in its understanding of the crime. Individuals and groups continued to work with various government agencies, hoping to bring into the purview of the law matters that had not been sufficiently discussed until then, or which came up in the course of prosecuting rape trials. The limited definition of rape as penile penetration, the refusal to consider other forms of sexual violence, through oral and anal means or through the use of objects such as sticks, bottles and so on, the absence of a legal position on child sexual abuse and child rape, the law's silence with regard to rape of women with disabilities, including mental disabilities, the continuing impasse over marital rape, in legal as well as social discussions, the complex question of gender neutrality when it comes to defining the victim, considering that queer persons could also be raped—all these were matters that figured in subsequent debates over the law and the need to render it more comprehensive. Procedural matters too were subjected to questioning: these included the place of interrogation, the absence of support for survivors, when interrogated or when examined in hospitals, the continued use of the 'two-finger' test to establish sexual conduct and character, the ignominy and humiliation that survivors were subject to in court when defence lawyers demanded multiple retellings of what they had endured, and the necessity for counseling and healing.

These formed the staple of feminist conversations and demands in different parts of the country well into the 2000s, and eventually fed into the Justice Verma Commission's recommendations for an amendment to the rape law, following the horrible and brutal gang-rape of a young woman on a bus in Delhi in 2012. The Criminal Law Amendment that was carried through in 2013 bore the stamp of these feminist discussions.

In the 1990s, though, when further reform appeared remote, feminists had to heed other concerns: for instance, feminist lawyers found to their dismay that court procedure, the attitudes of judges, judicial reasoning and the continued association of rape with issues of honour and chastity appeared to mock their efforts. Flavia Agnes, in her review of a decade (1980–1989) of legislation on violence against women, including sexual violence, was cautious, less than optimistic and critical of the women's movement's work in this respect. (She has since nuanced that review in very many ways, and continues to do so.) She noted that public—and feminist—outcry over rape was often difficult to sustain, or was not sustained as it was during the campaign period, resulting in judgments that sounded as if the law had not been amended. It became increasingly clear too that the role of the judge, as much as an effective law, was important. A review of judgments that Agnes undertook showed that progressive and sensitive judgments had been delivered in the past, prior to the passing of the 1983 amendment. The judge's understanding, argued Agnes, thus becomes crucial. For his or her reasoning, even if well-intentioned and calculated to punish the rapist, could set a discursive precedent that did not always represent progress or imply that rape was viewed as a crime against bodily integrity.

For instance, even progressive judges, and here Agnes quoted Justice Krishna Iyer, could err with respect to defining the crime: 'Youth overpowered by sex stress in excess. Hyper-sexed homo sapiens cannot be habilitated by humiliating or harsh treatment.... Given correctional course his erotic aberrations may wither away'. Agnes noted that this judgement was relied upon in several later judgements to reduce the sentences of young offenders. Secondly, sentencing could be on account of the judge's horror over how rape injures a victim's marriage prospects, or how her impaired chastity could result in her being continually stigmatized. Agnes referred to a judgment of the Kerala High Court in a case of gang-rape where the reasoning read thus: 'The court must compensate the victim for the deprivation of the prospect of marriage and a serene family life, which a girl of her kind must have looked forward to.' Agnes points out that this gesture notwithstanding, the court reduced the sentence from five years to three years while the stipulated minimum sentence for a case of gang rape was ten years.

Agnes' misgivings were not merely that: they were meant to provoke feminists into thinking through the distance that separated the normative word of the law and the conduct of rape trials. Further the review pointed to the important task that feminists had to undertake: the building of feminist jurisprudence.

Feminist practice with the law came up against another sort of limit, to do with child rape or child sexual abuse. Agnes' review in fact had raised the vexed question of establishing whether the

survivor was a minor or adult: for, if the former, even consensual
sex becomes rape; if the latter, the question of consent and character
invariably come into play. Child sexual abuse presented feminists
with particular difficulties. In dealing with a repeated instance of
abuse of an 8-year-old by her father, who was an undersecretary
in government of India, Sakshi, a Violence Intervention Centre in
Delhi had to come to terms with the bitter fact of having child abuse
defined at best, as an 'unnatural' act and therefore to be punished by
an ancient anti-sodomy law (Sec 377 of the Indian Penal Code); or
at worst considered an act that 'outrages the modesty of a woman'
(Sec 354 of the IPC) and therefore to be treated leniently. For,
while recognizing that the child had been wronged, the court could
yet not bring itself to suggest a judicial interpretation of the act
commensurate with the horrific nature of the crime. Commenting
on the Court's position, a Sakshi report noted:

> Renu's trauma found scant understanding in the law. Legally
> Renu was not raped because her vagina was never penetrated
> by her father's penis. All other violations of her various orifices,
> which were as or more painful, and equally or more humiliating,
> did not deserve to be understood as rape of her body. Instead
> the learned Additional Sessions Judged ruled that "Both the
> acts, i.e. insertion of finger in the anus and the vagina and
> putting the male organ into the mouth of the prosecutrix are
> acts which are against the order of nature. In order to constitute
> an offense of rape, there has to be the use of the male organ,
> which must find place in the vagina of the prosecutrix. The
> word, penetration does not connote penetration by a foreign
> object." (Naina Kapur et. al, 2000).

Subsequently Sakshi filed a public interest petition, asking for a
judicial interpretation of rape that would allow prosecution of
child sexual abuse. (Child sexual abuse was recognized as a crime
in India with the passing of the Protection of Children from Sexual
Offences Act, 2012).

These legal tales are fascinating, and not only in the Indian context. In Pakistan too feminists persevered in working with the law and however frustrating, it represented a dogged faith in republican values and a necessary antidote to cynicism and a sense of anomie. But I will not dwell on them, except to point out that the trajectory feminists in South Asia set out on possessed its own charge, but did not always lead them to places they wished to go—working with the law was effective in particular instances, but did not produce that sense of a movement forward, which feminist discussions about sexual violence, often conducted within their own precincts, desired. For instance, women's groups were invested in discussions to do with sexuality, sexual choices, female desire and the manner in which a culture of unexamined sexual coercion and violence was unmindful of, and violently antithetical to, women's sexual and emotional needs. But how was one to make such discussions public? Could women speak out on desire and not be termed wanton?

Yet during the 1980s, discussions of sexual violence proved productive in unexpected ways: I would like to draw attention to two aspects here—the manner in which they yielded an understanding of violence against women as such; and further, how they helped accentuate the notion that crimes against women were essentially violations of their civil rights, an argument that appeared particularly relevant as the country slipped into large-scale murder and mayhem from the mid-1980s onwards.

***

Even as the feminist campaigns against sexual violence took off, women began to protest and mobilize public opinion against the so-called dowry deaths. Families of brides that had been killed, particularly mothers, were an important part of such mobilizations. Theatre and music were utilized to communicate the appalling circumstances in which brides found themselves, and the tragic consequences that ensued, should their natal families not pay the promised dowry amount. Unlike the sexual violence campaigns, this did not require women to sort themselves out into the 'chaste' and the unchaste, or to agonise over whether the raped woman was at fault or not. While there was public derision, women could and did confront it, linked as they were in their processions and street theatre groups.

In the wake of protests against dowry and dowry deaths, the family as a site of violence emerged as a major feminist theme, and over a period of time, the structural nature of this violence was laid bare by feminist research. The killing of girl babies, the low caloric intake of female children, the care work and labour that even very young girls had to shoulder, the expectation that women should bear male children, and the contrary pressure from the State that they should have recourse to contraception: these and other related issues soon emerged as pertinent concerns. Marriage too was interrogated, especially the absence of rights within the institution, the problems that confronted many women when husbands were not reliable, including desertion and abandonment, domestic violence, at the hands of not only husbands, but the larger—marital—kin group, and the impossibility of saying no to unwanted or non-pleasurable sex within marriage. Sexual violence thus became one moment in a long experience of violence that women endured, and while many agreed it was possibly the worst, other forms of violence were no less terrible and as traumatic.

This also led to a widening of meaning of the term violence, so that it became possible to speak of the 'violence' of development, and of the capitalist economy. Sexual and economic violence came to be viewed in tandem such that it was possible to speak of the 'rape of women' and the 'appropriation of natural resources' in the same breath. It was not accidental therefore that at the third conference of women's movements in India, held in Patna in 1988, the following resolution was passed.

Women face specific forms of violence: rape and other forms of sexual abuse, female foeticide, witch killing, Sati, dowry murders, wife beating. Such violence and the continued sense of insecurity that is instilled in women as a result keeps them bound to the home, economically exploited and socially suppressed. In the ongoing struggle against violence in the family, society and the State, we recognise that the State is one of the main sources of violence and stands behind the violence committed by men against women in the family, the workplace and the neighbourhood. For these reasons a mass women's movement should focus on the struggle against State violence while building the strength of women to confront all those who use violence against them in the home or out of it (Chetna Gala, Gail Omvedt et al, 1988: 884).

Gail Omvedt noted that this was perhaps one of the few resolutions passed in the conference that did not see sharp divides amongst the various women's groups. In retrospect, it appears that while the resolution nimbly jumps from sexual violence to women's vulnerability at home, their economic dependence and suppression and their being victims of State violence, this last appeared the one phenomenon that women from different progressive political contexts would readily oppose. Thus as oppressor and grand purveyor of violence, or at the very least, an institution that did not respect women's rights, the State unified women even if only temporarily! Yet this did not yield a stringent feminist critique of the State or, to repeat an argument I have made earlier, feminist interventions in the cause of civil liberties. But the earnest rhetoric against the violence of the State served another function. It drew feminist energy away from what proved difficult and complex to negotiate: family, caste and kin networks, all of which kept women bound within their own life worlds, or forced them to confront the fissures that divided women.

The hold that family and community exercised over women's lives and what women stood to achieve by challenging these institutions had been a predominant feminist concern from the early days of the movement, as is evident in an essay by Madhu Kishwar published in *Manushi* in 1979. Significantly, the essay framed familial control over women as a denial of the fundamental rights guaranteed them under the Constitution.

Kishwar drew on the fundamental rights in India's Constitution to underscore the grave nature of these violations. In doing so, she returned us to the State, imagined here as an ideal Constitutional space and a source of hope and inspiration, and just as importantly to a discursive context to anchor our demands for justice and equality. Kishwar made it clear that she had necessarily over-simplified her description of families and what they do, and that she was aware that homes are as much about laughter and affection as control and obedience. But, she pointed out, this does not take away from the fact that families, including senior female members, restricted women's speech, mobility, choice of friends, vocation, work, matrimonial options, right to property and so on. Families, she suggested, are able to do this because they claim that their actions are being undertaken for women's good, their security and protection.

Elsewhere, Kishwar pointed out that the problem also had to do with the family model that had emerged as the norm, at least in many parts of rural North India. She described it as the well-endowed peasant family, which had moved out of tenancy into ownership of land in the wake of zamindari abolition; and which sought to upgrade its social status through regulating female mobility and insisting that women stayed within homes. While this was not always possible, since peasant production required female labour, this latter was invariably defined and marked as domestic, so that peasant women were not viewed as workers—for that would mean they were mobile and in the public eye, both of which were undesirable from the point of view of family honour. This ideology of the family, she argued, persists even in cities, for most migrants to towns and cities retain village-level linkages, and return home to find brides.

This juxtaposition of the family and women's—violated—civil rights is interesting, for it demonstrates quite unequivocally that for women to exercise their rights as citizens, the battle inevitably would have to begin at home, within the domestic sphere. Kishwar is quite forceful in arguing that unless women were equipped to deal with the family and community—through education, the setting up of women's committees, the guarantee of work, and through consciousness raising—they will not be able to gain control over their lives and rights.

I find her invocation of civil rights to frame and dissect women's status useful and interesting. With respect to challenging sexual violence, we have seen that it may not be enough to reform the criminal justice system and the law, or work to change the attitudes of judges (though feminists have been busy doing both). The language of protest needs to be republican, that is, it needs to be resonant with the concept of rights and liberties. Both citizens and State need to agree that sexual violence, indeed, all forms of violence against women are challenges to our existence as a sovereign democratic republic. Further, the register of civil liberties provides us with a narrative and vocabulary to speak of sexual violence in ways that refuse prurient attention, and by that token renders such speech fundamentally political.

These are matters that would emerge as central to feminist struggles in the twenty-first century as a new generation woke up to the cruel realities of community and caste diktats that annulled women's emotional and conjugal choices, and in some instances endorsed their being murdered in the name of family and community honour.

***

The question of civil liberties proved unavoidable in the 1980s for other reasons. The terrible Nellie massacre in Assam in 1983 which caused the rape and death of several hundred Muslims in that state; the anti-Sikh riots of 1984 which destroyed thousands of homes, caused an appalling loss of life, and resulted in horrific acts of rape; the torture and forced disappearance of hundreds of young men in the Punjab, through the 1980s and after, in the wake of the Indian State's campaign against the armed struggle for establishing the separate State of Khalistan; and the worsening communal situation across western and central India, which paralleled the rise of the Hindu Right and invariably took its toll on women's lives: these developments were brought to public attention and made the subject of wide ranging debates by civil liberties groups. Speaking the truth about the State's complicity in these instances, as well as the impunity with which it acted, in the face of challenges to its authority, appeared very important during this period.

Two reports are important in this context: the PUDR report on the anti-Sikh carnage in Delhi in 1984, and the report of the all-women fact finding team that visited parts of the North-east of India in 1982 to enquire into the depredations caused by the Indian army. The PUDR report makes it clear that violence, arson and rape, as had unfolded in Delhi following the assassination of Indira Gandhi were planned, and had the sanction of her party leaders and clearly showed the hand of government, whether police, elected members of local councils or bureaucrats, all of whom colluded with the murderous gangs, either by actively aiding them or by not heeding pleas for support and safety from the hapless Sikh population of the city. The report actually names those who led the mobs, and who directed the action, including rape.

The women's fact-finding team that went to the North-East was perhaps the first of its kind. Writing of that visit, Uma Chakravarti notes that the report not only documented instances of rape, but also sodomy. Despite the scale of the violence and the clear role of the army in having caused it, two members of the fact-finding team desisted from putting their names to the report—they could not bring themselves to sign a report which would be read as 'anti-national', in the event of it going public. In any case, the report was not debated in public and it would be almost another decade before the relationship between the Nation-State, feminists and sexual violence got taken up by feminist scholars and activists.

The collusion of the State with the perpetrators of deliberate acts of rape and murder of Sikh persons, and its recourse to rape and sodomy to subdue a recalcitrant and defiant population in the North-East of the country into accepting its version of nationalism, cried out for feminist analysis of the republic. This meant at that time—and now—that feminists outlined, for themselves and their political understanding, a critical position on the manner in which the republic's minority populations fared in the Nation-State, and on the question of national self-determination.

As we have seen, feminists have been under no illusion as to the role of the State in colluding with those who attack and assault women, or for that matter, the more marginal sections of our population as well as protesting citizens and rebels. On the other hand, feminist criticisms of specific State actions or particular instances of wrong-doing did not add up to a critique of the State. To advance such a critique, the idea of nationalism, sovereignty and security put forth and argued by the State have to be assessed critically—and from a feminist point of view. This latter ought not to be difficult, given the manner the State constructs its power and legitimacy through willful ownership, possession and destruction of what it considers to be rebellious bodies. Whether torture or sexual violence to which the latter are subject, these are fundamentally gendered acts and feminists in that sense have a fundamental stake in challenging the violent claims of State-driven nationalism.

Yet feminist critiques of the State did not prove incisive enough during this period. However, as parts of the nation became subject to successive waves of caste and communal violence in the 1990s, feminists were driven to outline such a critique, which, in effect, was of State impunity, particularly with respect to sexual violence.

***

Before I conclude this review of feminist efforts to seek redressal for sexual violence in law and in society, I would like to reflect on the variegated speech that emerged on account of such efforts: survivors' testimonies, available as affidavits, interviews or news stories; legal debates, which involved feminists, lawyers, civil rights persons, or judges; feminist appraisals and calls to action; in-group discussions amongst women activists; resolutions at conferences; articles, essays, books... What is perhaps not entirely captured—or captureable—in this rich medley of voices is the survivor's tenacity, the manner in which she stays with the case. To be sure, she is assisted by others, lawyers, feminist counsellors, family, sometimes community members, political leaders, even State personnel. Yet to stay alert to what is going on around her, to keep at the courts, even if a hearing is postponed yet again, to relive the facts of violence, to put up with the taunts of defense lawyers, to have to answer questions that are calculated to humiliate, and often, to do all of this in the course of a difficult everyday existence: this calls for profound courage and good faith. It is not that survivors do not give up in sheer exhaustion or that they expect dramatic results. But their insistence on accountability and justice is perhaps the most profound indictment of impunity, both of the State and civil actors that collude with the State, or whom the State often condones.

In this context I would like to recall the elation and sorrow that the survivors of the Vachathi episode exhibited when the trial court indicted over 260 officers of the state: tears, anger, disbelief, questions about reparations, reliving the past, and thinking back on all that they had endured for nearly two decades and through all this a sense of justice having won the day. The passage of time was marked for many of them by how some of them have moved on: for instance those who were but girls then were married with children now; others had endured other losses, some had moved away from the campaign, yet followed the details of the prosecution's case. In a sense, the mix of feelings that was on display that day or on other days when the judgment was commemorated in meetings, is not easy to understand in its entirety.

This is what perhaps ought to give us pause. For in noting our moments of struggle against sexual violence and impunity, we do not always stop to examine how women process grief and memory; often we do not return to those broken lives to follow their course of healing and reliving. Mathura, Rameeza Bee and countless others: who knows how their lives proceeded thereafter? Even if some of us took the trouble to keep up with individual fates, we have not recorded what happened to them; unless, of course they serve the interests of feminist pedagogy and politics. Thus, we remember Bhanwari Devi's struggle or the terrible violence visited on Soni Sori, but not perhaps of many others. The loss to our collective understanding, however, is immense. (Bhanwari Devi, a social worker from an oppressed caste was assaulted by dominant caste men, and when she filed for legal action, the ruling went against her, on the reasoning that respectable men would not have behaved as she claimed they did; Soni Sori, a teacher in the state of Chattisgarh has been subjected to untold police brutality and assault, with the State attempting justification of its actions on the grounds that she supported Left-wing militancy or Maoism and Maoist militants in the region.)

Before I conclude this chapter, I would like to recall Antje Krog's wonderful set of essays on deciphering a testimony given by a woman whose son was amongst those murdered during the apartheid years. She describes the very unusual nature of the testimony, the particularities of the language the woman used, which were not captured in translation entirely, and the manner in which she evoked ways of remembering and grieving that went beyond testifying against State impunity and the heroism of those who confronted the latter. She notes that if such testimony was not recovered for the justice archive, we stand to lose a vital part of the truth about apartheid-related violence, and which had to do with how communities process grief, loss and survival. It seems to me that we need to enrich our archive by looking beyond justice stories, and attend to the persistence of life, or equally the trauma that won't go away.

REFERENCES

Adulali, Sohaila. 1983. 'I Fought for My Life and …Won', *Manushi*, No. 16 (June-July); http://www.manushi-india.org/pdfs_issues/PDF%20Files%2016/18.%20I%20Fought%20for%20My%20Life.pdf (acessed 20 November 2015).

Agnes, Flavia. 1992. 'Protecting Women Against Violence: Reviewing a Decade of Legislation, 1980–1989', *Economic and Political Weekly*, XXVII (17): WS-19-WS-33.

Chakravarti, Uma. 2008. 'Archiving the Nation-State in Feminist Praxis: A South Asian Perspective' http://www.cwds.ac.in/OCPaper/uma%20occasional%20paper.pdf (accessed 16 November 2015).

Gala, Chetna, Gail Omvedt, and Govind Kelkar. 1988. 'Unity and Struggle, A Report on the Nari Mukti Sangharsh Sammelan', *Economic and Political Weekly*, XXIII (18): 883–886.

Gangoli, Geetanjali. 2000. 'Silence, Hurt and Choice: Attitudes to Prostitution in India and the West', Asia Research Centre, Working Paper 6; http://www.lse.ac.uk/asiaResearchCentre/_files/ARCWP06-Gangoli.pdf (accessed 16 November 2015).

Kapur, Naina Jasjit Purewal and Kirti Singh. 2000. *Sexual Assault Law Reforms, A Process Document—I*, http://feministlawarchives.pldindia.org/wp-content/uploads/SA-Bill-Pocess-Document.pdf (accessed 16 November 2015).

Kishwar, Madhu, 184 'Some Aspects of Bondage: The Denial of Fundamental Rights of Women,' in Madhu Kishwar and Ruth Vanita (eds.), *In Search of Answers: Indian Women's Voices from Manushi*, pp. 230–241. London: Zed Press.

Krog, Antje. 2014. *Conditional Tense: Memory and Vocabulary After the South African Truth and Reconciliation Commission*, pp. 39–117. Kolkata: Seagull.

People's Union for Democratic Rights and People's Union for Civil Liberties. 1984. *Report of a Joint Inquiry into the Causes and Impact of the Riots in Delhi from 31 October to 10 November.*

11

Feminist Dilemmas

Punitive Rape in Caste Society

Even as women's movements across South Asia mobilized opinion and undertook campaigns against sexual violence, sometimes by addressing the law, at other times challenging common sense, they had to come to terms with ever newer challenges. The decade of the 1990s proved particularly perplexing in this respect. New regimes of sexual and political violence emerged across the region, on account of changes in both national and global politics. Meanwhile, feminist responses were shaped by global conversations on the women's question, such as were occasioned by the 1995 United Nations Beijing Conference of Women, and the parallel NGO sessions that took place. In an earlier chapter I referred to the emergence of campaigns that addressed diverse realities under the rubric of violence, deploying terms such as 'Violence Against Women' (VAW) and 'Gender-Based Violence' (GBV). The Beijing Conference marked an important moment in the consolidation of such an understanding of violence.

The 'fit' between such phrases that acquired wide currency through the decade, and realities that made it impossible to speak of 'violence' without simultaneously invoking various other acts of brutal injustice against entire populations, was very uneven. On the other hand, campaigns undertaken in the name of VAW and

GBV made for programmatic interventions in particular contexts: they helped mobilize women into protest actions, encouraged them to speak their hurt in public, identified safe spaces for some where they could reflect on what they endured relatively freely, and where possible facilitated legal action. A critical and patient review of what was gained and lost on account of global campaigns against violence that sustained feminist work in very straitened circumstances awaits our attention; likewise we need to review how other social and political movements during this period in our various contexts addressed sexual and other violence against women, and the conversations that ensued or failed to ensue between feminists and other political groups critical of the social order.

In this and the two chapters that follow I take a close look at the 1990s in India, keeping the above reality in mind. The political everyday of Nation-States in the region acquired a density that makes comparison between States, even of the perfunctory kind that I have attempted to do, difficult. Until the 1980s, it was possible to map differences and similarities in terms of the historical progress of the post-colonial Nation-State in South Asia—from the nation-building years through the years of crisis and consolidation. The 1990s posed dilemmas that require us to examine national histories, both in terms of internal contradictions coming to a head, as well as external pressures, ensuing from a changed global environment—and these are invariably different for each of the States in the region. So, rather than link these realities, I propose to merely provide a very short description of what transpired in parts of South Asia during this period, and then go on to look closely at India in the 1990s.

***

In Pakistan, the legal and democratic register that feminists worked with as they challenged the Hudood laws eventually came to accommodate a range of other concerns, which cried for their attention. The growth of armed groups in nearby Afghanistan, particularly the Taliban, proved consequential for the women's question in the region. For one, the Taliban, which claimed to be guided by Islamic tenets, let loose a reign of terror, and the US, which had nurtured it in its early years, saw it fit to take against it. US troops landed in Afghanistan, and in the course of taking action against the Taliban, caused a culture of violence and impunity to take root. Women were the worst sufferers, caught as they were between the Taliban's misogyny, that did not hesitate to maim and kill women in the name of faith-based law, and the militarized politics inaugurated by the US, which transformed gender relations, led to the disruption of family and community life and caused a great deal of suffering.

Afghan developments spilled over into Pakistan: migration, the growth of an arms bazaar in the region, the influence of the Taliban on local faith-based groups, and the sudden eruptions of violence leading to deaths. Pakistani civil society had to respond to these events. For women's groups, the challenge translated into examining the effects of these developments on women's lives, and taking on board a set of circumstances, which in their interaction with older structures of control created grim regimes of sexual coercion and regulation as far as women in far-flung communities were concerned.

In Sri Lanka too, civil war had come to stay, and become a feature of everyday life: working to realize justice for women in particular circumstances of war and displacement, women's groups had to contend with not only war-time violence against women, including rape, but also with the impact of a militarized culture. In the Tamil areas, for instance, this meant having to reckon with forced recruitment of young people, including girls, into the ranks of the Tamil Tigers; tales of abductions of women and children; and of course the continuing violence of the Sri Lankan army. In these circumstances, it was not easy to prosecute cases of sexual assault, especially if they involved army personnel.

In Bangladesh, the conjuncture of the 1990s proved particularly important, for it helped break the grim silence around mass rape. International outcry over the brutalities that surfaced in the former Yugoslavia and in Rwanda had rendered the prosecution of rape as a wartime crime urgent. The setting up of the International Tribunal to try war crimes in the former Yugoslavia, and a similar transitional justice system which emerged in Rwanda, led to the making of rich international feminist jurisprudence to do with sexual violence—and also created conditions for victims and survivors to speak, without fear of being misunderstood and disbelieved. In Bangladesh, where the liberation war and the fate of the biranganas remained subjects of discussions at least of public rhetoric, questions of justice for victims and survivors and suitable reparations were not often or adequately raised. In the 1990s, inspired by the international outcry against conflict-related sexual violence, feminists in Bangladesh revisited a past whose ghosts had been barely laid to rest. This revisiting also helped critical reflection on other related concerns: for instance, the cruel fate meted out to indigenous Chakmas in the Chittagong Hill Tracts in Bangladesh where, in the name of crushing insurgency, Bangladeshi troops indulged in acts of extreme terror. This included violence against Chakma women, particularly those suspected of being combatants. Bangladeshi feminists worked hard to hold their Nation-State to account, and succeeded in drawing parallels between the deployment of sexual violence during the Liberation war against Bangla women, and the Bangladesh army's acts of rape against a section of their recalcitrant citizenry.

***

In India, the 1990s were the beginning of the Mandal-Masjid years—which saw a polarization of views and citizens on the basis of caste, gender and faith. I examine developments to do with caste in this chapter, and with religious identity in the next one. In both instances, I purport to show how fundamental matters to do with sexuality and sexual violence were to the expression of political worth, worthlessness, authority and resistance.

To begin the story of caste and gender in the 1990s, we need to go back to the Mandal Commission report. In 1978 a Commission was set up by government of India, headed by B P Mandal, to identify 'socially and educationally' backward communities—communities so identified were to be given preferential access in education and government employment. The Commission tabled its report in the Indian parliament in a year's time, but this did not become official until a decade later, in 1990, when a different government took it up and decided to implement it. This led to nation-wide protests by the so-called upper and dominant castes, who argued vehemently against affirmative action based on caste identities. Perversely enough, opposition to affirmative action claimed that it spoke in the name of denied equality. The opposition was also resolutely gendered in content: groups of girl students in Delhi and later on in Hyderabad declared in public that if the Mandal Commission's recommendations were implemented, they would not be able to find suitable husbands, since those who came into government service would necessarily be those who rode on the wave of affirmative action and not those who deserved their jobs, and came to them on grounds of merit. The subtext of course was that those who came to take their place in government on the basis of affirmative action would be men from the so-called 'lower' castes, whom upper caste girls could not be expected to love or wed!

This publicly expressed anxiety and disgust over social and conjugal mixing pitted articulate young women from dominant communities against subaltern men in ways that would prove consequential to the women's movements' understanding of social and sexual justice. For the moment, though, in 1990, such opinions appeared merely shocking to feminists who had assumed that a sisterhood invoked in and through a declaration of shared sexual vulnerability would constitute all women into democratic beings, committed to an integral politics of equality and justice.

Even as the Mandal Commission got to work in 1979, other matters to do with caste emerged as pertinent in parts of the country; especially violence against dalits. This was not only in contexts where dalits under the leadership of Marxist-Leninist parties waged class war and therefore incited rage and violence, but also where they had been a part of historical struggles against the caste order, as in Maharasthra and Tamil Nadu; and where they had dared assert their right to a decent existence in the context of accelerated development, as in politically volatile Andhra Pradesh.

Thus, during the Namantar movement (1978), that is, the struggle waged by dalits to have Marathwada University in Aurangabad, Maharashtra named after Dr Ambedkar, dominant caste Marathas targeted dalit lives, homes and villages and caused death and destruction. On the one hand, Marathas resented dalit political visibility and expression and deliberately targeted them; on the other, the unequal social and economic relationship between dalits and Marathas, particularly in rural Marathwada, helped anchor the violence. The local, contentious edge to Maratha-dalit relationships, occasioned by dalit aspirational and political mobility, proved a decisive factor in provoking dominant caste wrath.

In any case, whether violence against dalits was because they dared engage in class war, or an expression of caste authority that stood challenged, or both, it was fundamentally gendered—dalit women were targeted and raped in several villages, often brutally. While sexual servitude within caste-based economies demanded that dalit women be available to upper caste men, Dr Ambedkar's presence and inspiration had enabled dalits in Maharashtra to challenge such practices. Yet, when an exceptional situation of political stress and violence prevailed, upper caste men did not hesitate to lay claims to dalit women's bodies—it was as if the women were being punished for a politics of resistance and self-respect.

In spite of several decades of ideological resistance to upper caste—Brahmin—hegemony and the assertion of a putative Tamil identity that ostensibly did not heed caste, caste violence that targeted dalits persisted in Tamil Nadu as well. In 1978, in the city of Villupuram, men belonging to the ruling All-India Anna Dravida Munnetra Kazhagam (AIADMK) set fire to dalit homes and assaulted dalit women. It all started with a caste Hindu man abusing and attempting to molest a woman who lived with a dalit man. Following this, a group of dalit men sought out the trouble-maker and beat him up; whereupon he took his case to local powers that be, and with one thing leading to another there was a storming of dalit homes—arson, looting and destruction of houses of better-off dalits, as well as their poorer neighbours, followed. Local police stood by watching, even as the AIADMK member of the Legislative Assembly led a group of attackers.

Certain facts emerged from accounts of the Villupuram atrocities: dalit presence in the city announced a certain mobility and freedom, and while dominant caste vanniyars (counted among the most backward castes) stood cheek-by-jowl with them in accessing work opportunities, they also nurtured a sense of caste pride. Dalit mobility must have unsettled the vanniyars' sense of caste-based self-assuredness. Then again, local caste authority was both class and caste based, and not necessarily under vanniyar control; rather it rested with trading castes, but the vanniyars possessed the power of numbers and could be employed as shock troops in any given situation.

Caste violence in Tamil Nadu was not a new phenomenon. After all, the single largest murder of dalits in the post-independence era took place here. 44 dalits were burned alive in Kilavenmani in East Thanjavur in 1968, following several months of struggle for better wages, and for asserting their political allegiance to the Communist Party (CPM). Women were central to these struggles since they formed the bulk of the agricultural workforce for paddy cultivation, given their central role in rice transplantation. In the past, they had suffered sexual and social ignominy, and while communist presence in the region had put an end to the worst forms of sexual servitude, dalit women's situation remained vulnerable. However Villupuram marked a new development: it was an urban riot and further, it did not happen in the context of a protracted class war, as in many rural struggles across India, but with teaching dalits their 'place'.

'Showing dalits their place' underwrote several incidents of violence that took place in the 1980s in Tamil Nadu. For instance, in the early 1980s, caste violence broke out in parts of the Ramanathapuram district in south-eastern Tamil Nadu, following the conversion of a village of dalits to Islam. Dalit mobility, education, economic betterment, and political awareness instilled in them a resolve to assert their self-respect, and conversion seemed a fit response. This was of course resented by caste Hindus—and led to violence in different parts of the district. As I shall argue later, a sense of self in caste society is crucially dependent on negating the personhood of those lower in the hierarchy, and when the so-called lower castes rebel, castes higher up in the hierarchy are challenged in their very—caste-bound—sense of self, and so fight hard to punish the rebels and teach them their place. In all instances, social anxiety to do with dalit assertion acquired gendered attributes (as it did in Villupuram) and was almost always punitive in intent.

'Punitive' action against dalits was undertaken for other reasons as well: in Andhra Pradesh where militant Left political organizing had brought several hundred dalit labourers within the ambit of Naxalism, political restiveness was the order of the day through the 1980s and early 1990s. The same period witnessed what Dr K Balagopal has termed the political rise of the 'provincial propertied classes' (comprising land-owning peasants form upper shudra castes). Their political assertion, which targeted the Indian National Congress and its economic clout, which commandeered

State resources to their advantage, worked to render them a
formidable force in the region. Public expressions of their class and
caste identity at the level of village and taluq were ferocious—as
events that unfolded in the village of Karamchedu and Tsunduru
during the 1980s and 1990s demonstrate.

In July 1985, the village of Karamchedu in Prakasam district
of Andhra Pradesh witnessed ghastly murders—of Madiga (a dalit
caste) men and women by Kamma (a peasant caste) mobs, and
the rape of a least three women, two of whom were but girls. The
Green Revolution had catapulted peasant communities such as the
Kammas into economic prosperity and they were all set to claim
their political due in the state. Dalits continued to be landless for the
most part, but had grown politically trenchant, partly on account
of education and conversion to Christianity but also because they
were groomed by the Congress party as a constituency of voters
that would stay loyal to them. Given that the Kammas aspired to be
regional rulers, they saw the Congress as their enemy and the dalits
who dared to vote for the Congress as traitors who must be taught
a lesson. Further, Madigas, along with sections of the backward
castes and other dalit castes in the village, had resisted the more
coercive demands of the peasantry and this, no doubt, angered the
Kammas. Trouble broke out when a Madiga woman remonstrated
with Kamma youth on account of a local village quarrel: her
defiance became the occasion for the Kammas to round up a mob
of their own and descend on the Madiga settlement. Apart from
killing six people, the mob pounced on three women, including
one who had delivered a child only a few days ago, and raped them.

Close on the heels of Karamchedu, followed the atrocities that
unfolded in Tsunduru (1991): the alleged teasing of a dominant caste
girl by dalit youth was cited as a reason for the subsequent violence
that broke out in the village, claiming dalit lives and livelihoods.
The charge of teasing was preceded by the circulation of rumours
that insisted that dalit youth were lying in wait for dominant caste

girls as they walked to college; that dominant caste women who had taken to work on their fields, not wanting dalit men to do so, were approached by the latter who cited starvation and begged to work; whereupon the women relented and allowed these men to labour, following which they pounced on their benefactors and stripped them naked! Such rumours, as well as the structural and social contexts that shaped dalit lives—dalit assertion, for one, conversion to Christianity, education, their taking to government employment, and their not supporting regional political groups, and staying loyal to Congress (as in Karamchedu)—rendered them vulnerable to attack. In the event over 19 people were killed and several badly injured.

***

Feminist responses to the caste-gender conundrum that emerged in student reactions to the Mandal report and in punitive violence and rape directed at dalits were episodic and region-specific. I pick up the story from a context that provided the possibility for feminist conversations across regions. At the 1990 conference of women's movements held in Calicut, groups from Andhra Pradesh and Tamil Nadu coordinated sessions on caste and feminism, and pointed to the relationship between caste and gender identities; to the fact that the possession of women's bodies, rather the authority to claim and possess women from other, and often lower, castes was a crucial expression of dominant caste hegemony. As a group from Tamil Nadu pointed out, transacting caste and masculine status through laying claims on women's bodies had become the norm to such an extent that when dalits challenged the place assigned to them, they too had recourse to similar rhetoric: thus a dalit leader in Southern Tamil Nadu exhorted young dalit men to forcibly tie the taali (mangalsutra) around the necks of dominant caste women, to prove that they were 'no less' masculine.

In 1991, these concerns were discussed yet again at a National Workshop on Women and Development convened in Bangalore and attended by dalit women's groups—they became the subject of a self-conscious feminist conceptual response to sexual violence and the caste question (by Vasanth and Kalpana Kannabiran). Their essay, since published in the *Economic and Political Weekly*, dealt with the Tsunduru incident and with two other instances of sexual aggression and murder of dalits in Andhra Pradesh, and helped move discussions of sexual violence to a new terrain—one that feminists had not sufficiently engaged with, at least not in all parts of the country. I would like to focus on two important arguments that this essay advanced: the complicity of upper caste women in justifying the murder of dalits and the construction of manhood in caste society, which is based both on the capacity to possess and violate as well as the ability to shame and violate lower caste men and women but in different ways.

Vasanth and Kalpana note that when upper caste women of Tsunduru took to the streets after the gruesome murder of dalits, raising slogans about how their modesty had been outraged by the latter, rape became suddenly 'speakable': '...what would normally, by upper caste standards, be an unimaginable act, marching on the streets crying rape, now achieves respectability because upper caste women are crying out in defence of their endangered chastity' (Vasanth Kannabiran and Kalpana Kannabiran, 1991: 2132). The subtext was vicious: if dalits are granted rights like others that would open the door to the rape of other caste women. This conflation of a right with the 'right to rape' ironically enough reflected on cultures of manhood, as cultivated by dominant caste men. It is by laying claims to the bodies of lower caste women that upper caste men stand defined in their authority; not only may they dispose of these bodies as they wish, but in doing so, they also send out a signal to lower caste men that they cannot ever hope to protect their women. The potential emasculation of the lower caste man must be secured, it appears, before an upper caste man may assert his manhood.

In arguing this point, Vasant and Kalpana point to another instance of violation: a Golla (a lower caste, fitting into the Other Backward caste category) woman was paraded naked through the streets of her village in broad daylight by dominant caste men, who claimed that she had been instrumental in a girl from their community eloping with a Golla youth. Men from the Golla community averted their eyes, and Golla women shut themselves indoors. An old man tried to hand the woman his upper garment, but was beaten up. This poignant scene was framed by hateful taunting of Golla men by the aggressors: 'Open your eyes. Are there no men amongst you?' (*op. cit*, 2131)

The issues that this essay foregrounded were complex: On the one hand, there was the question of the complicity of dominant caste women in perpetrating sexual violence against dalit and other lower caste women, but the reality was also that dominant caste women operated within a territory overdetermined by the space of the household, family and kin network. On the other hand subaltern male activists, determined to challenge the caste order, sometimes had recourse to the same gendered rhetoric as the upper castes. In this context, feminists had to rethink their practice as well as their understanding of a putative sisterhood. Clearly they could not hope to claim or sustain solidarity with dalit women without challenging and fighting the casteism of dominant caste women. This would mean they challenge casteism and take the part of anti-caste movements, which invariably would mean they engage with the men in these movements as well. In effect, the challenge was to rethink the feminist project itself, and within it our understanding of sexual violence, keeping in mind the twisted sexual politics of the caste order.

Significantly, whereas class had become a feminist issue, caste had not. In the wake of the disenchantment experienced by many women who were politicized by Left movements but felt acutely the absence of debates around feminist concerns, several had gone on to enrich their understanding of class. Both in terms of feminist practice and research, much was said and done with respect to the specificity of female labour, especially the role that women played as subsistence workers and food-providers; the household as a locus of both production and reproduction; the role of marriage and family on the one hand and cultural practices of nurture and socialization on the other, in sustaining relations of reproduction. Curiously though caste, so crucially linked to labour, marriage and reproduction was untheorized. Rather it was understood within a generalized critique of gender roles, divisions and labour. Except for Gail Omvedt, who wrote insistently about the structural as well as social hold of the caste order and why feminists had to take that seriously, caste did not attract the attention of feminist thinkers.

It is not that feminists did not have to 'do' caste, as activists or indeed for that matter as scholars. When taking up cases of rape and sexual assault, working on issues to do with sanitation and labour, women's health concerns, or with women in prostitution, caste had to be dealt with. Caste was part of what feminist scholars researched when they worked on kinship and community. But caste as a category of political understanding and practice was as yet unavailable to feminists. Part of the problem was that feminists, who were articulate and present in a public sense, arguing, debating and writing in ways that held the ear of the State or the media, lived and worked in urban contexts, and did not view themselves as marked by caste. On the other hand, this was also a function of privilege, since to be 'unmarked' in the Indian context invariably meant that one was of a caste that could take its hegemonic or dominant status for granted, and 'stand in', so to speak, for humanity.

To return to the 1991 essay on Tsunduru: rich as it was in its insights, feminist practice with respect to sexual assault in the context of caste-based inequality and violence remained bound by the logic of what in feminist circles was referred to as 'case work'. While the individual instance was addressed, long-term strategies for challenging the sexual politics of the caste order and the violence that underwrote it were not developed. A younger generation of women politicized by the Mandal years, especially in Andhra Pradesh, Maharashtra and Tamil Nadu, would come to this challenge, with greater verve and imagination in the new millennium.

***

Significantly, in that decade of caste-related unrest and violence, the government of India took cognizance of rape as a crime that proceeded from a systematic denial of personhood—but not on account of feminist advocacy or argument. This recognition emerged out of an initiative to ensure that the civil rights of dalits were upheld, rather that the refusal of such rights was adequately punished. Given the punitive use of rape and murder by the dominant castes, which the state could not entirely ignore for various reasons, including electoral compulsions and the liberal good faith in the power of law exhibited by some of its own personnel, a new law was drafted to punish violent crimes to do with untouchability. This was the Prevention of Atrocities against Scheduled Castes and Tribes Act (PoA Act), 1989.

The lead-up to the act, according to P. S. Krishnan, former Secretary of the Government of India may be traced to a decision of the Home Ministry to monitor the commission of crimes against dalits. This decision was made in the wake of the Kilvenmani violence of 1968 (in Tamil Nadu when 44 dalit agricultural labourers were burnt to death) and the murder of a dalit boy, Kotesu, in the village of Kanchikacehrala in Andhra Pradesh in 1969, and took effect in the early 1970s. Information about such crimes as the above was gathered by the government of India from the States (for instance, information about the Villupuram violence against dalits in Tamil Nadu that I have referred to earlier was tended to the Centre and became the basis for an indictment of the working of the Protection of Civil Liberties Act in the state). In 1977, following the massacre of dalit agricultural labourers in Belchi, in Bihar—this happened in an era of acute class and caste war, which as we have seen was spearheaded by various Naxalite groups—the government of India decided that something more substantial needed to be done.

Accordingly in 1978, the government created a new post of the Joint Secretary in the Ministry of Home Affairs to deal with matters pertaining to the Scheduled and Backward castes. Krishnan was the first to be appointed to this post and he utilized his authority and position to insist on speedy adjudication of some of the more horrific cases, especially the Belchi and Pipra murders of dalits in Bihar. In 1987, five years after the creation of the post of Joint Secretary, Prime Minister Rajiv Gandhi announced that his government was committed to ending atrocities against dalits, and if need be would consider a new legislative enactment, with stringent penal provisions. Following this, Krishnan was made Special Commissioner for the Scheduled Castes, and in that capacity toured the country, collecting information on atrocities, their details, causes and consequences. After consultations with the law ministry the Act was framed, and passed in 1989 to become law in 1990.

In a sense, the PoA Act, like the amendments to the rape law which came into effect in 1983, was a much needed legal remedy. It is likely that the success of the Naxalites in mobilizing dalits into veritable class armies was read by the State as a warning of impending and continuous violence, and as an indication that dalits will not brook the sort of oppression that they were forced to endure. Also, as we have seen, the 1980s witnessed the consolidation of the civil rights movement that had come into its own in the Emergency years and after, and report after report had pointed to how violence against dalits and women was encouraged by the State's indifference and passive collusion with local class and caste authority. Whatever be the reason behind Prime Minister Rajiv Gandhi's announcement, the Act was passed. As those who are familiar with it know, it comprises a detailed list of enumerable and wide-ranging atrocities, including rape of dalit women, and all of these are explicitly linked to untouchability. That is, they are viewed as crimes committed by non-dalits who wish to practice untouchability with impunity.

An extraordinary Act by any reckoning, it revealed the coming together of two impulses: the will to uphold the rule of law in the republic, and moral anguish at all that was being done in the name of upholding caste identity and the hierarchical order of the caste system across different sites. It was an instance of legislation that was anchored firmly in the social order it wished to reform, punish and transform, even as it sought to challenge that order.

Feminists did not see the Act as providing a context for rethinking sexual violence, at the time of its passage; or as a tool to build feminist jurisprudence. Subsequently, except perhaps for the Vachathi incidents with which I begin this book, which saw the Tamil Nadu AIDWA approach the Commissioner of Scheduled Castes and Tribes to undertake an investigation, and which led to a filing of cases citing the PoA Act, direct feminist engagement with the Act has been almost non-existent.

***

Even as feminists appear to have been nonplussed by the challenges thrown up by punitive sexual violence, the decade of the 1990s witnessed the emergence of dalit women's groups. This announced the making of a feminist politics that directed attention to the caste and class basis for sexual oppression and which took on the cultural and social reasoning that attended it. In what follows, I identify certain figures and movements, so as to be able to condense a very complex history into certain moments that possess heuristic value. I am very aware that this is but a very sketchy attempt and more needs to be done, especially with vernacular archives, histories and texts.

Ruth Manorama, who was one of the women instrumental in the formation of the National Federation of Dalit Women in 1995, wrote and spoke eloquently on caste, gender and feminist politics. A well-known presence in the women's movement in Karnataka who had gained vast political experience organizing urban poor women in Bengaluru city, Ruth had consistently called attention to the interplay of caste and gender in matters of sexual violence. Familiar with the radical anti-casteism of the Tamil self-respect movement—Ruth is a Tamil speaker who works in Bengaluru—and drawing on Dr Ambedkar's writings, she linked sexual vulnerability, social vulnerability and cultural control to demonstrate how the everyday violence of caste was sustained and normalized by deeply internalized value systems, which in turn were sanctified by Hindu belief, custom and practices. She was thus critical of what she described as Aryan texts and scripture and noted that dalits, being pre-Aryan people, were not circumscribed in their daily life by these misogynistic world-views. She conceded that over time, dalit autonomy was compromised and dalits too came within the bind of the rules that frame the caste system, and some amongst them began to imitate the upper castes, and impose restrictions on what women could and could not do. However, there had always been an emancipatory tradition among dalits, she observed, that was opposed to the caste order and the beliefs that underlay it.

Ruth's views were not only her own, but widely shared by fellow activists: Fatima Burnad in Tamil Nadu, for instance, argued in similar terms. Yet in the feminist circles both moved in, these views were not debated, as they ought to have been. For one, this was a new theme in feminism: feminists had not sought to engage with the anti-caste traditions of religious critique, or with the atheism and antinomianism some of them advanced. For the most part, feminists and women's movements stayed with a secularism that rejected religion, but which did not see fit to examine religious precept and practice closely; or to re-examine cultures of feminism that assumed Hindu norms to be universal (something that Flavia Agnes called into question during this period). Further, feminists were more prone to consider religious dictum an instance of false consciousness, or a patriarchal world view, rather than as something that was consequential to the sustaining of inequality and social violence in caste society. Only with the rise of the Hindu right did feminists take to public criticisms of religion, but even then for most of them it was Hindutva, the concentrated political philosophy of the Hindu right, which appeared a problem. The non-brahmin and dalit rejection of Hinduism, the rich insights yielded by the histories of religious conversion in the context of caste and the adoption of resistant religious identities by dalits and lower castes were not part of the feminist domain of ideas; and if and when they were discussed, such debates unfolded in Christian feminist circles, as was the case in Tamil Nadu from as early as the 1970s.

On the other hand, dalit feminists, following Dr Ambedkar, saw themselves as the rightful inheritors of this dissenting and freethinking tradition. Besides, as far as dalits were concerned, Hindu notions of purity, pollution, right, wrong, touch, distance and so on were embodied in irksome and menacing quotidian practices; and these notions sanctified the latter, and provided justification for the cruelty that was routinely trained at them. As for sexual violence, dalit women activists understood it to be part of a continuum of violence that dalit women experienced: in a life-world where food, water, clean living spaces are routinely denied to dalit women, where their labour was exploited, and no protection available in their places of work, where to be in bondage to a landlord or petty trader was commonplace, and at all times they are viewed as sexually available, and humiliated in their bodily being, sexual violence emerged as not an exceptional act of violence, but the most concentrated expression of a fundamental animus against dalits.

Even as they announced a vision of oppression and freedom that was distinctive, dalit women took to mobilizing and organizing around some of their key concerns, which included the question of wages for women agricultural labourers, sexual harassment and discrimination at work places, bonded labour conditions, health issues, especially the manner in which dalit women, indeed as many working class women, were used as guinea pigs when it came to contraception trials, sex work, the problem of dedication of dalit girls to local temples which made them sexually available to upper caste men, the rights of dalit Christians, both within the community and without, and more. Depending on the region and the type of organization, specific issues were accorded priority. While dalit women's groups had emerged across southern and western India from the 1980s onwards, these had functioned on their own, or in alliance with regional women's groups. Now they came together in a coordinated network in the National Dalit Women's Federation. A similar national initiative emerged when the National Dalit Human Rights Campaign was begun, and a women's wing sprung out of it.

The fifth national conference of women's movements proved crucial for a sharpening of dalit women's and feminist political identity. At this conference held in Tirupathi in 1994, dalit and adivasi women argued and fought their case for better visibility of their concerns, more time devoted to discussing them, and insisted that they needed to organize separately. In fact at the conference premises a separate enclave emerged, and the force of dalit and adivasi opinion was such that the rest of the participants had to heed what was being said from within that enclave. This claiming of an autonomous space within the women's movement had in fact begun a few years ago. Conferences convened in Bangalore in 1989, and later on in 1991, brought together dalit feminists who sought to mark the essentially different nature of their experiences, and provide a radical platform to foreground the latter.

The search for autonomy proved to be an interesting yet fraught exercise—on the one hand, it found expression in the formation of the National Federation of Dalit Women, which sought to differentiate dalit women's concerns from those of all other women; at the same time, this exercise was not entirely divorced from the women's movement, and continued to engage with the latter, though not always on convivial terms. For its part, the women's movement was less than open to what dalit women had to stay, and did not seek to rethink its views on sexual and caste oppression. At any rate, the distinct nature of dalit women's concerns emerged with weighty resonance in the mid-1990s. The 1995 Beijing Women's Conference provided an occasion for dalit women's groups to foreground their concerns—in all the public hearings on violence against women that were held prior to Beijing, dalit women were present as victim-survivors, organizers and ideologues, and this led to the making of a marked discourse on violence against women, and one in which it became impossible to talk of sexual hurt without mapping such incidences of hurt onto specific economic, social and cultural realities. In other words, from being an act that sought to hurt and shame with impunity, sexual violence emerged as a veritable condition of existence for India's most marginal citizens. Even as the nature of public speech about sexual violence altered, it came to be enriched by an emergent body of scholarship and writing on dalit lives. (I return to discussing this in some detail below.)

In Pune, Maharashtra, particularly in the mid-1990s and after, dalit women's feminism was forefronted in the efforts that the Department of Women's Studies at University of Pune undertook: drawing on the work of Maharashtrian activists, particularly women in the Ambedkarite movement, a series of discussions, seminars, workshops and publications ensued through the decade of the 1990s which sought to build an archive and canon of anti-caste feminism in English, thereby opening a window onto the fascinating world of Ambedkarite feminism. These texts helped address aspects of dalit women's lives and realities, of which feminist groups may have known in conversation, but which were now available as startling literature, fable and argument.

Gail Omvedt's work had anticipated such a development, and in fact her understanding of violence, including sexual violence, was based on her deep knowledge of caste and the workings of caste. Elsewhere in Maharashtra too, there were activists deeply imbued with an Ambedkarite sense of the social and political contexts that shape our lives, for instance in Nagpur and Aurangabad, traditional bastions of Ambedkarite movements. These histories were recalled in the 1990s and after and found their place in two important texts, Sharmila Rege's *Writing Caste, Writing Gender* and Meenakshi Moon and Urmila Pawar's *We Also Made History.* Both these texts made available to English and non-Maharashtrian readers a rich, complex world of women's lives and consciousness that was startling in what it offered to the reader and scholar, by way of an understanding of inequality, oppression and violence, but also of resistance, hope and brisk organizing.

The 1990s also inaugurated the publication of dalit women's life stories, memoirs and autobiographies from across India in English translations—and these not only provided a comparative perspective on the nature of dalit women's lives, but also demonstrated the existence of an entire life world and history of protest and defiance, located both at home and in the world. Bama's *Karukku*, Urmila Pawar's *The Weave of My Life* and Baby Kamble's *The Prisons We Broke* have proved particularly influential texts for those of us invested in engaging with dalit lives and histories. Apart from making clear that dalit women do 'speak differently', as political thinker and Professor Gopal Guru put it, dalit women's accounts of their lives indicated that it may not be possible for feminists to construct sexual violence merely as an exceptional event. Dalit women's experiences indicated that stigma and shame were indivisible from the everyday life of caste society, and were built into not only the social division of labour that relegated dalits to the worse forms of manual and service labour, but also into material life, why, into our very structures of feeling.

From being served soiled food to being forced to make a living disposing waste, or tending to the dead, dalit lives were virtually ground into physical dirt and degradation on the one hand, and emotional and cultural emptiness on the other. It was small comfort that they were 'allowed' their cultural specificity or the practice of rituals and customs that made for sociability—for the very ground of dalit existence was a denial of personhood, of what I have referred to earlier as 'ontological wounding'. In this context, dalit women's speech about violence, even sexual violence, was not separable from their general reflections on a life of negativity imposed on them, and which they have always sought to resist. Viewed thus as a constituent feature of dalit women's lives, sexual violence appeared a condition that was unspeakable for reasons that feminists had not thought of until then. I would like to refer to moments in two narratives in this context, both from the Tamil context: Bama's *Karukku* and Sivakami's *The Grip of Change*. I owe the insights I record to a remarkable study on dalit women's lives, by the Indian Institute of Dalit Studies (2010).

In *Karukku*, a dalit girl who goes to pick firewood is dragged into a shed and assaulted by an upper caste man; she is shocked and confides in the women in her community, but they advise her to keep quiet, for it would be her word against his, and nothing would come of it except further ignominy for her. But the man acts, and against her. He summons the dalit panchayat head and tells him that he was witness to a young dalit girl doing 'dirty' with a young man, and that he had caught them both out. For this, he says, they have to be called to account and made to pay a fine. Unable to refute him, the dalit elder returns to the community and calls for a meeting. The young girl is forced to go down on her knees and apologize, while her father forks out the fine; the women stand around muttering at the injustice of it all, but it is the girl who earns the blame, as the panchayat head reprimands her and tells her that it is they who have to be careful for otherwise it is they who would have to reckon with a swollen belly. Bama narrates this episode with defiant energy, and makes clear that it is not shame that stops the dalit girl from preferring a complaint, rather the fact of her community being economically dependent on the upper castes, and under their social control that renders it impossible for her to speak; for her speech, in these circumstances, has no value. Even her community head cannot insist on a fair hearing for her, because in a sense, he is also rendered speechless.

In Sivakami's novel, a young widow is raped by a dominant caste landlord and forced to be his concubine; when she is submitted to further ignominy by being beaten by the upper caste man's wife's brothers, she seeks refuge in the home of a local dalit political leader. He intercedes on her behalf: he indicates to the landlord that he does not intend to press rape charges, but insists that a caste atrocity had been committed and needs to be recompensed. This strategic move also helps stall charges that could be foisted against the widow. Sivakami's tone is angry and even scornful as she narrates the life and times of this dalit man and his family. She sees him as a manipulative political leader, who is not particularly sensitive to the realities of dalit existence. However, in a note that she appended, a few years later, to an edition of her English translation, she wonders if she has been unfairly harsh on the dalit political leader: the character had been based on her own father, but this was not the only reason why she felt she may have erred in pointing to his corrupt and gendered politics. She had not sufficiently accounted for the fact that a man in his circumstances was necessarily circumscribed in his actions: his political universe was, after all, limited, and left him with very little room for manouevre. The realities of dalit existence being what they are, she ought not to have judged him harshly, especially at the time of the writing of the novel, when a new generation of dalit leaders had appeared on the historical stage.

In these two instances, sexual violence exists both as a condition of existence for dalit women as well as one they cannot hope to confront without compromising their means of survival and the interests of the larger community. Secondly, we see that the position of dalit men with respect to sexual violence cannot be read off their behavior alone. In all incidents to do with attacks against dalits, except when they are armed or part of strong political movements, men flee the scene of impending violence—in fact their womenfolk sometimes push them to flee—since to remain, awaiting upper caste goons, would mean certain death. For women, it means being raped, but they yet stay, hoping to salvage whatever they may out of raided and destroyed homes. Fleeing men experience conflicted emotions—they are mocked for being 'unmanly' by dominant caste men, and they feel their helplessness as well. If we are to analyse the dalit political leader's stance in this context, like Sivakami, we are bound to understand what he was up against: while he does not 'flee' in the literal sense of the word, he is not left with much choice in a system that requires him to keep with its norms, if he is to remain visible at all; or as in Bama's novel, if he is to continue to live and work. If in such circumstances a man exacts the maximum out of what he may, while pushed to the margins, his unfree situation calls for analysis and not merely condemnation.

Dalit feminists' complex politics of community and gender notwithstanding, dalit male leaders and ideologues have not responded with alacrity to dalit women's concerns. While they are not averse to addressing gender-related discrimination, like other men they demur when dalit feminists link the social and the familial, the political and the intimate. Thus, domestic violence within dalit communities remains, as in other political contexts, a feminist concern, and is not taken on as part of a larger anti-caste, democratic politics. Secondly, when it comes to long-standing cultural practices such as ritual prostitution, dalit male activists' responses are likely to be 'masculine' in perception, and not always attentive to the experiences of dalit women. For instance, in Arakkonam in northern Tamil Nadu, a dalit women's group has been working for some years with a group of women called the Mathammas, who are 'dedicated' to a local temple, which means that they ought to be available to dance during temple festivals; the subtext of course is that they are also sexually available to upper caste men.

The dalit women's group desired to fight this practice, but discovered unexpected obstacles. For instance, their attempts to influence State policy such that the Mathammas benefit from protective affirmative action was thwarted actually by young dalit men in the neighbourhood: these men, it appears, rushed to inform government that no such class of women exists (Fatima Burnad, personal communication). While this may be read to mean political rejection of a hated practice, and an assertion of (male) pride in the face of imposed community stigma, it works not through challenge but denial, and leaves dalit women to combat a custom that targets girl children, who are even kidnapped in some instances from schools and forcibly pledged to temples.

Once again, we realize that to speak of rape and other forms of sexual servitude, the conditions that structure speech often turn out to be decisive. What allows speech, what brackets it, what renders it a valued testimony, what mocks it and what makes for defiant action: in caste society, almost all the time, the odds are tipped against dalits, and dalit men as much as dalit women cannot hope to speak in critical and oppositional ways, as we know them. For dalit feminists, this poses a problem, and one they do not expect to solve easily. For one, they align and work with the larger political community of dalits but at the same time, they cannot desist from speaking out against patriarchy as they experience it, at home, their immediate familial and caste worlds and in political movements.

The larger feminist world, especially that which looks to understand caste, has not really sought to comprehend the dalit feminist predicament, and some of us hasten to criticize dalit patriarchy without really heeding the double-voiced discourse of dalit women. In fact this would also become the ground for dalit feminist criticisms of the Indian women's movements, and of feminism as such, that both were essentially 'caste-blind'.

This latter is evident in the writings of a new generation of dalit women, especially those who inherited the militant and resonant activism of the 1990s and came into their own in the early twenty-first century. For this generation, not only local histories, but new transnational solidarity networks have provided spaces and contexts for rethinking their experiences. Much like Beijing 1995, the 2001 Durban conference against all forms of racism and xenophobia helped focus dalit concerns in an international context. Also the active interest taken in caste-related violence in India by groups such as Human Rights Watch during this time helped bring newer dimensions to the analysis of sexual hurt: the horizon set by the legal and ethical imperatives of international law and jurisprudence. The National Campaign on Dalit Human Rights which begun in 1998 as an initiative that reviewed the workings of the PoA Act, 1989 was active in Durban, and helped set a new militant tone for discussion to do with rights in a failed republic. A women's wing emerged from out of this campaign, the All India Dalit Mahila Manch.

Every region has in fact seen a new generation of dalit feminist activists writing, speaking and protesting. In some places, the decisive—and contentious—role played by the Church, whether Catholic or Protestant, has been central, particularly in Tamil Nadu. In other places, the neglect of the gender and caste question by progressive movements, especially of the Left, has led to a recalling of other pasts that dalits can own up to—this is particularly evident in Kerala and Andhra Pradesh, for instance—and has produced rich and argumentative writing and argument. Drawing on the autonomous traditions of dalit organizing in Karnataka, symbolized in the Dalit Sangharsha Samiti, dalit feminists in that state have held their own for several years now. The efforts of dalit feminist activists, politicized by these varying circumstances, have received a fillip by an emergent generation of dalit feminists, active in university spaces; and their stringent and often brilliant cultural interventions, such as those of Jenny Rowena, for instance, have forced non-dalit feminists to acknowledge their own sins of omission.

There have been occasions when women's groups have made common cause with dalit groups in protesting atrocities against dalits, yet the frisson between dalit groups, including dalit women's groups and feminist groups, persists. For instance, when the Khairalanji incidents (2006), which saw a family of Maharashtrian dalits cruelly butchered and the women of the family subjected to gruesome sexual assault and murder, took place, it was argued that feminist groups—in Mumbai, for example—did not respond with the urgency that was required; and especially at a time when dalit groups across the state were active in demanding justice. Whether such a charge was warranted or not may be argued, but the fact remains that there has not been a studied feminist response to Khairalanji or other such incidents. Such responses have been more forthcoming in the second decade of the 21st century, it must be admitted, but we still have a long way to go.

As noted above, if feminist lawyering had taken cognizance of the opportunity presented by the PoA Act, and worked closely with dalit groups in addressing the increasing incidence of atrocities against dalits, meaningful and productive conversations around caste and gender might have emerged. Secondly, when sexual coercion and violence to do with ritual sex work were challenged by dalit women's groups, the women's movement was stuck with its own ambiguous position on sex work, not wanting to deny the dignity and agency of women in sex work, and yet being all too aware of the structural violence that defined it. Dalit women had a more unequivocal position on the subject: they argued that many women engaged in sex work were from communities that had been burdened with caste-imposed prostitution, and that female agency in this context cannot be affirmed without paying heed to a caste-based division of labour which relegated some sections of women to sex work.

It may be argued that sexual violence is not reducible to caste-based violence, and that it does happen randomly—for one, the rapist is not one kind of person; neither is there one sort of victim. Yet, it appears important that feminists grasp rape in caste society as a 'founded' event, and one made possible by the existence of caste itself. I will return to the question of sexual violence and caste cultures in the last section of this book, where I discuss social and civic impunity.

***

I wish now to address the question of caste, gender and sexual violence from another angle, of how gender plays out in the context of relationships between different caste groups, including dalits in the context of a rapidly changing economy.

In many parts of India, given the logic of agricultural development and the periodic crises that it has thrown up, the relationship between caste status and property on the one hand and caste identity and labour on the other has been unsettled. Peasant castes, which used to labour on their lands as well as on the lands of feudal tenure-holders, have come into their own in some parts of the country, whereas in other parts they have partially moved away from agriculture into industry and the professions. Dalits continue to remain landless for the most part, or possess small holdings, and many have left their rural homes to seek education and work in urban India. Further, in the rural hinterland as well as the moffusil, electoral politics has opened up opportunities, by way of enabling particular castes to access local office, government contracts and real estate. These changes have proved consequential for women's lives, given that in some parts of the country, such as Tamil Nadu for instance, women from these castes have greater access to education and to diverse forms of employment. Women have become more mobile than before, which in turn has affected community and caste self-perceptions to do with status and honour.

Conflict, contestation, strategic alliances and unstable social relationships have thus come to define life in these contexts, especially from the early years of the twenty-first century. In a volatile economy where social certainties are in disarray and political life has uneven outcomes, existential concerns fold into gender concerns. This has been the case where men from peasant or artisanal castes have felt disempowered for a variety of reasons: uneven economic growth, for one, and for another, bewilderment in the face of lower caste and female mobility. In such contexts, men from these castes have drawn on their caste authority to do two things: police social behavior, including of women from their own castes, and women from castes lower in the hierarchy; and insistently differentiate their history and status from those they hold to be beneath them.

One important expression of this will to differentiated status is an angry opposition to intercaste marriage. Should women from a peasant, artisanal or trading caste seek partners outside approved marriage circles or should aspirational dalit men be seen in the former's company, punishment is swift and deadly. If the girl is a legal minor, the man she is intimate with could be and is charged with statutory rape and with abduction. If she is not a minor, both she and her partner are hounded and harassed, and sometimes done to death. Dalit girls too bear the brunt of the sexual and caste anxiety that backward communities exhibit: they are sexually assaulted and 'shown their place' when they show signs of defiance or wanting to better their lives.

Importantly, at least some feminists have sought to engage with these concerns—as is evident in the detailed report on violence against dalits in Haryana published by the group Women Against Sexual Violence and State Repression. The report notes with grave concern: 'Those who are struggling on the ground are well aware that resisting the caste system and working towards its annihilation necessitates going beyond protests against caste atrocities. The myriad ways in which caste is tied up to marriage, family and property, and the cultural and social tyranny it brings in its wake are compounded today by the deepening social and economic inequalities. This complex dynamic cannot be tackled without the forging of a common front and concerted action by all democratic groups and social movements.' It also affirms that feminists need to consciously be part of this common front: 'WSS holds that it is incumbent on feminists, women's movements and democratic rights movements to join the Dalit movements and Dalit feminists in confronting and questioning the apathy and silence that shroud the issue of sexual violence against Dalit women in Haryana' (Women Against Sexual Violence, 2014: 36).

There have been other responses to this process of gendered change: the sexual violence against and social death imposed on non-dalit women who seek to marry outside their caste confines, or who ignore internal gotra restrictions, has become a cause of concern to feminists engaged in addressing the issue. The phenomenon of what is often called 'honour' killings, but which Uma Chakravarti has rightly characterized as custodial violence, since they take place in familial custody, has pushed feminists to speak of sexual violence in new ways. For this is not only assault but actually sexual death, so to speak, since this is a form of violence that both literally and metaphorically annuls female sexual choice. Further, the gory ways in which the woman who transgresses caste boundaries to be with a partner or lover is dealt with ought to qualify as torture, which as I have noted confounds sexual and other forms of bodily violence.

***

While the centrality that feminists accord to caste has come somewhat late, in a related instance but the product of a different history, feminists have demonstrated that they could engage with structural inequality and difference and engage in conversations across social, religious and gender divisions. Feminist interventions in the context of communal violence, especially the kind that we have seen since the 1990s have been remarkably productive and in some senses exemplary. It remains a puzzle that what we achieved with the minority question, we failed to do, with respect to the caste question. Let me therefore now turn to the Masjid issue, which unfolded in tandem with the Mandal issue in the 1990s.

REFERENCES

Anonymous, 1978. 'The Villupuram Atrocity', *Economic and Political Weekly*, XIII (41): 1721–1725.

Balagopal, K. 1985. 'The Karamchedu Killings: The Essence of the NTR Phenomenon', *Economic and Political Weekly*, XX (31): 1298–1300.

Balagopal, K. 1991. 'Post Chundur and Other Chundurs', *Economic and Political Weekly*, XXVI (42): 2399–2405.

Balasubramaniam, J. 2014. *Villupuram Atrocity: Physical and Symbolic Violence against Dalits*. http://baluyash.blogspot.in/2014/07/villupuram-atrocity-physical-and.html (accessed 22 November 2015).

Chakravarti, Uma. 2003. *Gendering Caste Through a Feminist Lens*, Kolkata: Stree.

Chowdhry, Prem. 2008. 'Enforcing Cultural Codes: Gender and Violence in Northern India; in Mary John (ed.), *Women's Studies in India: A Reader*, pp. 292-296. New Delhi: Penguin Books.

Dalit Panthers Manifesto, http://ir.inflibnet.ac.in:8080/jspui/bitstream/10603/14528/15/15_appendicies.pdf; (accessed 22 November 2015).

2010. *Dalit Women: Rights and Citizenship in India*, Final Report, Delhi: Indian Institute of Dalit Studies.

D'Costa, Bina. 2016. 'Journeys through Shadows: Gender Justice in the Chittagong Hill Tracts' in H. Hossain and A. Mohsin, (eds.), *Of the Nation Born: The Bangladesh Papers (Zubaan Series on Sexual Violence and Impunity in South Asia)* New Delhi: Zubaan.

Dube, Leela. 2008. 'Caste and Women', in Mary John (ed.), *Women's Studies in India: A Reader*, pp. 466–474. New Delhi: Penguin India.

Kannabiran, Vasanth and Kalpana Kannabiran. 1991. 'Caste and Gender Understanding Dynamics of Power and Violence', *Economic and Political Weekly*, XXVI (37): 2130–2133.

Manorama, Ruth. 2008. 'Dalit Women: The Downtrodden Among the Downtrodden', in Mary John (ed.), *Women's Studies in India: A Reader*, pp. 445–451. New Delhi: Penguin India.

Omvedt, Gail. 1993. *Reinventing Revolution: New Socialist Movements and the Socialist Tradition in India*, pp. 64–66. London: M.E. Sharpe.

Perera-Rajasingham, Nimanthi. 2008. 'The Politics of the Governed: Maternal Politics and Child Recruitment in the Eastern Province of Sri Lanka' in Radhika Coomarasamy and Nimanathi Perera-Rajasingham (eds.), *Constellations of Violence: Feminist Interventions in South Asia*, pp. 121–148. New Delhi: Women Unlimited.

2014. *Speak! The Truth is Alive: Land Caste and Sexual Violence Against Dalit Girls and Women in Haryana*, Delhi: Women Against Sexual Violence and State Repression. https://wssnet.files.wordpress.com/2014/07/wss-haryana-report-compiled.pdf (accessed on 22 November 2015).

12

After Such Violence

Feminism confronts the Hindu Right

The Masjid issue began with the Hindu right—comprising various constituents of what has been described as the Sangh Parivar—claiming that the Babri Masjid, a mosque in the city of Ayodhya in Uttar Pradesh was originally a Rama temple and had to therefore be restored to that status. Such claims had been put forth even at the time of independence, and an idol installed within the mosque premises, but at that time Prime Minister Jawaharlal Nehru ordered the locking of gates of what eventually came to be called, rather deceitfully, the 'disputed structure'. This latter was a mosque in the 16th century and remained one until the 19th century, when a group of Hindus claimed that these were the premises where the Hindu god Rama was born, and began to offer worship. The matter went to court, and colonial government declared that the inner premises were to be left to the Hindus, and the outer to the Muslims. Until the 1940s, this was the situation, and after the locking of the gates, there was a lull.

By the mid-1980s, the Hindu right had become politically ascendant; it re-visited the Masjid dispute and with the active connivance of the State, smuggled in an idol and commenced worship. Soon, hectic efforts to mobilise people to build a temple in Ayodhya in place of the mosque were initiated, with L K Advani of the Bharatiya Janata Party (BJP), the premier party of the Hindu right, undertaking what was called a 'rath yatra' to rouse public opinion and render them complaisant with this demand. The yatra left behind a trial of blood, and was responsible for rioting, violence and death across the country. On December 6, 1992, a mob headed by Hindu right-wing leaders stormed the mosque and brought down its ancient dome. This dramatic and horrifying act of vandalism and violence produced very destructive consequences—resulting in the death of thousands of Muslims across the country. The violence visited on Muslims proved gruesome—horrifying stories of rape were reported in many parts, particularly Surat in Gujarat.

Feminists had to confront phenomena which would remain a staple with Hindu right mob politics—savage forms of sexual assault that appeared systematic and deliberate. While Hindu-Muslim riots are not new phenomena and researchers have indexed those that happened since independence, the killings that happened in the wake of the campaign to construct a temple in place of the Babri Masjid were deliberately undertaken, and with the intention to terrify the Muslim population at large. In earlier riots too, women had been targeted for sexual violence and in some instances, riots had broken out over matters pertaining to women—cross-faith love, instances of felt insult to women's honour, alleged instances of rape of women from either community by men of the other community—but those of the 1990s unfolded as morbid spectacle, calculated to prove a political argument.

***

Earlier riots happened due to a mix of reasons. In their compilation of riots in post-independence India, Violette Graff and Juliette Galonnier call attention to the following: rumours about mistreatment of Hindus in Pakistan; election-related intimidation; economic prosperity of Muslims in places where they were a

minority; ostensible lack of respect shown by Muslims to Hindu
holy books or icons; instances of Hindus feeling beleaguered in
essentially Muslim spaces, such as Aligarh Muslim University;
the alleged theft of a relic relating to the Prophet Mohammed in
Kashmir; and a host of other reasons, including the proactive role
essayed by the Rashtriya Swayamsevak Sangh (RSS) and Shiv Sena,
arch right wing groups, in fomenting acts of dastardly violence,
especially in western and northern India. I call attention here to
some important moments in the history of mass violence to do
with religion—to better locate the deliberate and planned violence
against Muslims that was acted out in the 1990s.

   The RSS and Shiv Sena were particularly active in the riots
that engulfed Ahmedabad in Gujarat in 1969. Hindu communal
organizations had become increasingly vocal in the city, and
following the 1965 war with Pakistan, anti-Pakistan feelings ran
high. Following specific instances of anti-Muslim sentiment that
went public, large-scale rioting began in the context of Muslims
undertaking an annual pilgrimage to a shrine located next to a
Hindu temple. In the madness that followed, Muslims homes and
neighbourhoods were targeted, houses torched, and businesses
destroyed; women raped and children killed. The pattern of
violence was chilling: Muslims who tried to flee were caught and
brutally tortured and killed. Some were pulled out of trains, and
violence spread from the city to the districts. This riot proved a
foretaste of what Gujarat would experience in the 1990s and 2000s.
The Jaganmohan Reddy Commission appointed to enquire into the
riots pointed at the preplanned nature of the violence, and noted
that electoral rolls had been utilized to identify Muslim homes and
businesses. The Congress government was blamed for not doing
enough to stop the riots, for the delay in announcing curfew and
for being guardedly indifferent—in fact the Congress calculatedly
played the Hindu card, so to speak, in a year when they felt they

would lose the Hindu vote. The Commission also blamed the RSS for its role in the violence.

The Ahmedabad riots became the pretext for full-scale violence in the weavers' town of Bhiwandi in Maharashtra the following year (1970), when the Shiv Sena set about celebrating the birthday of the Maratha ruler Shivaji, who in popular lore is hailed as the Hindu king who dared take on the mighty Mughals. As in Ahmedabad, several lives were lost. In both cities, Muslims comprised a majority of those killed—in almost all riots this continues to be the pattern, with the Muslim dead vastly outnumbering Hindus who die.

The rape of Rameeza Bee and the killing of her husband in custody sparked off violence in Hyderabad in 1978, and the city saw more instances of violence related to inter-community tensions through the following decade. For a mix of reasons, ranging from anger over Pakistan to local circumstantial grievances, some places in Bihar, and in Uttar Pradesh, Biharsharief, Aligarh, Meerut and Moradabad were sites of tension, mayhem and death in the first half of the 1980s—with government playing a grim and dirty role in Moradabad, when men of the Provincial Armed Constabulary ran amuck and killed several Muslims.

Given the public visibility gained by the Bharatiya Janata Party (BJP) when it was part of the coalition that opposed the authoritarian rule of Indira Gandhi during the Emergency years (1975–77), Hindu political identity was affirmed and consolidated by the late 1970s. In Maharashtra, the Shiv Sena had become associated with a ferocious Hindu populism, drawing its support from a discontented urban underclass; its politics of hate played out in any number of violent incidents involving Muslims in Maharashtra during the 1970s and after.

***

What was significant in all this, especially in the 1980s, was a public show of Hindu grievances, orchestrated by the RSS and its affiliates—

and typically these had to do with a gendered perception of what came to be viewed as the 'Muslim problem'. It was proclaimed that the Muslim population was growing at an alarming rate, and that Muslim polygamy was to blame, and that the ulema, or Muslim religious leaders, were exhorting Muslims to have more children. This demographic argument gestured towards the conversion of dalits to Islam in Meenakshipuram in Tamil Nadu; and at a Hindu Sammelan held in 1981 in Uttar Pradesh, Hindus were exhorted to take stock of their imperiled (sic) condition. An Ekamata Yatra, carrying holy water from the Ganga crisscrossed the country, and sent out a message to Muslim converts to return to their original faith. In retrospect, this appears an anticipation of Advani's rath yatra of the 1990s.

It is not surprising then, following such public proclamations of Hindus under siege, that the Babri Masjid was claimed by the RSS as a site for a future Ram temple in 1986. Rajiv Gandhi, who took over as Prime Minister in 1984 following Indira Gandhi's death, presided over this process of ushering the Hindu right to the centre stage of politics and history. Earlier, in 1986, his government had assented to the passing of the Muslim Women's Protection on Divorce Act following the famous Shah Bano case. Shah Bano had filed for maintenance from her estranged husband, who had thrown her out and taken a younger wife. She filed under criminal law, under Article 125 which dealt with alimony; whereupon her husband divorced her and claimed that henceforth under Islamic law he was not entitled to maintain her. She filed a petition in the High Court in Madhya Pradesh, and the court awarded her alimony, but her husband took his argument to the Supreme Court, where his petition was eventually dismissed and the High Court decision upheld.

The Supreme Court declared that there was no discrepancy between Section 125 and Islamic law. Further, one of the judges in his pronouncement referred to the Constitutional injunction that

India ought to move towards defining a uniform civil code that would apply to all religionists. This led to protests from groups of Muslims, who feared that their community interests would be sacrificed to Hindu majoritarian ones, even as articulate Muslim women joined their fellow feminists in demanding justice and rights for themselves. As matters appeared to go out of hand, Rajiv Gandhi backed the passing of a new act that guaranteed Muslim women alimony during the iddat period, that is, for 90 days after being divorced. This act was seen by the Hindu right as one of 'appeasement' of Muslim fundamentalist opinion. In order to stannch the growing appeal of the Hindu right, Rajiv Gandhi's government agreed to the opening of the locks of the Babri Masjid and for Rama worship within its precincts.

It is important that we read the sequence of events that saw the Hindu right lock horns with Muslims in the 1980s in terms of its underlying gendered logic—for this logic would eventually lead Hindu men to berate Muslim men for being 'backward', with regard to Muslim women's rights, and Muslim women for being fecund mothers. They would conjure up a spectre of Muslim 'hordes' overrunning Hindustan, presided over by lascivious Muslim men. Whatever the political and economic contexts of rioting in the wake of the Babri Masjid dispute, the force of hatred directed against women and the violent murders that claimed both Muslim men and women in the riots, cannot be understand outside of this structure of sexual and demographic anxiety. Such anxiety was carefully cultivated and propagandized and deployed deliberately to incite Hindu men to act on their sense of 'manhood'.

***

Such exhortations to Hindu manhood possess a hoary history. Hindu masculinity emerged as a desirable attribute in the 1920s in the discourses and practices that were set in motion in northern and north-western India in the early twentieth century. Mediated by the Arya Samaj's shuddhi and sangathan programmes, these notions came to constitute Hindu political common sense, and became a feature of the public propaganda of the Hindu Mahasabha and other Hindu organisations, and eventually of the RSS and its brotherhood in saffron. Charu Gupta's work alerts us to the salient aspects of this desired masculinity.

Charu Gupta draws a detailed picture of the economic, social and political circumstances that obtained in the United Provinces in the decades leading to the 1920s; while upper castes continued to hold superior rights in land, and were active in state service and also in the intellectual sphere, the region's transformed economies saw upwardly mobile shudra (backward caste) peasants and dalit workers court higher varna status and respectability. While this made for contentious caste relationships, it nevertheless enabled the emergence of a diffuse constituency of Hindus, which defined its claims to authentic Hindu-ness through a redefinition and regulation of Hindu women's lives. Gupta argues that educated and articulate dominant caste women, however modest their number, were seen as posing a threat to the 'unity' and 'sanctity' of the Hindu home—and this provoked into existence a tendentious discourse on women's proper place, role and function in Hindu society. So much so that even communities whose women worked in public spaces in the city, in shops and markets, for example, were keen on confining them to the household.

Those who spoke and wrote thus betrayed great sexual anxiety; part of this had to do with the fact that they had to reckon with the presence of assertive women, and part had to do with their sense of being inadequately Hindu. Thus the arguments to do with women's proper role unfolded within a discursive and political framework that positioned Hindus as victims of colonial rule, which, it was said, had deprived them of manhood; Hindus were therefore asked to regain their lost virility. The Hindu Mahasabha made the restoration of Hindu manhood one of its central objectives.

One of its stated aims was 'to 'improve the physique of the Hindus and promote martial spirit amongst them by establishing military schools and organising volunteer corps'; and its chief slogan was 'Hinduise all politics and Militarise Hindudom' (Charu Gupta, 1998: 721).

Further, it was argued that Muslims were all set to overpower Hindus through forcible conversion and luring Hindu women to liaise with Muslim men. Demographic arguments were deployed in this context, conjuring up an image of an over-fecund community. Gupta points out that the Moplah rebellion in Kerala (1921), which essentially was a peasant conflict whose political expressions drew on religious identity and imagery, the Khilafat agitations (1919–1922), which brought Muslims into the heart of nationalist politics and the vibrant discourse around the question of Islam in the modern world that raged across West Asia, were all melded together to suggest an imminent Muslim threat to Hindus. The Arya Samaj's Shuddhi campaign accelerated on this account in the 1920s, and its proponents made it clear that to 'return' to Hinduism was to regain one's lost—and pure—status, and one's emasculated manhood. For this, Hindus had to unite, and organize: 'The protection of Hindu community is the most important question at present... We have to stop producing emasculated and weak Hindus... We have to search for new ways to make the Hindu community powerful... This is no time to argue for caste divisions... We have to bring together all parts of the community to make it a solid whole' (*op. cit*, 729).

Organized Hindu manhood was to set itself certain important duties, the most fundamental being the protection of Hindu women and children; in essence this meant protecting Hindu women from Muslim men, who were portrayed as lascivious and without morals. Hindu women were thus exhorted to keep away from anything to do with Muslims or Islam. Gupta notes that 'Clear-cut and detailed instructions were issued to Hindu men and women in this regard. Men were told never to let their women board "ekkas" driven by Muslims, not to keep Muslim servants, not to invite Muslim prostitutes or singers on joyous occasions, not to buy any household items from Muslims, etc. Women were specifically warned not to let any Muslim selling bangles inside the house, never to touch a "tazia" as she would soon become a widow, not to visit any maulvis, "pirs" or "melas". Further, if any woman ever got lost, she was advised never to take help of any Muslim but go to the nearby Arya Samaj' (*op.cit*, 731).

Clearly the criss-crossing and syncretic cultures of the everyday, which structured women lives and in which they freely circulated, were to be exchanged for membership in a putative Hindu community. Here women had to consent to be protected on the one hand, and on the other, be ready to wield the sword or dagger to defend their chastity and honour. Even as the Hindu woman was asked to refashion herself, she was fed stories of imminent abduction, rape and violence by Muslim men. Newspapers during the 1920s and well into the 1930s carried stories of Muslim men abducting Hindu girls, and over and over the message that the Hindu public sphere sought to convey was this: beware of Muslim men, for they are out to convert Hindu women. The Hindu widow was seen as particularly vulnerable, given her status within her own community and outrageous arguments were advanced in this regard: 'Our sexually unsatisfied widows especially are prone to Muslim hands and by producing Muslim children, they increase their numbers and spell disaster for the Hindus... Muslim "goondas" are especially seen outside the houses which have Hindu widows... You yourselves say, would you like our Aryan widows to read "nikah" with a Muslim?' (*op. cit*, 733).

Charu Gupta sums up the Hindu manhood project this: 'The central argument being grounded by the Hindu communal organisations was that to protect "our" women, sangathan was a must. First the image of a ferociously intolerant "other" was constructed and then the Hindus were invited to become equally ferocious. Thus, the justification for Hindu male prowess was provided by pointing to the sexually predatory Muslim male and the vulnerable Hindu woman' (*op. cit.,* 731).

There was a further twist to this propaganda: just as how the Hindu widow's problematic sexuality was seen as an incitement to conversion efforts, the dalit woman's 'unclean' body and being were marked out for disapproval. In effect the dalit woman became a negative measure by which upper caste—and aspirational shudra—women were to judge and regulate their own behavior. dalit women were seen as inherently promiscuous, given to loose talk, capable of luring upper caste men, and given to filling the heads of young Hindu upper caste women with wrong notions about marriage and domesticity. On the other hand, they were seen as potential converts to Christianity and the dalit woman convert was portrayed as giving herself airs. That dalit women's presence in public spaces, their labour within upper caste homes and their boldness of demeanour and readiness to convert caused deep anxiety to Hindu men is evident. To ensure that Hinduism does not lose out on its labouring classes, the upper castes were entreated to treat dalits better!

***

I have dwelt at some length on the making of Hindu masculinity in late colonial India because it provided a set of arguments, images and tropes for the Hindu right to deploy at will. The imprecation to Hindu men to get virile acquired a particular edge, when aligned with the shrill patriotism of the years leading to Partition. Further, Hindu masculinity and its other, Muslim (sexual) depravity, became constitutive of Hindu nationhood as such. This is why, to this day, a political position that challenges this combination of manhood, Hinduism and nationhood invites the charge of being, among other things, 'effete'—this is evident in the rhetoric of the Shiv Sena or the Bajrang Dal, which look for and find their adherents in the shrill malcontents of the street and bazaar. Anand Patwardhan's films on the Babri Masjid dispute capture this politics of menacing and at the same time absurd machismo of the right; except that the fact of it appearing absurd does not mean that it cannot kill, maim and destroy.

For feminists, the riots of the 1990s were thus as much about Hindu manhood as they were about the tragic fate visited on Muslim men and women. The first indication of what they were up against was Surat 1992, where sexual violence and death became, as I have noted above, the stuff of spectacle: a disturbing story filed in *Manushi* soon after the events contains grim details of what Muslim women experienced during those trouble-filled days. The public shaming, gang rape and murder of Muslim girls and women, the murder and burning of Muslim men and children in fires stoked for that purpose, the humiliation visited on Muslim religious leaders, the attempts to force the latter to utter the names of Hindu gods, the looting and destruction of Muslim shops, the public speeches of Hindu religious and movement leaders that broadcast hatred and vile abuse against Muslims and exhorted Hindu men to kill and rape, the indifference of the Police in most places, the role played by legislators belonging to the BJP—these pertain to not only Surat 1992, but also Gujarat 2002 (and in fact were evident earliest in the 1969 riots I have referred to above). It is as if a script for a ghastly demonstration of humiliation, rape and murder had been put in place; one that could be rehearsed acted out over and over again.

To be sure, the material conditions that obtained at the time of these riots determined certain patterns of behaviour: the political economy of riots has been well studied, and we know that ideology is not always the sole determining force, and that contentious political and economic interests are played out during these fatal moments in time. Also, political conjunctures that anchor particular instances of communal violence influence their trajectory. In the 1990s, the

Masjid dispute was brought to bear on the political energies that the Mandal Report had unleashed; and a potential radical critique of caste that could emerge from that context of protest was countered by an appeal to Hindutva that cut across caste lines. Significantly, in the 1990s, the so-called shudra castes did not, in unison, pick up the Hindutva gauntlet, especially in Uttar Pradesh and Bihar, given the tough anti-Hindutva stance of the dominant political parties in both states. On the other hand, the Hindu right was hard at work as it sought to draw support from these castes, as also from some dalit castes across the country, which worked to its advantage in Gujarat in 2002, when sections of dalit and adivasi communities participated in the violence.

Yet, across space and time, howsoever riots are constituted, we are left to reckon with the ubiquity of sexual violence; and this, as feminists have argued, is not merely an instance of identities writ large on women's bodies, but that this violent inscription of identity has been constitutive of the destructive politics of the Hindu right, especially for the period we are concerned with. This is why, in the 1990s and 2000s the violence that was on display pushed the limits of what may yet be done to women's bodies. As Tanika Sarkar went on to write in the wake of Gujarat 2002,

> ... (it was) as if the most gruesome elements from all the annals of mass destruction have been pulled together to form a whole' (Tanika Sarkar, 2002: 2872). This cruelty, evident not only in brutal acts of rape, but of the murder and burning of half-alive and dead Muslim women, points to the manner in which sexual violence became the axis on which an entire sequence of horrific acts turned: 'Hindu mobs swooped down upon Muslim women and children with multiple but related aims. First, to possess and dishonour them and their men, second to taste what is denied to them and what, according to their understanding, explains Muslim virility. Third, to physically destroy the vagina and the womb, and, thereby, to symbolically

destroy the sources of pleasure, reproduction and nurture for Muslim men, and for Muslim children. Then, by beatings, to punish the fertile female body. Then, by physically destroying the children, to signify an end to Muslim growth. Then, by cutting up the foetus and burning it, to achieve a symbolic destruction of future generations, of the very future of Muslims themselves. The burning of men, women and children, as the final move, served multiple functions: it was to destroy evidence, it was to make Muslims vanish, it was also to desecrate Muslim deaths by denying them an Islamic burial, and forcing a Hindu cremation upon them; a kind of a macabre post-mortem forced conversion. (Tanika Sarkar: 2876).

The pervasive use of sexual violence to apocalyptic ends was such that a report that recorded the experiences of children during the violence noted with sorrow how the word rape had become one that children appear to know instinctively, even seven and eight year olds. Most of them had seen their mothers, sisters or grandmother assaulted and a child defined *Balaatkaar* thus: 'a woman's clothes are taken off, she is killed and burnt' (Kavita Panjabi et. al, 2002: 65).

***

Feminist responses to Gujarat 2002, as indeed to all riots since the 1990s, have been concerted and consistent both in the regions where violence happened and in terms of working through national strategies for addressing the problem. Sitting down and speaking with women about what they had endured, counseling children, building bridges of peace and trust with Muslim community leaders, with whom they could not hope to have much in common when it came to the question of women's rights, taking specific cases to court, and undertaking immediate as well as protracted relief work—these have been some of the ways in which feminists, working on their own with victim-survivors and with other groups, addressed events whose meaning eluded rational understanding.

Importantly, feminist conversations with Muslim minority communities have not been defined only by matters to do with gender justice, particularly those that emerged as pertinent in the context of the Hindu right's shrill demand for a uniform civil code. Invested as many feminists are in the making of a gender-just civil code, they have yet consistently disdained the idea of a 'uniform' code. Given the menacing rise of the Hindu right, they have rightly distanced themselves from that objective and taken nuanced positions: from outlining a case for reform of Muslim personal law to arguing for a broad-based egalitarian civil code that covers both private and public domains, with the provision that if a person so wishes, he or she can choose to be governed by the laws of their community. Further, given the sustained work that feminist groups have done across the country with respect to communal violence and its effects, the relationship between feminism and faith, in this context an embattled minority faith, has been productive.

To return to Gujarat 2002: for many of those who undertook work on matters to do with justice or rehabilitation after the violence, it has not been easy to come to terms with what they witnessed, or came to hear of, from fellow feminists and other friends in Gujarat: the planned and deliberate nature of violence, for one, and the manner in which hatred against Muslims was consciously cultivated and nurtured through appeals to Hindu sexual insecurity. Perhaps what was most galling was the role played by Hindu women, some of whom literally stoked the fires that burnt Muslims, by supplying their cooking gas cylinders for the purpose; and others who pushed half-burnt bodies into the fire. Fed on tales of Muslim women having extremely fertile wombs, Hindu mothers, feminists realized, could be made to feel enraged. Further, they could be made to look on Muslim women with contempt, because they accept polygamy and the venalities of 'triple talaq'. While the role of propaganda was evident, equally on display was the sexual othering of Muslim women, and the affirmation of Hindu womanhood through a castigation of the Muslim other, and a strategy that merely rewrote the script of caste. The Hindu women who acquiesced with the sexual politics of Hindutva were given to viewing their lower caste counterparts in exactly the same way: as a source of potential sexual danger, and a symbol of the unregenerate nature of the lower castes.

Finally, for all the work that feminists had done on sexual violence, Gujarat 2002 posed a conundrum: in the fact of hatred such as this, what does one do? How does one even define criminal intent or come to grips with a sexual politics that is so profoundly ugly, perverse and destructive?

As always, there was the problem of speech: those who witnessed acts of brutality that beggared understanding and language had to battle forgetting and fear in order to lay claims to justice; those who had been victims of outrageous sexual violence did not, could not speak of their experiences in the face of what their daughters or other female kin had undergone; and, in the interest of bearing witness to the suffering of others, kept quiet about their own; then there were those who had tried to gain the ear of the State, either by trying to file a complaint, or through appealing to a policeman to heed their plight, and had been cruelly rebuffed.

Feminists who came as part of fact-finding teams or on relief missions were shocked at the widespread denial of what Muslim women had endured and in many cases not survived. While complaints of sexual violence do suffer this fate even in 'normal' times, the systematic nonchalance on display in Gujarat, each time the matter was brought up, spoke volumes of a politics that was not merely one of denial, but one which had thoroughly naturalized the commission of these acts, that neither the perpetrators, nor those who authorized them to act in the ways that they did, felt the need to acknowledge what had happened.

A BJP woman MP, Maya Kodnani, as a feminist report on the violence notes, appeared almost bemused when asked about the bestial violence that Muslim women had been subjected to:

she dismissively said that she had heard something about it, but there have been no confirmed reports. A police officer in one of the districts was not indifferent, but clearly did not think that this was a question that ought to detain him from carrying out what, to him, was more important: the maintenance of law and order. The Gujarati vernacular media was silent on the matter, in fact did not even gesture towards it; and yet, it gave room for the circulation of groundless rumours about the violations committed by Muslim men on Hindu women, especially on board the Sabarmati Express train, of which some coaches burnt at Godhra station.

The burning of the train in fact became a context and reason for ideologues of the Hindu right to defend the vile acts they had unleashed: they argued that Muslims were behind this deadly arson, and that this was what had caused violence to break out in the first place, in other words, 'spontaneous' Hindu anger, justly retributive, was what led to unexpected acts of violence in Gujarat in February and March 2002. The media picked up on this argument about retribution and added its own–salacious tales about how Muslim men had impaired the honour of Hindu women.

There was yet another concern that feminists had to address: While news of what women had suffered was available and taken note of in all fact-finding reports, only one, published by feminists, connected the experiences of women to the overall politics of Hindutva. Women's groups in Gujarat had been vocal on this issue, and insisted on a framework of understanding that grasped the deliberate use of sexual violence as both ideology and strategy. How was one to do this? This was not easy, especially for those engaged in prosecuting these cases. For one, they had to reckon with an indifferent criminal justice system that was politically compromised: medical personnel could not speak their minds about the actual status of wounded and hurt bodies, except under cover of secrecy, or when they felt assured of support; police had failed to file appropriate First Information Reports, or even if they did, would not register cases under relevant sections; it was next to impossible to hold to account senior officers, in the police and other departments concerned with the delivery of justice.

Secondly, victims and complainants who came forward to speak could not be guaranteed safety, since their tormentors were at large and continued to threaten them. Then there was the problem of speaking and continuing to live in a community. For Muslim men, devastated as they were, did not find it easy to handle the tales of horror that women in their households had been subject to, and in their trauma did not always find it easy to sympathise with or support women. In such circumstances, some women preferred to stay silent. Then again, it was common knowledge, at least to lawyers and rights activists, that rape cases are the hardest to prosecute, given the way matters to do with evidence are addressed within the court system, and if there was a choice of getting a conviction out of a murder case, those engaged in the fight for justice noted tersely, they would rather work with that—since justice was the need of the hour.

Feminists around the country decided that they perhaps ought to mobilize their own intellectual and legal resources to both mark the immense and tragic gravity of what had happened in Gujarat; as well as think of appropriate legal measures that would help them engage with the situation. It was clear to many of them that they ought not to lose sight of the fact of mass violence and ought to locate sexual violence within that framework. It was also evident that it may not be enough to bring individual perpetrators to book. That was tough enough, but what was as important, if not more so, was to fix 'command responsibility', to create a set of legal measures that would make for a recognition that these were willed political crimes, that they were part of a strategy to deprive Muslims of their fundamental rights, push them into civic non-existence, and most important, to decimate them, as a community.

Eventually a team of feminist lawyers, writers and civil rights activists, many of whom had been active in international tribunals, and forums that engaged with mass violence—in Yugoslavia, Rwanda, Algeria, Sri Lanka—was put together. This team visited Gujarat, listened to depositions, read reports that were already available and prepared a detailed document of what had transpired, and what ought to be done. The report is significant for many reasons. It helped frame the events in Gujarat within the context of crimes that have been acknowledged as crimes against humanity and as genocidal crimes. It positioned the acts of sexual violence that had taken place within the purview of international jurisprudence, which had evolved out of the hearings of crimes committed in Bosnia and the rest of former Yugoslavia. In a context where law and justice appeared to falter, it brought in a universally-held normative context for the State to re-examine its own Constitutional commitments. More than anything else, it made it clear that sexual crimes are not to be viewed in ghettoized legal terms, rather they have to be viewed as systemic, deliberate and emanating from the directives of authority held in impunity. In other words, it is not only the 'doer' of the crime who is to be held responsible, but also all those who have created the conditions for him to act in the manner that he did.

The members of the international team as well as their Indian counterparts were under no illusion what their work would actually amount to, and whether it would help bring about relief and justice for victims. Yet, it was clear that such work was wholly necessary, if only to challenge the utter impunity with which civil society and State had behaved in Gujarat, and to keep alive a politics of recognition. Meanwhile, women's groups in Gujarat, lawyers working on particular cases and civil rights activists continue to work at the immense and unfulfilled task of justice-seeking and healing. This has not been easy, since the Hindu Right continues to be in power in Gujarat (at the time of writing this section), and has systematically sought to dissuade and threaten victims from going to court.

***

Feminist efforts to rethink sexual violence in the context of mass crimes, and in relationship to attempts to systematically deny their civil rights, particularly their right to life, liberty and livelihood were put to use in the framing of legislation that addressed these and other related concerns. The result was that the Communal and Targeted Violence Bill that has been drafted—but not passed in Parliament—contained sections that drew on the experiences of activists in Gujarat, 2002; and also on older memories of things gone wrong in the republic. The Nellie massacre in Assam in 1983; anti-Sikh violence unleashed in Delhi in 1984, the Cauvery riots in which minority Tamil speakers were targeted and attacked in Bengaluru city in 1991; persistent attacks on dalit and adivasi villages and settlements, accompanied by acts of public shaming, rape and murder by dominant caste armies and in some cases State-supported militias at all times, but particularly in the period starting with the 1970s: in each of these instances, political parties were active in fomenting hatred, State machinery collusive with dominant community and political leaders, and sexual attacks on women an integral part of the violence. In almost all instances, witnesses were not forthcoming since they feared for their lives, the criminal justice system lackadaisical and unwilling to prosecute cases brought to its notice, and even if individual perpetrators were sometimes awarded sentences, those who actually presided over the destruction, be they political leaders or their bureaucratic supporters, were not ever brought to book.

Keeping these facts in mind, feminists worked with lawyers and legal personnel to insist on certain clauses: an entire section was devoted to defining sexual violence and how it ought to be addressed in the context of mass violence. Apart from rape, gang rape and mass rape, which target women, various sorts of sexual acts committed on either men or women were sought to be penalized. While drawing on existing definitions of sexual violence, new provisions were suggested, which included acts such as removing a person's clothes or any other form of conduct that is calculated to cause a person sexual indignity. Given the nature of mass violence, it was urged that judicial cognizance be taken of the circumstances under which sexual assault happen, and that delays in reporting it, absence of medical evidence or lack of corroboration of the victim's testimony ought not to be cited in ways that would affect the victims' case adversely.

Witness protection, fixing of command responsibility, including of non-State actors, penalizing hate speech, charging State personnel with dereliction of duty, and the drawing up of a charter of reparations are some of the other features of the bill that feminists, among others, wanted included in the Bill. Most important, of course, was the Bill's proviso that recognized that acts of violence against minorities in every instance are targeted; that is, such acts are not only deliberate, but calculated to hurt, cause humiliation, deprive a person or persons of a sense of personhood and most importantly deprive them of their rights as citizens. (Interestingly, feminists who worked on the Bill were influenced by the PoA Act, and drew liberally from its spirit.)

While the Bill is yet to see the light of day, discussions around it enabled feminists establish connections between sexual violence and systematic and targeted violence against embattled minorities in every instance. The Bill reflected an understanding that exceptional violence does not pertain only to specific acts of targeted hurt, but also to everyday contexts—the inclusion of acts of violence against dalits and adivasis within the scope of the Bill is proof of this understanding. This is significant, given that of the many populations being targeted systematically, dalits and adivasis resident in central and eastern India are the most numerous. In the name of development, they are being alienated from productive resources and are subject to various degrees of coercion. Adivasis have fled their homes in Chattisgarh, where a concerted war is being waged against them by the Indian State, which has made it clear that it is on the side of Capital and 'development' under the latter's auspices. They have fled either to the central Indian forest and joined up with the Maoist insurgent group that has taken hold of vast swathes of forest territory; or fled Chattisgarh to live in camps in neighbouring Andhra Pradesh and Telengana. Women have been the worst sufferers in this regard and been the target of state-directed violence, including rape.

The elaborate provisions on dereliction of duty and command responsibility in the Communal and Targeted Violence Bill point to not only to acts of omission, but insist on acts of commission as well—that government personnel actually assist in targeting minority populations. Punitive action against erring State personnel, clearly meant to be corrective and cautionary, is advanced as an antidote to impunity.

For civil rights and feminist activists, such action that brackets and thwarts impunity appeared necessary for another reason: in the light of the routine abuse of authority by the Indian Armed Forces in Kashmir and in parts of North-east India. The republic, in a sense, had to be saved from the State, and the sovereignty vested in citizens differentiated and in some instances protected from the institutions meant to guard it. In the event, democratic interventions in these regions, especially by women's groups, have helped produce a much-needed critique of the Nation-State, indeed of the sexual politics that underlies its practice of impunity. I examine these developments in the following chapter.

REFERENCES

Graff, Violette and Juliette Galonnier, *Hindu-Muslim Communal Riots in India I (1947–1986)*, Online Encyclopedia of Mass Violence, [online], published on 15 July 2013, accessed 8 August 2015, URL: http://www.massviolence.org/Hindu-Muslim-Communal-Riots-in,736, ISSN 1961-9898

Hindu-Muslim Communal Riots in India II (1986-2011), Online Encyclopedia of Mass Violence, [online], published on 20 August 2013, accessed 8 August 2015, URL : http://www.massviolence.org/Hindu-Muslim-Communal-Riots-in,738, ISSN 1961-9898

Gupta, Charu, 1998 'Articulating Hindu Masculinity and Femininity: 'Shuddhi' and 'Sangathan' Movements in United Provinces in the 1920s', *Economic and Political Weekly*, Vol. 33, No. 13, March 26, pp. 727–735

Hameed, Syeda S., 1992 Ruth Manorama, Malini Ghose, Sheba George, Mari Marcel Thekaekara, Farah Naqvi, *How has the Gujarat Massacre affected minority women—Fact-finding by a Women's Panel*; http://www.outlookindia.com/printarticle.aspx?215433

Mander, Harsh and Farah Naqvi, 2011 'When equal protection matters most', *Indian Express*, 21 July http://www.indianexpress.com/news/when-equal-protection-matters-most/820147/0

Panjabi, Kavita, Krishna Bandopadhyay and Bolan Gangopadhyay, *The Next Generation: In the Wake of the Genocide: A Report on the Impact of the Gujarat Pogrom on Children and the Young*

Peer, Gazala, 2011 *Prevention of Communal and Targeted Violence (Access to Justice and Reparations Bill, 2011: An Insight*; http://www.manupatra.co.in/newsline/articles/Upload/864BE18B-8FEB-4EAA-972E-EA1340F8E669.pdf

Threatened Existence: A Feminist Analysis of the Genocide in Gujarat, Report by the International Initiative for Justice (IIJ), December 2003.

Sarkar, Tanika, 2002 'Semiotics of Terror', *Economic and Political Weekly*, Vol XXXVII No. 28, July 13, pp. 2872–2876.

Shah, Kalpana, Smita Shah and Neha Shah, 1993 'The Nightmare of Surat', *Manushi*, No. 74–75 (Jan.-Feb.-March-April), pp. 50–58.

13

A Wounded Republic

Disciplining Our Borders

In the northeast of India and Kashmir, the armed forces exist, it appears, to repeatedly remind citizens just how unfree they are. The national self-determination struggles in both regions, which go back to the decade of Indian independence, have been termed seditious, considered criminal and those engaged in them not always worthy of dialogue. In turn, those willing to endorse the Indian State's position have been nurtured into loyalists, leading to the persistence of internecine strife in these regions. In this chapter I examine, albeit briefly, developments in the Northeast, particularly Nagaland, Manipur, Assam—and on the other side in Kashmir, in the context of conflict-related sexual violence, and the possibilities for justice and healing in these traumatized spaces. I focus on particular moments in the long and tortuous history of civil strife in these regions, rather than the overall nature and timescale of the strife in question.

***

Before I consider specific histories, I would like to point to the issues at stake, by looking at two regions and the manner in which the Indian State has dealt with them—Kashmir and Nagaland.

In Kashmir, a largely non-violent struggle took to arms in the wake of systematic erosion of the autonomy guaranteed under Article 370 of the Constitution of India. Following independence, several Indian states that had not been part of British India but were under native governance, 'acceded' to the Indian Union, giving into a mix of persuasion and coercion that was deployed by the newly independent nation. Kashmir's situation at this point in time, in 1947, was complex. A Muslim-majority state, ruled by a Hindu ruler, Hari Singh, it was home to democratic discontent, which had been met with brutal violence. Kashmiri democrats insisted on their right to self-determination, but meanwhile, Hari Singh refused to concede to their demands, even as he delayed acceding to the Indian Union.

An invasion by tribal militia, supported by Pakistan in October 1947, proved to be a turning point, and resulted in Hari Singh hastily signing the instrument of accession. Indian troops meanwhile marched into Kashmir. A full-fledged war between the two barely independent nations of India and Pakistan was brought to an end under UN auspices. Much of Kashmir remained with India, except for a part that had been occupied by Pakistan, and where rebels punished by the erstwhile ruler of the state had gathered. More important, a UN resolution insisted that the future of Kashmir be decided through an impartial plebiscite—Kashmiris would thus decide whether they desired to accede to India or Pakistan. India, meanwhile, effected an amendment to its Constitution by promulgating Article 370, which ensured special status and internal autonomy for Jammu and Kashmir, with Indian jurisdiction in Kashmir limited to defence, foreign affairs and communications.

Elections were held in Kashmir in 1951, with the UN warning that this would not constitute a plebiscite. Veteran Kashmiri democrat Sheikh Abdullah won the elections and took office. The good Sheikh veered between insisting on the plebiscite and reluctantly agreeing to the terms of accession signed earlier. This did not please the Indian State, which lost no time in substituting its own men in office, even as it put the charismatic leader behind bars and ensured that he stayed out of politics. Meanwhile, even as India and Pakistan retained their claims over Kashmir, the region's constitutive claims to autonomy were not conceded by either country. While elections continued to be held over the years, it was evident that they were rigged in a manner favourable to parties that supported the government of India's stance. As India loyalists were returned to power serially, in sheer frustration the young took to arms. Given the duplicitous yet scrupulously 'legal' manner in which Kashmir has been forcibly accommodated into the Indian Union, Uma Chakravarti has rightly compared Kashmir's status to that of a wife kept locked within a forced marriage!

Armed militancy may be traced to the late 1980s (though the Jammu and Kashmir Liberation Front [JKLF], which did not speak the language of faith-based identity, but of the claims of Kashmiriyat or the distinctly Sufi-inspired syncretic culture of the region, was founded in 1977). A slew of militant groups emerged in the valley, some supported by the government of Pakistan, which was equally concerned about the Kashmiris's desire for self-determination and appeared to want to regulate it in a manner that would serve its own purpose. Pakistan was particularly worried about the politics of the JKLF and wanted to neutralize its appeal and so supported parties whose understanding of nationhood and identity was narrow and closed. In the event, as armed groups confronted each other and the Indian State and army, rampant violence restructured the nature of the struggle, rendering it very bloody. The region continues to be volatile, and the demand for 'azaadi' or freedom remains as resonant as all those decades ago, and as we shall see, the Indian State's brutal response continues with impunity.

I turn now to Nagaland. Since the 1940s, Naga nationalists have demanded autonomy, leading to a state of independence.

On the eve of Indian independence, they insisted on their right to self-determination, but agreed that they would work towards national independence under the 'protection' of the government of Assam, which governed their territories in British India. This was to continue for a specified period, after which they would decide their national fate. However, as with Kashmir, this decision was continually deferred, given the Indian State's opposition to it ever being made. Meanwhile, the Indian State made it clear that Naga autonomy was speakable only within the Indian Union and not outside of it. Naga nationalists began a series of non-violent protests, which were met with armed presence. The Indian Armed Forces moved into the region in the 1950s, and have not left since. Naga nationalists meanwhile set up what they called the Federal Government of Nagaland in 1956, with its own armed wing, which soon earned the hostile attention of the Indian Armed Forces. This resulted in close army control over and surveillance of villages, and the beginning of protracted guerilla war.

In the 1960s, sections of the Naga nationalist leadership were lured or persuaded, as the case may be, into accepting position and office in the newly created state of Nagaland; protests by those still committed to national self-determination continued and were often met with cruel acts of repression, including terror acts against civilians and violence against women. In 1975, the government of India proposed the Shillong Accord. The Accord invited recalcitrant armed Naga insurgents to surrender their arms and enter mainstream politics within the Indian Union, with the proviso that issues they considered germane would be discussed in the days to come (incidentally, that day never dawned, according to critics of the Accord). Those who refused the terms of the Accord persisted with their demand for an independent Naga nation, forming the National Socialist Council of Nagaland; whereas those who accepted the Indian State's offer agreed to work within the terms it had outlined. A state of civil war appeared imminent, and

this vested the Indian Armed Forces with insuperable authority and
rendered it immune to civilian control or accountability. To this
day the situation continues, though peace accords are signed from
time to time. Meanwhile, Naga nationalists insist on the historical
justness of their cause—and are supported by their fellow Nagas
from the hills of Manipur.

In Kashmir and Nagaland, unfreedom is underwritten by thick
rhetoric about the territorial integrity and sovereignty of the nation,
the need to be vigilant against acts of terror calculated to sabotage
the latter, and the exemplary role reserved for the armed forces
in this respect. Whatever the actual provocation in both places,
whether covert action by insurgents demanding the right to secede,
or overt action by citizens by way of sit-ins, hartals and meetings,
the response on the part of the State has been to deploy the army.
Even when the cause of provocation is the army's own behaviour,
the forces are expected to—and do—marshal such dissent into
quietude.

Illegal arrests and detentions, torture and interrogation of
suspected agents of sedition who are then 'disappeared', extra-
judicial killings sometimes ending in mass burials, and a relentless
surveillance of the civilian population continue to shape daily life
in these regions, in greater or lesser measure. As far as women
are concerned, this has meant that they are subject to searches,
questioning; their homes may be broken into, their children
detained; and their persons, their bodies, meanwhile become
available to the armed forces to use as they will.

While I have dwelt on the situation in Kashmir and Nagaland
specifically, the description of the role of the armed forces is
extendable to other parts of the Northeast, that is, wherever
nationalist claims are made, either through peaceful means or armed
violence. The nature of grievances, the character of militancy, and
the justness of claims may be differently accented in different places,
but the presence of the State, particularly the role it is authorized

to play is singular in all instances, and constitutively gendered in its expressions.

***

Earlier, we saw how in 1971 two groups, one from Nagaland and the other from Manipur wrote letters to Premier Indira Gandhi drawing attention to the army's depredations, particularly brutal sexual assault of women, including girls. Such acts remained in place and in the 1980s the troubles in Nagaland came to national attention, partly on account of a women's group—East District Women's Association, which had been formed in 1974 in direct response to sexual assaults perpetrated by Border Security Force (BSF) soldiers—inviting a civil rights and women's team to visit the region (I have referred to this earlier); and also because in 1982 and 1987, two dastardly acts of sexual assault on civilian women were committed by the Indian Armed Forces which called out for critical attention—the one in Ukhrul valley in Manipur, and the other in Oinam in Senapati district of Manipur. Both instances of assault were legitimized as reprisals for Naga insurgent action, which caused the death of army personnel in these places. These so-called reprisals were not unlike earlier acts only now the brutality was captured in international human rights reports, particularly those of Amnesty International.

Even as the rest of India, indeed the world, took note of the Indian Army's actions, local resistance, especially of women, was singular and pronounced in the context of Oinam: for instance, in the exemplary courage displayed by the Women's Union of the Manipur Baptist Convention. Members of the Union pressurized Church authorities who were not warm towards the insurgency to assist with prosecuting the case against the Assam Rifles, the division of the Indian Army that had caused several deaths, tortured people, including children, brutally assaulted women and older people in Oinam. On the Union's insistence, a room in a girls' hostel was

made over into a space for recording witness statements and the
Union subsequently filed a case in the High Court, seeking justice
for those who had been subject to sexual violence and humiliation.
The Naga People's Movement for Human Rights was particularly
active in this prosecution process and supported the Women's
Union's efforts, and along with other groups a rally was organized
to protest the assault on women, and the organizers demanded a
repeal of the hated Armed Forces Special Powers Act (AFSPA)
which facilitated and encouraged impunity in the region.

While the prosecution has met with several roadblocks,
the struggle of Naga women persists, for these are not the only
instances of injustice that have to be combatted. Indeed since the
1970s, women's groups have been engaged in dealing with the
consequences of conflict, including sexual violence, the destruction
of homes and families and the consequent transformation of
everyday life and relationships. Women's groups have thus worked
in multiple terrains, including sometimes with State organizations,
where it was warranted. However, as the conflict wore on, and the
prospects for peace appeared evermore remote, militancy bred
its own discontents, which resulted in internecine conflict and a
politics of suspicion and attrition. For those engaged in working
on issues to do with sexual assault, their problems have not only
redoubled but also thrown up fundamental challenges.

Dolly Kikon, whose work I have quoted at the beginning of this
book, has pointed to the trauma that Naga society has been subject
to over the years and the multiple sources of silencing that women
who have been assaulted and sexually hurt have to negotiate. In
Kikon's words, a 'dysfunctional militarized and violent culture'
has evolved over the last two decades, with the Army controlling
and regulating the terms of political conflict, pitting one insurgent
group against the other, as well as one tribal community versus
the next. Sexual violence, she makes clear, has to be seen in this
context, as both constituting militarized culture as well as being

constituted by it. Questions to do with culpability and justice on the one hand and with trauma and healing on the other, unfold within such a culture and are seldom resolved.

Kikon calls attention to the impact of such a culture on everyday life, and relationships through an examination of what appears to be the most visible symbol of decades of conflict: the so-called ceasefire zones. Since 1997, Naga insurgents have been confined to these zones, and from this location, they interact with the State, their families and the general public. Significantly, these zones are viewed as refuge spaces by those who are harassed by the army, or are fleeing this or that insurgent group; or who simply have nowhere to go, with their tales of sexual and other forms of injustice, which they have suffered in their homes, or as a consequence of the conflict. By their very nature, notes Kikon, these spaces are deeply traumatic and are not easy to negotiate; yet, ironically enough, they have become places that are expected to offer custody and care to the young and the abandoned.

Kikon narrates in detail a rather hair-raising story of an insurgent who repeatedly raped his daughter: her narrative unfolds as an unmaking of consciousness, both of the rapist and his victim. The brazenness, lack of conscience and utter perversion of spirit that the former exhibits on the one hand, and the sheer helplessness of his child (whom Kikon calls Beth), on the other, bereft of familial support, unable to pursue justice either through State protocols or the systems set up by insurgents, having to reckon with the threat of assault by others who see an assaulted girl as easy game—the unravelling of the social order is not only evident, but appears a scenario from which there can be no easy exit. Kikon notes:

> Beth's case brought multiple worlds of the insurgents, family, and the state agencies together. Beth's maternal family, particularly her maternal aunty who was her guardian was a member of a Naga insurgent organization, while Beth's father belonged to a rival insurgent camp. This division in the

family created deep anxieties beyond the family connections. The state agencies like the police were apprehensive to get into an 'internal' matter where rival insurgent groups were involved. Beth's case is an important example because the violent act transgressed the boundaries of the family, the political as well as the legal jurisdiction of rival insurgent groups, and the state agencies as well. Yet, none of these institutions sought to hold the perpetrator—Beth's father—accountable and deliver justice for the victim (Kikon, 2016).

Kikon's analysis is extremely thoughtful and she does not seek easy answers: she is deeply committed to the freedom, justice and peace process in Nagaland, and is therefore rightfully critical of the Indian State's presence and its actions, but she refuses to be drawn into a false choice, between the justice of the State, which is so hard to access, and the justice of the insurgent groups, which is often summarily delivered and raises more questions than answers. In the course of a meeting with women activists, some of whom were from insurgent groups, Kikon had the occasion to discuss the stance taken by insurgent groups with respect to sexual assault. She learned that groups handed out capital punishment to those suspected of such crimes. This is disheartening, notes Kikon, especially when the Naga collective, as she terms it, is engaged in coming to terms with a culture of silence and impunity with regard to sexual violence; the insurgents' responses, she observes, are not based on a discussion of justice or the principle of rights, rather they appear to have been taken 'to save the image of the organization' (*op. cit.*).

Kikon is reflective about the so-called collective as well: she reasons that it has been equally structured by violence and trauma and this is evident in how it responds to the predicament that children like Beth find themselves in. Beth was sent away for a while, but then returned to go to school in the city where there was no guarantee she would be kept safe from her father, and sure enough, was assaulted again. When she tried to run away to her aunt's house, she was called back to look after her younger siblings, and meanwhile her father was never caught or brought to justice, though a case was registered with the police. Clearly, reasons Kikon, a shared and diffuse sense of impunity is in place in this militarized world:

> The multiple structures of authorities ranging from state institutions, cultural groups, and insurgent organizations in Naga society often overlap....The members belonging to various Naga armed groups from the camps and the Naga public regularly cross paths... (Beth's) father's frequent travels between the ceasefire camp and the home to rape his daughter without any inhibition allows us to trace the culture of impunity and the courage of the perpetrators who inhabit multiple spaces of authorities and cross from one jurisdiction to another regularly. Here, the physical and political boundaries between the ceasefire camp and the home were broken down allowing the father to not only interrupt the lives of the householders but also systematically inflict sexual violence and psychological trauma on his child (*op. cit.*).

***

A similar sense of reflective anguish about the reality of women's lives, during the heyday of conflict or times of violence and the after-life of these experiences, has been captured by Xonxoi Barbora in his writings on Assam. Assam too had witnessed an armed struggle for national self-determination, which persisted even after Assamese nationalism went mainstream and a section of nationalists went on to contest elections and command authority (not unlike in Nagaland). The United Liberation Front of Assam, an armed political movement committed to national self-determination, however persisted in waging war with the Indian State, which as in Nagaland, denied its justice claims and retaliated with various acts of brutality.

The justice claims of Assamese nationalism notwithstanding, it has proved deeply problematic, given the manner in which it conceptualized and engaged with populations that were not 'Assamese', especially with Muslims in the region, many of whom, it claimed, were illegal settlers from Bangladesh. Assertions of identity have since remained deeply conflicted and for other reasons as well, given the emergence of various tribal armed groups, each with their own claims on political autonomy and distributive justice.

In this complex and embattled context, what may be considered redeeming and life-affirming? Is it possible to understand life worlds in the region, beyond what is posited by the historical and social claims of conflicted groups and identities? Barbora suggests that women's experiences in the region, not only of violence but of endurance as they negotiate life in makeshift refugee camps and other provisional spaces, could help leaven and ultimately re-position narratives that invariably end up being about conflicted identities. In these latter, violence is always a function of ethnic or linguistic difference that has gone wrong or turned perverse, and sexual violence in particular is always already an instrument of State (army, police) terror. There is a sameness to these tales, notes Barbora, which points to their having emerged out of a context, defined by the State's unilateral refusal to heed democratic demands in diverse contexts; and in each of the latter, conflict with the State has sought to mirror the State's own viciousness such that alternative political projects stand compromised.

A visible sign of these failed projects—of ethnicity, nationalism— is the camp, argues Barbora, whether it is the ceasefire camp or the refugee camp set up in the wake of inter-community or inter-group violence: 'These (political) projects, while pretending to question the State, end up miming its worst qualities of exclusion through violence and coercion. In many ways therefore, camps are a visceral reminder of the failure of political visions charted out by activists and entrepreneurs alike' (Barbora, 2016).

Barbora observes that the privileging of ethnic and other differences as causes for conflict overlooks other reasons, and that it might be more pertinent to 'problematize the lack of the universals that we take for granted in other parts of the country: democratic values, peaceable-ness and a political desire for representation and equitable distribution of wealth' (ibid.). On the one hand, this means returning to the State and the political conditions that prevail and interrogating them, especially from the point of view of widespread impunity; and on the other, this requires framing the problem of impunity itself in terms of sexual violence against women, and women's experiences in engaging with it, and living beyond it. This would help us redraw the map of the political space, as such, and indicate how the collapse of the political is accompanied by and mirrored in the remaking of gendered experiences and spaces; and how the one cannot be addressed without paying heed to the other. To attend to women's experiences then would mean asking a set of very different questions about identity, conflict and violence. What forms could such an understanding take, though? This is a more difficult question to address. I would like to conclude this section by examining, in this context, a set of events from Manipur.

***

Manipur too has been home to political discontent—resenting the terms of its integration into the Indian Union. Historically, the Meitei community that resides in the valley regions of Manipur was drawn into Vaishnavism, and thereby suffered disconnect with its pre-Hindu past. However, within the region that we call Manipur today, the Meitei are the dominant community, and their concerns and views influence both mainstream and dissident politics and culture in the state, including those advanced by Manipur's insurgent movements, which are dominated by Meitei nationalists. Of the latter, the People's Liberation Army is the most important and has declared its commitment to securing a socialist and independent Manipur.

In contrast to the valleys, where the Meitei dominate, the hills of Manipur are home to Christian Naga communities, who for a while now have demanded that they be made part of the state of Nagaland. Various Naga groups have been active for decades in the region, in tandem with insurgent groups in Nagaland.

In Meitei society, traditionally, women take on protective social roles, even militant ones, as was evident in early twentieth century struggles in the region. In post-independence India, and in the context of militancy and the culture of anomie that it sometimes fosters, women have been engaged with urgent social concerns, to do with alcoholism and drug addiction among young people. The Meira Paibis, or women 'torch-bearers' of Manipur, those that literally guard home, hearth and village are particularly well-known. In the wake of the Indian Army's presence and continued violence against insurgents, they have emerged as grave witnesses to an ugly conflict. As with the Naga, Meitei women too have been subject to harassment, humiliation and violence by the Indian Army, whose actions are protected by the Armed Forces Special Powers Act.

The Meira Paibis have protested army violence consistently, and one instance has become justly famous. This had to do with the rape and murder of Thangjam Manorama in 2004. Manorama was picked up by men from the Assam Rifles on a charge of being associated with the People's Liberation Army. She was raped, tortured and shot dead, with bullets emptied into her vagina. A few days after her death, a group of Meira Paibis stationed themselves outside Kangla Fort, the Assam Rifles headquarters, and stripped their clothes off. In all their naked dignity, they confronted the army with the startling demand, 'Indian Army Rape Us, We are Manorama's Mothers'. This unsettling yet eloquent defiance bears looking at in some detail—for what it tells us about the power of dissent and witnessing, and also about the inscription of either on bare bodies.

The baring of the body by the Meira Paibis signified many things: for one, it overturned the cult of furtive secrecy that is associated with the female body; and dispelled the widely held notion that terrible things done to the body may not be talked about. Secondly, it took on symbolic meaning, standing in for all those assaulted bodies, denied dignity and worth—nakedness in this instance refused sexual inscription and by the same token called attention to how women's bodies are sexualized through acts of brutal violence. Finally, even as they protested thus, the Meira Paibis re-possessed their bodies as sheer materiality, as bodies that registered affliction and hurt, and which demanded justice as a right, on this account. In another sense, their call to justice appeared a sacrificial ritual: holding the banner, marching down the streets, offering themselves as witness to Manorama's innocence, indeed the innocence of all women who had been thus hurt, they dared authority to do its worst. This is political dramaturgy of the highest order, and a wager.

A similar sense of ritual informs the fast undertaken by Irom Sharmila Chanu for several years against the continued retention of the AFSPA in Manipur. She too offers her body, as witness and sacrifice. Her refusal of food, is, in effect, a refusal of the right to life; in circumstances where such a right is routinely violated, she denies it to herself, in the hope and faith that her act would persuade the Indian State to reconsider its refusal to protect its citizens, in fact its role in actively denying them their right to life. The State remains caught in a quandary. It has to prevent Sharmila from achieving her end, from completing her sacrifice, and so seeks to force-feed her. On the other hand, it does not behove its authority to grant her a hearing. This creates a political impasse; yet, this disjunctive moment allows us to measure the extent of the State's impunity, mark its bewilderment at an act that embarrasses its resolve.

When women thus offer their bodies up as evidence of the State's complicity in acts of sexual violence, the narrative does turn, for now we realize that the only shame that needs to be acknowledged is that of the State itself. Yet, this is not perhaps the narrative turn that Barbora has in mind: for it does not recast the terms of debate, though it certainly causes the debate to falter. The naked female body or the sacrificial body cannot stand in for the multiplicity of bodies seeking justice, each marked by its particular history and context. In other words, there is no one female body so to speak—a fact that became painfully clear, when, the Meira Paibis turned hostile to Naga demands for greater political and cultural autonomy.

The Meitei and Naga have not always worked in concert—though armed groups from all sides forge contingent and strategic alliances—given their specific nationalist claims. However, women from both communities have borne the brunt of retaining a sense of life and home in not dissimilar ways. Tangkhul Shanao Long, the Naga women's group that has been active in Manipur since 1974, when it was formed after a disturbing suicide of a young woman raped by Border Security Force men, is as committed to securing the social good as the Meira Paibis are, and does take on a similar protective role. Likewise, the Naga Mothers Association has been active since it was founded in 1984 and as committed to peace, justice and the rebuilding of communities. It is somewhat dismaying therefore to note that ethnic loyalties and affective sentiments preclude the making of wider solidarities amongst women.

Neither the Meira Paibi nor Tangkhul Shanao Long are 'feminist' in their politics, in the secular sense we understand the term; rather they are vibrant, organic collectives that seek to extend women's nurturing, mentoring role into the public sphere. This is true also of the Naga Mothers Association. Paula Banerjee reports that in one instance when there was a standoff between the Assam Rifles and the Naga insurgents, the women of the Tangkhul Shanao Long literally interposed themselves between the two and attempted to defuse the situation. Yet, it appears that given the fact that in the face of identity-related concerns, the great universals, especially of democracy and the right to representation, have not been granted their due, even cultures of nurture remain ridged by identity and attendant notions of exclusion and inclusion.

***

If, it seems, that the situation in the Northeast is dispiriting and alarming at the same time, in Kashmir, matters have not been very different. The presence of the Indian army in the region, again protected by the AFSPA and other acts, including the Public Security Act and the Disturbed Areas Act, has meant that Kashmir is retained by force within the Indian Union. Starting from the 1980s, the region has emerged as perhaps the most militarized in the world, with over 6,00,000 troops, working out to a ratio of one solider for every 10 civilians. Preventive detention, torture, harassment of entire village populations, forced disappearances, particularly of youth, and sexual violence persist in the valley. Kashmir's Pandits, the Hindu community that has lived in the region for several hundred years, have since been displaced, both on account of militant pressure and the active encouragement of the government of India, which desires to tar the Kashmir nationalists with the brush of fundamentalism. Thus the rich, layered and ecumenical culture of the state has slowly been reduced to its vestiges.

As in the Northeast, the rape of women remains a side history, in terms of how it is understood and dealt with. However, civil rights reporting on the region has recorded the widespread use of sexual assault as a weapon against populations suspected of being supportive of 'terrorism', from across Pakistan or locally. The numbers are staggering and the dismal record of justice very discouraging. I shall return to discussing this in some detail, but for now I wish to note that there are other forms of indignity that women have been subjected to: the forced disappearances of loved ones has meant that they wait for news in a state of perpetual uncertainty and meanwhile have to engage with State agencies, not only to know the fate of their family members, but also to avail of reparations, such as these are.

Worse is their civic and conjugal status if the disappeared happen to be husbands: and thus there has emerged the phenomenon of 'half-widows', who live in a twilight zone, not sure if their husbands are alive or dead, and yet carrying on a life where they are absent. It does not help that Muslim personal law, as it is applied in the valley, has no clear position on the half-widow—that is, there is no religious directive as to how long a woman is to wait for a disappeared husband before she remarries. Secular governance has also very little to offer them: for one, if they are to avail, say, of a widow's pension they have to prove to the concerned authority that the disappeared men were not militants, and this is obviously not easy. Secondly, should they actually access reparations, they have to reckon with the fact of the disappeared man's natal family laying claims to what may be had from the State.

The status of the half-widow is perhaps matched by that of the man who is detained, tortured and returned to society: typically such torture targets his genitalia, and renders it literally useless. His 'masculinity' deterred and destroyed, the man cannot be a husband, and fulfill his duties as a man and prospective father. The violation of the marital tie, of conjugality, is perhaps the most visible symbol of the unraveling of community that the Indian Armed Forces and the State have caused to happen. The secondary status of women in marriage and the family render conjugality problematic in any context, yet it is a fundamental social tie, a civic expression of permissible intimacy. The systematic targeting of home and family with a view to unsettling a community is therefore a thoroughly gendered crime whose gravity must be acknowledged.

Women have not been quiet victims in the valley. They have supported the struggle for azaadi, or freedom from Indian rule, been part of demonstrations, and remonstrated with State authorities when the men in their families or neighbourhood were arrested or interned. There are women's groups in the Kashmir valley of various ideological persuasions, including decidedly Islamic ones. One of the more prominent faces of untiring dissent is that of Parveen Ahangar who has been instrumental in the forming of the Association of Parents of Disappeared Persons (APDP). Searching for her missing son, in jails in Kashmir and other parts of India, she came to formulate a strategy of protest and more important witnessing. One of the more moving depictions of the APDP's work—by Shahnaz Khalil Khan—notes that members meet every month and sometimes sing verses from the *Yousufnama*, or 'Joseph's story', the lamentation of Jacob (Old Testament), for the disappearance of his favourite son after he was sold into slavery by his jealous brothers. Such remembering is particularly poignant given the ubiquity of loss in the valley, and its affective power defines resilience that is anguished but nevertheless unwilling to forget—in essence, an evocative symbol of how memory about hurt and injustice is kept alive, not through bitterness, but through deep and profound sorrow that yet seeks justice.

There are angrier voices, of women's groups that support azaadi and secession, though none of them appears to have political weight when it comes to making decisions, whether within formations of which they are a part or in a more general sense. While women's presence, role and work are necessary aspects of political life in Kashmir, these are seldom considered politically resonant or significant. Some watchers of the Kashmir scene go so far as to suggest that male-headed militant groups position the grieving mother and the raped woman as icons of suffering and martyrdom, to the exclusion of all that women are and do— since these images best indict the Indian Armed Forces' violence.

That women also position themselves thus, in particular contexts, is also true. However, there is undoubted power and energy to such imaging, and in a context where authority gets away with much, these representations of martyrdom are certainly of more than instrumental significance.

Again, we return to the question of what is speakable: the grieving mother is an eloquent icon; the raped woman, less so, nevertheless, her damaged personhood stands in for a greater loss, of honour, identity, sense of community and importantly, she is the ultimate victim of insuperable and illegitimate authority. Yet, none of this makes it easy to speak of rape, or of how women, and men, come to grips with it.

***

As in the Northeast of India and elsewhere in the country, rape in the Kashmir valley is not simply an 'occurrence'. It is a punitive act, sometimes programmatically and at other times randomly directed at women. However it is not the only sexually outrageous act: men in detention, and as I have pointed to earlier, during interrogation, are willfully sodomised and hurt, and their genitalia, equally willfully damaged. Sexual torture as we know by now is constitutively gendered.

Seema Kazi in her work on gender and militarization in Kashmir reminds us that—and as we well know, from numerous other contexts—rape in the context of anti-insurgency operations is not a side-effect, nor is it only meant to terrorise women. It is a political act committed with impunity, which derives not only from unchecked authority, but also from the sexual prerogative that men have given themselves in this regard. As such it becomes a weapon in a battle that men wage with other men, in this instance, the soldier with the so-called militant. The desired end in this battle is to emasculate the militant, or his supporter, and render him helpless. This is most evident, when an army man rapes a woman, because her brother or someone known to her is—ostensibly—a militant. It is as if by assaulting her, the army is laying claims to enemy possession, as if her body stands in for territory that is theirs by right.

Ananya Kabir's characterization of Kashmir as a 'territory of desire' is worth bearing in mind, in this context: in Indian cinema, from the 1950s onwards, Kashmir emerged as a landscape of desire, a place that welcomed honeymooning couples. This was as true of say Tamil cinema as it was of Bollywood. Visually exotic and suitably faraway, Kashmir was a landscape of fantasy for many of us, growing up in southern India, during the 1970s. That we did not wish to lose our access to this desirable faraway space was made evident in Tamil film-maker Mani Ratnam's *Roja* (1990s) where a young woman from a remote southern Tamil Nadu village pits herself against militancy, as she searches for her husband who has been held captive by the so-called terrorists. An unfulfilled honeymoon is the occasion for the unfolding of this sentimental and dangerously chauvinistic drama.

If an obsessive relationship to Kashmir that is at once aesthetic and political drives acts of sexual violence, women bear the effects of this obsession in particularly painful ways. For one, it is an obsession that plays itself out relentlessly—the sheer number of rapes reported in the valley testify to this—and secondly, this repetitive act has emerged, in essence, as a rather morbid one, seamless in every sense with the death that accompanies it. It is not only that women are rendered 'socially dead' by acts of sexual violence, but often, they are made witness to the deaths of their loved ones. Or acts of rape are followed by acts of murder. Anthropologist Cynthia Mahmood notes that the number of dead that washed up by the river on the other side of the Line of Control is notched up on a blackboard, and that on the day she visited that eerie spot, it stood at 476.

Then there are women who are raped and murdered, as happened in Shopian, where two young women related by marriage were found dead, and floating down a river. The Indian army and government have bent over backwards to prove that the women were not raped or killed and a Central Bureau of Intelligence inquiry—which took the part of justice in Vachathi—decided to abide by and affirm the State's impunity in this instance.

In any case, acts of rape have not been acknowledged by the Indian government, as is evident from the rape of 40 women in the village of Kunan Poshpora, which happened in 1991. In fact, a senior journalist who was part of a team that visited the village to enquire into the incident affirmed the official position that no such incident ever occurred and that it was 'a massive hoax orchestrated by militant groups and their sympathisers and mentors in Kashmir and abroad...for reinscribing Kashmir on the international agenda as a human rights issue' (Kazi, 2007: 203). The case was reopened after twenty years and more, when a younger generation of women filed a public interest litigation to re-examine the events of that time, but the women of Kunan Poshpora are yet to be heeded.

The Indian army's responses are not merely exercises in denial: the army appears to want to either coddle soldiers or to shrug their behaviour off as being in the nature of things. One of the officers that Seema Kazi interviewed asserted that a soldier who is part of a campaign is not likely to think of sexual assault, in fact this would be the last thing on his mind: 'A soldier conducting an operation at the dead of night is unlikely to think of rape when he is not even certain he shall return alive,' proclaimed Lt. General D.S.R. Sahni, General Officer Commanding, Northern Command when asked to answer charges of rape by military forces (Kazi: 204). This benign affirmation of the soldier's vulnerability in the face of imminent death and by that token a refusal to acknowledge that he could rape, though, is offset by what another officer had to say about his men. Kazi records that, in a moment of rare candour, a senior officer of the Central Reserve Police Force admitted to a writer: 'Who do you think joins the [paramilitary] forces...? Do you think you'll be able to pick up a gun and kill? Could you stay away for months from your family earning just a few thousand rupees, risking your life every day? No you wouldn't. Only a brute would or someone desperate. We get the worst—the rogues, the thugs, and then we have to play with them, giving them lead and reining them in. It is not easy.' (*op. cit.*, 205)

This 'admission' reeks of elitism and betrays the contempt that officers have for their men, in essence for those from marginal groups that join the forces. 'The worst' in this definition are 'criminalised' men but the implication is also that these desperate beings are what they are, because they are essentially lower class and caste brutes. What is of course not acknowledged is the role that senior officers play in authorizing torture, and sometimes supervising it themselves. Or that they prefer to look the other way, should complaints of rape come to them; or as sometimes happens, are not averse to seeking sexual favours from women who have been trafficked.

While political groups are not averse to producing evidence of rape to bolster their case against the Indian forces—and this is not only true of Kashmir, but other embattled contexts, where rape becomes a mark of utter victimhood—they also do the opposite: they decry women who report rape. It has been pointed out that armed groups in Kashmir have not desisted from considering raped women dishonourable, and worse, as having 'given in' to the enemy, in short as mukbirs or collaborators.

***

Women's as well as men's responses to rape in the valley are marked by a sense of wistful sorrow, humiliation and helplessness. A woman who is assaulted, if she is young and single, is viewed as damaged for life, and cannot expect to be loved or married. Kazi quotes a young woman who endures such an existence:

'Whenever I received a proposal of marriage, the neighbours would inform people who came with the proposal that the military had visited my house. These people in turn would speculate about the nature and timing of my torture and the fact that I was alone with ten to fifteen military personnel in the middle of the night. Others would feel apprehensive, fearing similar treatment at the hands of the military if I married into their family. As a daughter-in-law, they feared I could be subject to further physical abuse by the military that would be very humiliating and dishonourable for my husband and his family. None of the men considered me worthy of marriage' (Kazi: 206).

When a wife is raped, she can expect to be left alone but in the event that her husband stays with her, both face problems. Bashrat Peer in *Curfewed Night* tells the story of a woman who was subject to sexual assault on her bridal night, but whose husband insisted on staying with her. But he had to confront a social world that would not leave speaking of 'the woman who was raped.' In Peer's account, the young woman is viewed as a bearer of ill-luck and shunned by all, except her husband.

Many feminist commentators on Kashmir have been critical of how Kashmiri men have responded to the problem of rape. Writing of how Yasin Mallik of the Jammu and Kashmir Liberation Front acknowledged that women have been assaulted by the Indian Army, and suffered 'torture and stigma', Seema Kazi observes: 'That this "torture and stigma" is subsequently inflicted by Kashmir's society (apart from the military) is an issue that Yasin Malik fails to address' (Kazi: 209). Kazi however is sensitive to the semantic and existential problems that underwrite this reluctance to deal with torture and stigma that is re-inflicted on the raped woman by a thoughtless social order. She notes in this context that while we hear of men and families that will not countenance raped women or empathise with them, we hear less of the helplessness and bewilderment that men experience and goes on to record what a former member of the JKLF that she interviewed had to say in this regard:

For me it is not fighting and dying for the cause that is daunting as it is based on the idea of freedom... it is part of the struggle for freedom.... But when the military use women to humiliate us and the family and the community, it is not possible for me, or for any of us to bear this denigration... soldiers rifle through young women's rooms, take out their clothes and taunt their brothers and fathers... we can only watch and do nothing. There are among us those who have taken up arms, who subsequently heard of their sisters' detention at military camps. That is enough to break anyone. It is easy to pick up the gun as the desire for freedom runs deep and strong within... yet it is very difficult, almost impossible against the risk and danger of sexual retaliation at women. I cannot fight if my sister is humiliated or raped... (long pause) I have not spoken about this to anyone. (*op.cit.*, 157)

Women from the valley are not unaware of what the men in their families and in the larger community endure and live with, and while they are clearly distressed by how social norms can be unforgiving, they yet seek to negotiate a passage to dignity in rather mindful ways. As we have seen with respect to dalit women, they are in a double bind: the men who are reluctant to put by questions of honour when speaking of rape, are men they live with, men who have themselves undergone sexual torture and degradation. Their helplessness is evident to them in a way that it can never be for an outsider, just as their aggression or indifference hits closer than what we imagine.

Women's sense of justice persists through their suffering, and they have struggled hard to keep the memory of wrongdoing alive, should they find an enabling context and forum to speak of what they endured. The fact that the women of Kunan Poshpora did not demur from approaching the courts again speaks of their resolve to fight for justice.

***

As always, then, the challenge for feminists is twofold: to heed women's experiences, without losing sight of the incalculable damage wrought to marginal communities, or communities whose rights have been systematically denied, and who have suffered torture and death for daring to resist the armed might of the Indian State. The noting of such damage requires, in effect, learning to 'speak' in ways that accounts for the anguish that an entire population undergoes, even though responses to that damage may be varied and some not likely to elicit feminist sympathy. Further, it requires a sustained critique of the Nation-State, including of the sense of belonging that it seeks to impose on all of us; and in this context, of the ethical bankruptcy and cynicism that inform State policy, and the impunity that is protected by an instrumental deployment of legislation.

To do all of this, and yet demand better laws and greater accountability from the State might appear a misnomer—but clearly this is also what is required of those of us who wish to prise apart the republic from a narrowly defined and tightly held nationalism—and national structures—that do not mind killing or authorising the death of its own citizens by the thousands and hurting thousands of others to keep its borders 'inviolate'.

Feminist work in this context is not absent, and we have begun to work at bringing together aspects of our experiences that have remained apart: for instance, Uma Chakravarti and Nandita Haksar have both been writing and speaking of the need to keep together discourses of civil liberties and rights and feminism. Yet, testifying against the Nation-State is not easy. If women from the borderlands do so, they are conveniently termed seditious, and if those from within the nation's 'defined' and 'settled' regions do so, then they are termed traitors.

I would like to refer, in this context, to Nandita Haksar's provocative and brilliant book, *Hanging Afzal, Framing Geelani*, which addresses the republic, so to speak. The attack on Indian

Parliament in 2001 and the subsequent arrest and incarceration of Syed Ahmed Geelani, Afzal Guru and two others are the events that define the book's narrative horizon. Nandita Haksar defended Geelani in court, and based on her experiences of that time, she reflects on the nature of Indian democracy, secularism and justice in a series of letters that she addresses to various people whose opinions, acts or the absence of action on their part, when warranted, raise questions about the future of these values in India. Amongst those she seeks to converse with are former Prime Minister Manmohan Singh whom she approached to speak of the condition of political prisoners in Tihar Jail; jurist Upendra Baxi, who had not raised his voice against the obvious travesty of justice that was on display during the prosecution of Syed Ahmed Geelani; Bipan Chandra, doyen of the old parliamentary Left, whose views on secularism and nationhood are subjected to critical appraisal by Haksar for being inadequate and formulaic; Barkha Dutt, the journalist, symbol of a new era of media, when opinions are sought to be made and unmade on television; Om Prakash Mehra, who produced the feel-good film *Rang de Basanti* and attempted to capture a young generation's attention with a film that was both entertaining as well as anodyne in how it portrayed a nation's ills; Syed Bismillah Geelani, Syed Ahmad Geelani's brother with whom Nandita worked when handling the former's case, and with whom she argued passionately, about patriarchy and an ecumenical approach to faith; and finally young comrades, inspired by struggles for justice.

Each of these conversations seeks to extend our understanding of democracy, calls for us to be vigilant and vocal in challenging the Statist version of the republic and insists we relook older verities. Through these conversations Haksar also builds a case for thinking of the nation differently, acknowledging its multi-ethnicity, insisting on the need for freedom and openness in forging relationships even while asserting linguistic and faith-based affinities, and most of all, working towards freedom from patriarchal and caste injustice. In all instances, she positions democracy as the best guarantor against all those ills that flow in its absence, particularly those that women experience, from discrimination and neglect to sexual violence.

I wish to recall the one conversation that seems apposite to the concerns explored thus far in this book: the one that speaks of an impossible friendship, in this instance between Nandita Haksar and Bismillah Geelani. Nandita recounts the circumstances in which they met, the friendship they reluctantly forged, as they worked together to ensure that Geelani had a fair trial. She notes the impasses that mark their comradeship, to do with Nandita's unease with the teachings of the Jamat-i-Islami, which undoubtedly have influenced Bismillah, particularly the organization's views on women and its sectarian interpretation of women's place and functions in social and familial worlds; and with Bismillah Geelani's disquiet over her origins, being from the Kashmiri Pandit community that sees Muslims as enemies, rather than as fellow sufferers, and with her feminism. She invites conversation on all these matters, speaks of how important it is to reach out and sustain relationships that share a vision of justice and freedom, though those who are in such relationships may disagree on the principles that underlie these important values.

The tone of the conversation that engages Bismillah Geelani is interesting: for it suggests how we may speak of differences, and quarrel with positions we cannot accept, in a spirit of fraternity, and we also realize the importance of political understanding that allows us to do this, and which, in turn, is held in a spirit of generosity and openness. For feminists looking to engage with dalit concerns, or those that animate the struggles of ethnic and faith-based minorities, there are important lessons to be learnt here. It is significant that as she gestures towards a politics and comradeship that will make for productive work for a common cause, Nandita Haksar imagines these not in instrumental terms; she does not use words that point that way, words such as 'strategic alliances', or 'united front', for instance. Instead she deploys a language of affect, of speech that strives to be critical yet open and affectionate even, principled yet generous.

REFERENCES

Asia Watch & Physicians for Human Rights (A Division of Human Rights Watch), *Rape in Kashmir, A Crime of War*; https://www.hrw.org/sites/default/files/reports/INDIA935.PDF (accessed on 22 November 2015).

Association of Parents of Disappeared Persons. 2011. *Half-widow, Half-Wife: Responding to Gendered Violence in Kashmir,* http://www.jkccs.net/wp-content/uploads/2015/02/Half-Widow-Half-Wife-APDP-report.pdf (accessed on 22 November 2015).

Banerjee, Paula. 2008. 'The Space Between: Women's Negotiations with Democracy' in Paula Banerjee, (ed.), *Women in Peace Politics,* pp. 201–217. New Delhi: Sage.

Barbora, Xonzoi. 2016. 'Weary of Wars: Memory, Violence and Women in the Making of Contemporary Assam' in U. Chakravarti, (ed.), *Fault lines of History: The India Papers (Zubaan Series on Sexual Violence and Impunity in South Asia),* New Delhi: Zubaan.

Haksar, Nandita. 2007. *Hanging Afzal, Framing Geelani: Patriotism in the Time of Terror,* New Delhi: Bibliophile South Asia.

Jahanara Kabir, Ananya. 2009. *Territory of Desire: Representing the Valley of Kashmir,* Minnesota: University of Minnesota Press.

Kazi, Seema. 2007. *Between Democracy and Nation: Gender and Militarisation in Kashmir,* A thesis submitted in partial fulfilment of the requirement for the degree of PhD, London School of Economics and Political Science, The Gender Institute http://etheses.lse.ac.uk/2018/1/U501665.pdf (accessed 22 November 2015).

Khalil Khan, Shahnaz. 2012. *Framing women's terrestrial and online discursive landscapes in Jammu and Kashmir.* https://www.iaaw.hu-berlin.de/de/medialitaet/upload/pdf_ghs_report_skk_10_05_12 (accessed on 22 November 2015).

Keppley Mahmood, Cynthia. 2000. 'Trials by Fire: Dynamics of Terror in Punjab and Kashmir' in J. A. Sluka (ed.), *Death Squad: The Anthropology of State Terror*, pp. 70–90. Philadelphia: University of Pennsylvania Press.

Kikon, Dolly. 2016. 'Memories of Rape: The Banality of Violence and Impunity in Naga Society' in U. Chakravarti, (ed.), *Fault lines of History: The India Papers Vol. 2 (Zubaan Series on Sexual Violence and Impunity in South Asia)*, New Delhi: Zubaan.

Nag, Sajal. 2012. *A Gigantic Panopticon: Counter-Insurgency and Modes of Disciplining and Punishment in Northeast India*, http://www.mcrg.ac.in/PP46.pdf (accessed 22 November 2015).

1986. *The Naga Nation and its Struggle against Genocide*, A report compiled by International Work Group for Indigenous Affairs, Copenhagen: IWGIA. http://www.iwgia.org/iwgia_files_publications_files/0166_56_The_Naga_nation_and_its_struggle_against_genocide.pdf (accessed 22 November 2015).

Parratt, John. 2005. *A Wounded Land: Politics and Identity in Modern Manipur*, New Delhi: Mittal Publications.

Peer, Basharat. 2010. *Curfewed Night*, Scribner, pp. 144-151

John Thomas, John. 2010. 'Church, Politics and the Limits of Theology' Ph.D. dissertation, *Missionaries, Church and the Formation of Naga Political Identity, 1918-1997*, pp. 264–321. Jawaharlal Nehru University, Centre for Historical Studies. http://shodhganga.inflibnet.ac.in:8080/jspui/bitstream/10603/31360/11/11_chapter%206.pdf (accessed 22 November 2015).

Part lll

Part III

14

Everyday Lives and Exceptional Violence

We continue to fight for justice in matters to do with sexual violence and the impunity that its perpetrators rely on frustrates us, as we seek to bear witness and claim justice. Yet, we continue to speak, in varied tongues; at the same time, such speech is never adequately or critically mindful of all that affects our lives as women. In and through such speech, wild and tame, programmatic and nuanced, co-opted or ignored, as the case may be, we try to keep alive our sense of hurt, anger and sorrow, and our desire for justice and redressal. This 'we' is not just the articulate 'us' that is visible or voluble—it includes hundreds of us who patiently go to the courts, suffer through several adjournments, do not mind preparing yet another affidavit and wait out the outcome, sometimes for decades. It includes too those who seek quick or militant political solutions, as well as those who imagine that if they are in the precincts of power, their chances of getting just redressal are better.

Speaking as we did in and through various historical contexts, we have challenged the impunity of State and society, and claimed voice and expression even at times when there have been attempts to silence us. One has only to think of countless witnesses who have fought hard to keep their memory of assault alive, often at tremendous psychic costs to their well-being, just so to be able to secure justice. I would like to invoke, in this context, the case of Bilkis Bano from Gujarat. Gang-raped (during the 2002 carnage of Muslims) when pregnant and a key witness to the murder of her kin and little daughter, Bilkis survived through the kindness of strangers, including fair-minded bureaucrats. With the assistance of a human rights support network with which she came into contact when in a refugee camp, she countenanced being cross-examined in court. Bilkis' deposition was coherent but it is evident that she was under great strain. This is not surprising, if we are to consider what the criminal justice system expects of a witness.

In the course of the deposition, she is asked to identify a set of objects, pieces of cloth, slippers and bangles. Each object, carefully preserved within an envelope is shown to her, and she then identifies it, as such-and-such's footwear, odni, bangle... The poignancy of this act, and the strength of the woman who had seen her loved ones die and now had to identify what was theirs once—these literally leap out of the dry legal phraseology of the deposition. But at times Bilkis pauses; she does not remember, she says, cannot remember. She falters while describing what was done to her. The deposition is also interrupted when she requests time to go and feed her child— this last detail, indicative of the persistence of everyday life, the pull of duties and responsibilities that cannot be put by, tells its own story, a story that is both pragmatic and tragic, and not a particularly consoling one. Considering she was pregnant when she was raped, and then went to have more children, this act of nurture appears almost miraculous.

Yet the resilience of the witness, and our heroic attempts to sustain speech after sexual violence are only part of the story. For we are still left with that residue of sadness which refuses to go away, and which is an expression of our bewilderment in the face of such evil. Bilkis Bano's deposition, to be sure, conveys a sense of hope, but yet it is hope haunted by persistent sorrow. Further, acts of extreme violence exhibit a brutality that defies context and meaning: howsoever we explain and reconstruct the sequence of events that lead to extreme violence, in this case the brutal rape that Bilkis suffered, the details of that brutality exceed all attempts to comprehend them. Then again, the rape of children and young persons, not only in situations of extreme terror but in everyday contexts, and by those that are ostensibly their guardians and protectors, casts our interpretative certainties into disarray. Likewise, random acts of sexual violence, that is, rape by strangers, often chilling in their seemingly motiveless malignity baffles us.

While we may not ever have satisfactory answers as to why and how such evil acts persist, we may yet want to ask questions about the kind of cultures that permit their commission with impunity. By this I don't mean the particular or contingent culture of sexual violence that overwhelms a society at a moment in time; but more durable practices to do with the body, which might not appear problematic or exceptional in an everyday sense, but which are not entirely unrelated to gross acts that destroy bodily integrity.

While throughout this book, I have referred to various expressions of sexual culture in the Indian context, in what follows I would like to bring them together and produce an argument that helps us view the exceptional in terms of the everyday—this is necessary if we are to achieve that recognition of suffering which alone can thwart impunity. In other words, I intend to draw the contours of social and cultural conditions that produce misrecognition. In the Indian context, this would require us to examine the semantics of touch.

***

In caste society in India, touch mediates social relationships in fundamental ways. For one, it has to do with how we mark and value food, and how and with whom we exchange it. Touch in these contexts is a token of acceptance of certain bodies and the exclusion of others. Exclusion is not merely an act of separation,

but encodes a sense of revulsion as well. Secondly, touch also has
to do with our sense of boundaries: the so-called untouchables are
expected to live beyond the pale of the social order, and forced to
bear responsibility for disposing of what that order rejects and what
it expels from within its boundaries, from waste to death. Thirdly,
within the social order, that is, within communities that are not
thus exiled, there is a further coding of touch: a subtle hierarchy of
who has the primary right of access to various material and spiritual
goods, including political office and educational choices.

Lastly, touch is regulated in ingenious ways when it comes to
sexual intimacy. In a context where to touch or not expect to be
touched marks social position and status, desire is scrutinized, and
some kinds are considered appropriate and others illegitimate.
Thus, an upper caste or dominant caste man is deemed to possess,
and sees himself as possessing, unfettered sexual right—over the
bodies of women in his own family and community, as well as of
women from social groups that are subordinate to and economically
dependent on his own.

Men from castes that are not particularly differentiated from
those below them, including the so-called untouchable castes,
because they still perform common labour alongside them, or are
engaged with them in an everyday economic sense, possess what
may be called ambiguous rights: thus men from say peasant or
artisanal backgrounds, who occupy the middle of the caste order,
and who are not yet economically or politically powerful might well
expect to have relationships with women from castes placed lower in
the hierarchy as a matter of right. But this right may not be easy to
enforce, given their lack of secular authority.

Men from communities that are deemed the lowest, including
so-called outcaste communities, possess no sexual rights that they
may assume at will. As we have seen, even the right of conjugal
access is not something they may take for granted, since the women
in their families, as much as them, were (are) deemed the property

of upper and dominant caste men. Their continued humiliation—as men, robbed of their 'protective' role—implies that they cannot exercise sexual authority as a matter of right. It is another matter that dalit domesticity is also embattled, and that dalit women experience violence at home as well. But socially and culturally, dalit men are denied the public sexual authority that comes with masculinity.

As far as women are concerned, the logic of touch is inverted. Women from upper and dominant castes are to be protected and are also enjoined to guard themselves—from the possible sexual attention of all men, and to forge conjugal ties with their own caste men. Over the decades, women from these groups have become educated and are mobile; protection in these changed circumstances translates into self-defined abhorrence of touch from any but their own kind. For the most part, upper and dominant caste women thus guard their caste status as zealously as men.

Women from castes that are neither at the top nor the very bottom continue to be subjected to 'protection' and are also expected to protect themselves. Women from peasant, artisanal and small trading communities who occupy this middle rung of the caste order have always been mobile, being workers in the field and assisting in shops or trades. With peasant and small town society in the throes of transformation—from the late 20th century onward—on account of various factors, including the retreat of agriculture, these women's lives have opened up, with many going into higher education or seeking work outside their home towns. Thus, they are more likely to come into contact with men from different castes including those below them, than upper caste dominant women, who mostly circulate within their own caste-class contexts. Policing of women from communities that are ranged between the dominant and the entirely subordinated casts, their mobility and relationships is therefore more insistent: punishing those who make cross-caste marriages take place within this social group.

Working class and caste women, particularly dalit women, are deemed sexually available, as we have seen, and suffer ignominy, anger and repression of the worst sort. At the same time, they also exhibit defiance and have been visible in the public sphere more than any other class of women.

Given these rules and rights that sustain our caste order in its inequality, sexual touch is either coercive or furtive in its expressions. Unfettered sexual authority cannot but be violent, whereas the strictures on who can touch whom legitimately, creates a culture of public secrecy around sexual matters—who sleeps with whom, when he or she is not meant to, is a public secret but one that is not countenanced as socially 'speakable'.

In everyday life, these codes, to do with food, love, sex and status act in intertwined fashion and translate into acts and practices that shape our subjectivities, particularly our sexual selves.

***

Food in caste society separates and orders within a hierarchy not only of cuisines, but also people. Meat-eaters are deemed less 'pure' than those who are vegetarians. Amongst the former, there exists a division between beef-eaters and non-beefeaters. Beef is associated with dalits, since across India, dalits had traditionally been enjoined the task of skinning and disposing of dead cattle—and consuming them. Therefore beef is to be shunned by others. Over a period of time, food taboos have altered and across India, most people eat most things; yet the cultural meanings associated with food remain in place and are invoked to affirm—and denounce—caste identities. Thus, from time to time, beef becomes taboo, the killing of cows is criticised, butchers threatened, and beef stalls shut down. More generally, in such contexts, vegetarianism is upheld as a virtue, predictably by dominant upper caste ideologues. This happened in the early twentieth century, under the aegis of the Arya Samaj, and was also reiterated by Gandhi. In post-independence India too beef—and also meat-eating in general—remain the subject of contentious arguments. As dalits became politically assertive, they upheld their social and cultural practices as equally valuable and beef-eating in some instances has emerged as a mark of proud subalternity.

Yet beef, both literally and metaphorically, occupies a marginal space in our public imagination. In a state like Tamil Nadu, for instance, beef stalls seldom advertise their presence vocally. Nor are they particularly visible. It is almost as if it is shameful to admit to selling or eating beef. This visceral contempt for the food that dalits alone were supposed to eat does not stop there. It extends to and feeds into the contempt that is imposed on dalits; in particular instances, non-beefeaters assert their caste superiority precisely on this account.

This displacing of lowness on certain types of food and those who eat it may be seen as the basis for the more general and pervasive contempt towards food meant for the poor. Remains, old food, rotten food—not only dalits but the working poor were fed with what was clearly not consumable by anyone else. Significantly, when it comes to State provisioning, whether through the public distribution system or the free midday meal scheme in schools—as in Tamil Nadu—this contempt frames policy. Rice that is distributed for free is often of the most inferior variety; and food cooked for poor children is neither edible nor nutritious, as it ought to be. This is for the most part, and there are no doubt exceptions. This public contempt for the poor, deriving as it does from long-held cultural notions of good and bad food and who deserves what kind of food, is seldom understood as having to do with our attitude towards caste and the cultures of eating that the caste order has constituted over the centuries. But clearly there is a connection. Even within the public provisioning system the principle of caste separation persists. In Tamil Nadu, for instance, parents of children have sometimes protested at a dalit cook being employed under the midday meal scheme. While such protests have been set to rest by bureaucratic directive and court decision, they indicate that the politics of food is well and alive.

Further, the political culture of provisioning the poor, especially in places like Tamil Nadu where it has enjoyed a long history of populist patronage, produces a concomitant subjectivity: the citizen who waits for a 'welfare handout' is viewed either as an abject victim, or as intrinsically lazy, not willing to work, and opportunistic. One can see how the logic of lowness, with respect to food is reiterated at different levels of the food network, so to speak. Ultimately, and since it does not address the inequalities that undergird the experience of hunger, this logic works to diminish the personhood of the hungry poor. The flipside of this manner of viewing the poor is that those who actually labour to keep hunger at bay, and make bold to claim what is duly theirs, for instance grain or water, are not offered adequate State support; either by way of consistent wages, or State protection when they assert their right to life and livelihood. While the pliant subject is provisioned in a limited sort of way, the defiant subject is punished.

A study of violence against dalit women in five states across India (since published as a book) lists the reasons for their being targeted and attacked, including sexually assaulted. Of these, a significantly large number has to do with women insisting on their right to a life free of hunger. Assault and attack followed when women and their families tried to access water rights or the public distribution system (PDS) ration shop on equal par with dominant castes; asserted their rights to own land; tried to access forests or other common property resources; questioned dominant castes for destroying, or for their cattle destroying crops; when women won a contract to cook school midday meals and when women questioned the delay or part-payment or under-payment or non-payment of wages. This list is by no means exhaustive, but it helps build a map of everyday India, where touch and food determine so much else, and remain central to who therefore suffers the consequence of violent touch.

There is a further subtext to this: in the popular imagination, the poor and the hungry are viewed as piteous victims, but at the same time, hunger as a condition is seen as something that need not deter a person from achieving a higher purpose. Thus, it is commonplace to claim that even to assuage the pain in one's stomach, one ought not to do such and such low thing; thus, moral worth is measured by how the stomach's claims may be put away, indeed not heeded. This line of reasoning is particularly insistent when it comes to discussions around sex work: sex workers are often berated for choosing to heed the claims of the stomach, rather than their honour. Death, they are often told, is preferable to such a dishonourable life. On the other hand, should a sex worker's life take a suitably tragic turn, she is forgiven all, because, after all, it is said now, it was hunger that drove her to this profession. In all this, what is conveniently forgotten is the systematic nature of trafficking, abduction, confinement and violence that keeps the system of sex work in place. Forgotten too is the sex worker's complex sense of her own location and labour. Most important, the manner in which the experience of hunger and the impositions of the caste order combine in sex work is often forgotten—neither caste-mandated sexual labour nor its secular forms figure in the popular imagination.

Truth be told, women who challenge this sort of mandated sexual labour are the ones who also face sexual assault: popular morality plays an important role in erasing this out of the purview of the social imagination. As the study I have referred to above notes, sexual violence against dalit women has also to do with their refusal to be sexually available; and when they attempt to hold men, responsible for their being coerced into sex work, accountable. In this context, I would like to recall the moving life of a woman who was coerced into ritualized sex work, but who fought caste-imposed sexual stigma and hunger valiantly until her moment of tragic death.

In an obituary she wrote for Devi, a woman dedicated as a Mathamma or ritual temple dancer, S. Anandhi paints a picture of a life that was unjust in every way: dedicated as a Mathamma when little, forced to dance for dominant caste patrons, for a living spurned by the man she lived with and had children by, working to organize Mathammas and facing community disapproval and contempt, accused of being an alcoholic and amoral, being tormented by a partner whose family she helped support through her labour and finally being thrown out of her house by her son— Devi's life was hard, but she was a tough, intelligent woman who never gave up fighting for her dignity, her freedom, until that fateful day when she committed suicide.

In a life such as this, food, hunger, caste, sexuality and survival are all closely linked, and injustice and violence combine to keep these categories of experience yoked together. Mandated to exchange sexual labour for survival, trapped within an economic logic, underwritten by caste, and subject to unstable and often violent sexual and intimate relationships—one can see how a wide arc connects the politics of food, sex, violence and survival in caste society.

***

I come now to another feature of everyday life in caste society: the social organization of space. In rural India, neighbourhoods are divided into dalit and non-dalit settlements. The lines of division are clear and may not be breached easily. In small-town and urban India, while these divisions are harder to enforce as a matter of routine, they are nevertheless present—dalits find it hard to access housing in mixed neighbourhoods, while upper and dominant castes seek to remain exclusive, by making it evident that they will not countenance non-vegetarians and Muslims which often translates into keeping all but the elites castes out. Poorer neighbourhoods often house dalit homes, and while there is greater mixing in these, there are also clearly demarcated dalit slums.

As with everything else, women are expected to sustain these spatial boundaries and ensure that caste differences remain in place. How do women experience boundedness? For one, sociability is not easy to sustain across castes. To be sure, friendships are forged across caste lines and women do associate with each other while labouring, or in festive spaces, such as fairs or the cinema hall. Yet, social solidarity is not easily possible unless there is a political movement that brings them together—this is not unknown though even within horizontally organized groups, tasks and responsibilities may remain segmented on the basis of caste, with dalit women performing less cerebral functions than others. The experience of women's groups has also demonstrated how hard it is to organize dalit and non-dalit women together, and often separate sectors have to be established, one in the main village, as it is and the other in the dalit settlement.

Secondly, spatial boundaries being social ones, they are consequential both in a symbolic as well as a material sense. I have referred to this several times in earlier sections of this book but will repeat it here: dominant caste women affirm their difference by characterizing women from castes below them as incapable of 'feminine' virtue, and as given to promiscuity. Their sense of self is thus shaded by sexual anxiety on the one hand—the notion that dalit women will lure their men away from them—and caste pride on the other. We have seen too that upper or dominant caste women are as likely as their men to condone violence against lower caste and dalit women. Dalit women, on the other hand, have to negotiate sexual vulnerability on a daily basis; their sense of bodily integrity is constantly under threat, particularly when they are also economically dependent on the dominant castes. Apart from physical violence, a dalit woman may expect to be abused verbally almost as a matter of course, and in the coarsest possible fashion.

A study of the first information reports filed under the PoA Act in Tamil Nadu in the mid-1990s reveals that atrocity-related offenses are also insistently verbal—humiliating and denigrating references to dalit women's bodies, amounting to hate-speech are legion, and characteristic of dominant caste everyday speech. While the dalit woman's sense of self is thus fraught, it is also resistant: in fact much of the violence she experiences is on account of her stout refusal to surrender her dignity.

Thirdly, spatial (and social) boundaries, as we have seen, are sexual boundaries as well and romance in caste society is thus haunted by what is not permissible. As I have noted above, 'improper' touch and romance can and do lead to violence and while women and men have resisted codes to do with appropriate marriage and touch, they have also had to pay for their transgression. Should the woman be from a higher caste than the man she loves, and if he happens to be a dalit, men from her community punish not just her or her lover, but his entire community, and tellingly enough target dalit neighbourhoods, destroying their means of livelihood, their homes and more. In some instances, the woman's family may even prefer complaints to the local police that their girl was abducted and subjected to sexual violence. Pratiksha Baxi points out how courts sometimes abet this, either by claiming that no father would make such a complaint, and so therefore it must be true, and the lover has to be convicted; or they argue that the complaint is false, and is being lodged to save the family from embarrassment, for the girl is known to be promiscuous.

In contexts where political movements supported intercaste marriages, mixed marriages did survive familial and caste disapproval and eventually concerned families did make peace with each other—as was evident in villages in Dharmapuri district in Tamil Nadu in the 1970s, when the Naxalite movement was active in the region.

As far as dalit women are concerned, sexual boundedness works differently: for one, they are deemed sexually available, as we have seen, so there is no safety to be sought for within the caste community. Further, should they fall in love with other caste men, the passage to marriage is not only a rough one, but it may not even lead to marriage. But it can and does lead to sexual mortification and violence.

Within their own caste spaces, women are likely to be valued or not, depending on the economic and political status of the caste in question, since the women's question is often bound with a caste's sense of its own worth. Yet women also make spaces their own in any number of ways. Dalit women's life narratives contain fascinating accounts of how this is done—through acts of care, nurture, through skillfully negotiating male authority and violence, and seeking to hold on to their dignity in contexts where the homes are attacked and their sexual vulnerability is heightened. Even when men flee violence, women remain, to reclaim what may be reclaimed. As dalit lives are transformed, the space of the home becomes defined in other ways, through signs of progress, better living and by icons that reflect a heightened political sensibility. The Bhotmange household, before it was destroyed in the infamous Khairalanji violence of 2006, was one such space—complete with pictures of the Buddha and Dr Ambedkar. In fact, the rape and murder of Surekha and Priyanka Bhotmange were occasioned not only by specific differences and tensions, but also by the clearly changed nature of their living spaces, their social confidence, and obvious Ambedkarite politics.

Spatial differences and tensions, writ large by caste inequalities, produce particular sorts of bodies, docile, rebellious and fraught. While women experience these processes in particular ways—and are scarred by it—these processes remain central to the making of male subjectivity as well. For instance, the sexual authority that dominant caste men assume derives from a territorial and proprietary sense—the control they have over land, capital, trade and labour grants them impunity. On the other hand, their need to subjugate the laboring classes and the gratuitous violence they expend and justify in the name of caste pride are not reducible to their class arrogance alone. Dominant caste selfhood, it seems, is affirmed chiefly through the humiliation and 'emasculation' of lower caste and dalit existence. Anti-caste radical thought—from Periyar to Dr Ambedkar—has pointed to how the caste order makes self-respect impossible and refuses mutuality and fraternity. When viewed in this light, dominant caste masculine violence may be seen as an expression of a fundamental inability to be fraternal. This inability expresses itself in and through violence, and worse, does not see itself as suffering from a lack, but rather experiences a sense of fulsome selfhood precisely on this account.

The sheer perversion of this phenomenon is made evident when upper and dominant caste men are confronted with dissent and rebellion. When dalit assertion threatens to breach territorial and social boundaries, dominant caste men respond with verbal as well as physical violence. Verbal abuse in this instance is telling, since it betrays great anxiety over dalit 'intrusion' into spaces from where they have been kept away. Thus, some of the more common forms of abuse are directed at dalit self-worth—to the circumstances of their birth, the characterization of dalit men as not 'men' but actually 'faggots', and boastful references to how dominant caste men have access to dalit women. Abusive references to dalit women's genitalia and sexuality also abound. A warped sense of personhood, expressed in and through a bully's swagger, dominant caste masculinity is shot through with a fundamental sense of unacknowledged 'lack'. To name dominant caste masculinity in these terms is not to diminish its capacity for violence, but rather serves to underscore its fundamental instability and illegitimacy.

Lower caste and dalit 'male' selfhood expresses itself differently; while we have considerable literature on the humiliation imposed on dalits, we do not nearly have enough on how dalits, particularly men, have sought to come terms with the ghettoization of their lives, and the spatial boundaries that come with it. There is a rich history to be mined here, and I would like to merely flag snapshots from that history, which is layered, diverse and complex. My examples are from the Tamil context. In Tamil Nadu, it is not unusual for assertive political men, individuals as well as groups, to proudly flaunt the symbols of their self-worth, be it a party flag, inspiring phraseology that appears on a local wall, or the images of leaders they cherish. This goes back to the heyday of the Dravidian movement which writ its presence large on the streets and public forums of the state through the practice of a distinct iconography. The innumerable statues of Dr Ambedkar that we see dotting the Tamil landscape as well as the gaily unfurled flags of several dalit political parties speak of dalit spatial politics that is assertive and marked by its own symbols. Space has proved pertinent in other contexts as well, as when it comes to demanding equal rights and honours in places of worship—going beyond temple entry, such assertions are about sharing space and rights. Dalit men have been active in spearheading struggles that have to do with a competitive use of space: if dominant castes seek to assert their presence through commemorative events and festivals that speak caste pride and superiority, dalits, as is evident from practices in Southern Tamil Nadu, stage counter-events, which privilege their heroes, especially those who have challenged upper caste arrogance.

However, in spite of political change, economic growth and burgeoning social confidence, dalit lives continue to be marked by experiences of loss and alienation that come with the attenuation of selfhood that caste practices impose. An anomic sense of self in racialized societies, in the USA or South Africa, has been the subject of discussion and debate. In the Indian context, we need to think through this anomie, especially the sexual politics that constitutes it, and which it does not entirely slough off. Thwarted, beaten down, mocked at for not being men enough, forced to flee homes and neighbourhoods, living in entrapped environments, particularly in cities, whose space may be freeing in a social sense, but are oppressive nevertheless in their grinding poverty—what kind of masculinity emerges from out of these spaces, and how does it expend itself? Underclass violence, including sexual violence, cannot be separated from the contexts and details of underclass life, and feminist thought is yet to fully grapple with this phenomenon.

***

I examine next the question of sexual touch, to what might be called the semantics of desire in caste society. I have touched on this theme now and then in the preceding pages. In what follows, I would like to examine how 'normal' sexual and conjugal behavior is produced in caste society. It seems to me that the 'normal' is always already outrageous, as I have argued, and I would like to demonstrate why this is so.

Desire in caste society emerges as most problematic when it has to accommodate what it ought not to: whether it is same sex love, or queer romances or intercaste relationships. Mixing of things that ought to stay apart poses a threat to the social order, in which differences are constantly reiterated and rearranged within a persistent hierarchy of power and authority. Yet mixing does happen and is silently allowed its existence—except when it demands public acknowledgement, in which instance it leads to tension, resulting in violence.

I would like to consider in this context two Tamil texts that deal with 'mixing'. The first is *Mathorupagan*, a novel by Perumal Murugan translated into English, as *One Part Woman*, and which centres round a peasant caste (Gounder caste) couple in western Tamil Nadu and their desire for a child. Though they are in love and sexually obsessed with each other, the woman, Ponna, still does not get pregnant. This rankles, since all that she touches on the fields on which she and her husband labour literally blooms, and contrasts starkly with her own barrenness. The novel engages with the minutiae of her attempts to get pregnant; the narrative veers towards a crisis, when, on the advice of her mother and mother-in-law, she decides to go on a pilgrimage to a temple to which barren women go of a festive night. As they make the pilgrimage round they are 'allowed' to choose a man for themselves, and if they get pregnant by him, they are seen as being blessed with a 'child given by God'. Ponna chooses such a man, and meanwhile, her husband comes to know of it, and kills himself. He is troubled by her decision, the narrative makes clear, not only because she could actually bring herself to sleep with another man but also because the latter could, literally, be anyone, including a dalit!

The novel is set in the early 20th century, and was based on a practice of which the author heard, while researching into the history of the temple that is featured in the novel. Repeated references to 'god's children' in neighbourhoods around the temple intrigued him; in attempting to understand what that meant, he came to know of this perhaps apocryphal, perhaps real practice. The point is, he uses this liminal festive moment, which allows a breaking of caste barriers albeit for the purpose of procreation, to call attention to the hypocrisies that structure caste-based sexuality. If retaining caste is all about ensuring the 'purity' of one's progeny, a practice that allows one to bend the rule, in the interest of sustaining lineage is surely worthy of understanding for what it tells us about practices that belie strictures to do with touch.

Sexual love that cuts across caste differences is also the subject of Durai Guna's short story *Oorar Varaintha Oviyum* (A Painting by the Villagers), which is essentially about punishment meted out to a dalit young man for having dared to help himself to sacred ash at a temple festival, when he ought to have known better. The young man's parents help him leave town quietly rather than face up to the punishment. The crux of the story, though, is the actual moment of transgression. The dominant castes who object to the transgressive act arouse the wrath of a group of young dalits who beat them up. As matters threaten to get out of hand, an elder from the dominant community counsels restraint, arguing that the scuffle between the two communities is somewhat pointless, since they are, after all, on intimate terms: for, are not men from the dominant caste found with dalit women, and who knows, some children growing up in the dalit settlement could well have been fathered by dominant caste men. The short story passes on to focus on the punishment that is eventually handed out to the erring young man, but meanwhile, we get a glimpse of how the forbidden persists in and through restrictive sexual codes.

Significantly, both these texts were subject to angry criticism, and their authors threatened with dire consequences, should they not apologize for what they had dared to write. In the first instance, it was argued that the 'honour' of Gounder women had been wounded; whereas in the next instance, it appears that the real-life counterparts of characters featured in the short story had been hurt by the writer helping himself to their experiences. In the event, though, it became clear that to speak of what may not be spoken of, even if it happens, was the real crime. It is not that castes do not intermingle, or that intimate sexual relations do not happen across caste divides. But these matters are not to be spoken of, since it is this complicit silence that helps to perpetuate notions of high and low castes, and to sustain fear of miscegenation.

It could be said that public silence around 'inappropriate' sexuality too is of this kind: that transpersons exist and are in sexual and intimate partnership with men or women is known, even grudgingly tolerated. Same sex love and queer sexuality are not unknown, yet neither is to be spoken of. For to speak of love and pleasure that are not linked to appropriate procreation, but which may be varied and possible with unlikely partners, is to admit to the possibility of life beyond caste, property and progeny and heterosexual love. Silence, in such contexts, marks the limits of the permissible, but this does not mean that what is not permitted does not ever happen. But we are not allowed to name or acknowledge what must remain in the deep shadows.

***

The semantics of touch in caste society, whether it has to do with food, space and sexuality is calculated to produce unfreedom of various kinds. With respect to food and space, even if boundaries that keep castes apart and insistently reproduce hierarchy are transgressed, such transgression as we have seen is violently folded back into the terms of the caste order. Resistance meanwhile continues, and while it is thwarted, it 'succeeds' on account of its very possibility, which shows up the exercise of sexual, caste and class authority for what it is.

When it comes to touch, we see that what is allowed and what is forbidden are curiously linked. Thus the forbidden is not pushed away, in fact it is continually performed and as a punitive or cautionary measure, so evident in the manner dominant caste men seek to sexually possess dalit women, as if the very fact of untouchability requires to be enacted through acts of violence that wound the dalit body in an ontological sense. If the forbidden is to be consciously assumed, relished and possessed in defiance, as happens in intercaste relationships, it has to stay silent. If we dare speak of the forbidden in critical terms, or seek out a language and register, occasioned by political, social or cultural protest, which asserts the transformative value of forbidden gestures and acts, then violence follows, so that the forbidden may be pushed back into the shadows.

What help maintain sexual routine are hypocrisy and a commitment to unfreedom, both of which are enormously productive. For instance, where sexual objectification—of women—is the norm, women have to, and do, accommodate it, and meanwhile seek to exercise whatever dignified agency they might in negotiating their fate. In Saba Dewan's film *The Nacch*, which features the famed dancers at the Sonepur cattle fairgrounds, we see how they assess and manipulate male sexual interest and anxiety. They are watchful, pleasing, yet they keep their distance and retain a performative edge in all their transactions. They are protected from fawning men by a fence that holds back the milling crowd that comes to see them dance: in a telling shot we see aroused men, held back, flushed, excited, and ready to act out their fantasies, and on the other side of the fence are the women who have to skillfully negotiate this moment, without harming themselves.

This is a stunning visual portrayal of sexual objectification: the woman is not a poor victim who cannot help herself; neither are the men watching them all socially powerful. Both men and women, we realize, act out roles in an endless game that keeps excitement at fever pitch, even as their sexual selves remain thwarted and compromised by the fantasy they both submit to. The Sonepur dance routine mocks at sexual certainties built around the good and the forbidden, yet it is, itself, a symptom of a sexual condition that is fraught and unfree.

***

Our habitual sexual cultures, and the notions of tactility that underwrite them, teach us to consistently misrecognize sexual violence as legitimate, and challenge it only when it destroys what we are taught to consider inviolable. Perversely, inviolability has to prove its worth by suffering destruction and hurt. Unless we unpack notions of the good and forbidden, which are writ large on the bodies of women, and looped around the vertical axis of caste divisions, we are not likely to acknowledge suffering that inheres in sexual hurt.

REFERENCES

Anandhi, S. 2013. 'Remembering Lakshmi, Devi', *Economic & Political Weekly*, XLVIII (11): 32–33.

Anandhi, S. 2013. 'The Mathammas: Gender, Caste and the Politics of Intersectionality in Rural Tamil Nadu', *Economic and Political Weekly*, XLVIII (18): 64–71.

Baxi, Pratiksha. 2014. *Public Secrets of the Law: Rape Trials in India*, pp. 234–282. Delhi: Oxford University Press.

Britto, M.A. 2007. *Vankodumaiyum Satta Amalaakkamum* (Atrocities and Law Enforcement), Dr Ambedkar Cultural Centre.

Guna, Durai. 2014. *Oorar Varaintha Oviyam* (A Painting by the Villagers), Keelanda Veedu.

Irudayam, Aloysius S.J., Jayshree P. Mangubhai, Joel G. Lee. 2012. *Dalit Women Speak Out: Caste, Class and Gender Violence in India*, New Delhi: Zubaan.

Murugan, Perumal. 2014. *One-Part Woman* (translated from the Tamil *Mathorupagan*), New Delhi: Hamish Hamilton.

Sabrang. 2005, http://www.sabrang.com/bilkees/bilkisdeposition.pdf, (accessed 8 July 2014).

Anand Teltumbde, Anand. 2014. *The Persistence of Caste: The Khairlanji Murders & India's Hidden Apartheid*, New Delhi: Navayana.

In Place of a Conclusion:
Towards a Recognition of Suffering

In a sexual culture that is unfree, and where touch is coded and overdetermined, women's lives are necessarily fraught and burdened. As we have seen, though, whenever history has afforded moments for rethinking the social order, women, amongst others have interrogated and rearranged existing social and sexual arrangements. Their speech has been crucial when it addressed the many disabilities imposed on them, and the silent and not so silent sexual violence they endure. Such speech was of course neither easy nor entirely free. It had to gain the ear of society and the State, and therefore constructed itself carefully, through a series of silences or elisions, on the one hand, and permissible and sharply argued words on the other. The law provided both a context and register for such speech, as did the political imagination and discourses of revolutionary movements against caste, landlordism, and capital. Women also learned to articulate their experiences of hurt and assault through a language of affect and virtue. Eventually when women came to speak in the name of a feminist understanding of violence, they had recourse to language that united the personal with the social and political worlds, and matters to do with sexuality assumed significance. Sexual violence became a political crime and problem, and not merely a condition that women had to battle.

Yet, the deliberate use of sexual violence, as punitive action and to underscore the ideological projects of right-wing Hindu fascism and the assertion of dominant castes in a democracy that had taught the subordinate to resist them, has proved challenging. Likewise, the use of rape as a tactical weapon by the Indian Armed Forces, and against its own citizens, caused great political anguish for feminists who wished, at all times, to abide by the promises inherent in the Constitution and a State that had inherited the legacy of an anti-colonial struggle. They, therefore, had to connect with other registers and practices of protest and critique, and while these projects are ongoing and requiring of constant revision, they have remained in place, and insisted on foregrounding women's defiance of sexual and political authority.

***

The greatest challenge though has been to define oneself as a worthy sexual subject. Sexual violence, as we have seen in any number of instances, is premised on a notion of who is rape-able and who is not; and therefore has recourse to practice that damns you if you are indeed rape-able and does so; and damns you if you are not, in that you are raped anyway, only it is not considered an offence. Thus the dominant caste 'chaste' woman as well as the lower caste 'sexually available' woman are both subject to sexual violence just so that men in whom sexual—and social—authority is vested can affirm the terms of sexual and social relationships, as they deem fit. In such a context, how does one position one's sexual self? Women in political movements have claimed other selves, of the peasant, the worker, the dalit labourer, the adivasi insurgent, the ethnic-nationalist, only to find that their sexual selves precede them, and in the event, their bodies are viewed as trophies, to be possessed and handed out, or wrested and held aloft in triumph over the enemy.

Feminists grappling with the conundrum of the woman who is either a good sexual victim or a bad sexualized woman, who cannot hope to elicit social attention or sympathy, have addressed it by affirming female sexual agency; and sought to thereby rework the terms by which women's sexuality is damned. Thus they have upheld the dignity of the sex worker and the professional dancer; they have tried to frame women's sexual lives in terms of their own sense of what such lives entail, rather than impose on them a moral and social grid which in any case does not answer to the women's experiences. This has been a contentious process, since sexual labour in the Indian context is also caste labour, and for lower caste and dalit feminists, there is nothing to be recouped here, rather, they argue, the terrain ought to be abandoned altogether. Further, the celebration of female sexual agency must not be at the cost of ignoring the complex inscriptions of female sexuality in caste, commerce and poverty. Jenny Rowena, responding to the feminist excitement over the film *The Dirty Picture*, a bio-pic of the actor 'Silk' Smita who played the vamp in many a film, notes that feminist enthusiasm in this instance has been at the cost of appraising Smita's social context. She was from a working class and a lower caste, and this fact is seldom foregrounded in the film, argues Rowena. Further the actor who played her was appealing enough, being light-skinned and obviously 'upper caste' in her demeanour, and this detracted attention away from the actual conditions in which Smita worked, and the manner in which her body was framed by the camera. The point is, as Rowena has made evident in this and other essays, the feminist gaze cannot afford to separate the sexual from all other identities.

Another option has been to eschew the sexual altogether and portray women as defiant political subjects, as we find in the histories of Left-wing militancy. This is problematic too, since the woman's militant's politics has not spared her sexual violence or humiliation, and sometimes within her militant own ranks, she has had to confront either, as we have seen.

In this context, it appears important to heed the nuanced ways in which women from diverse contexts, who live with and endure sexual subordination and violence describe their condition. The sexual, it is evident, from a perusal of women's narratives, is not separable from other aspects of their existence, and for most women, the violence that seeks to break their bodily integrity is of a part with much else they endure: the refusal of their personhood in the name of class, caste, faith, ethnicity and sexual orientation. The reduction of the worlds of which they are a part, to a condition of subjection and humiliation, is the defining context for their own experience of hurt, and unless this is addressed by feminists, the latter's understanding of sexual violence cannot be complete.

In previous sections of this book, I have reiterated this argument; I wish now to relate it to a politics of recognition, of recognition of suffering with which I began this book. Such recognition, it seems to me, cannot ever be complete unless we are able to understand and name the denial of personhood that precedes and follows sexual violence. For instance, today we are prone to criticizing the South African TRC for its oversight regarding sexual crimes. This is fair criticism and cannot be otherwise, yet it may not be possible or desirable to either consider sexual violence in South Africa outside of the context of apartheid or reduce it to a series of acts that unfolded in the apartheid era. The assaulted body is a historical body, and cannot only be reduced to its 'sex'. It has to be accounted for in terms of its bodily being, in other words, its ontology, which, in the case of apartheid was denied, occluded and punished.

The assaulted body is also a material body and this cannot be forgotten either. As Rhonda Copelon has warned us in her writings against the use of the term 'genocidal rape' with respect to crimes committed against Muslim women in Bosnia, the crime is grave, but rape ought not to be considered consequential only because it unfolded within a politics of numbers to do with ethnicity and identity. The suffering and hurt female body, or indeed other hurt bodies, are all too real and cannot be read as 'texts' or as emblems of particular national histories. It is important, therefore, to recover materiality, and in such a way that we are able to mark the diverse ways in which a body is already defined to be 'disposable' before it is actually hurt and assaulted. Ontological wounding is what is at stake here, and we need to recognize it for what it is without losing sight of the body's inexorably historical and material existence.

That said, we have to also reckon with the problem of rape as the ultimate crime against women—and howsoever we seek to counter this argument, we are still left with the fact of the experience of violence being not granted voice or speech, unless we fight to speak. And to speak requires a sense of how all speech with respect to rape is always already overcoded, in legal, medical and cultural registers that the claims of the hurt body are always hard to sustain on its own experiential terms—unless we actively choose to pay heed to the latter. The challenge is to 'hear' and decipher the many languages of hurt and suffering.

I would like to bring in a rather distressing short story to illustrate what I mean. *Lizards' Colony* by Mahmoud Saeed, an Iraqi writer, in exile in the United States of America, features an Arab female interpreter called into translate for the US army. She is literally— and sexually—'broken into' her task and made to witness horrible acts of torture in the course of an interrogation—and meanwhile she has to 'translate' what the victim attempts to convey. She is not quite clear as to how and when she was sexually assaulted, and suspects it happened during the first day of work, when she was drugged and raped. Her body still bearing the marks of what was done to it, she waits upon a particularly brutal interrogation scene. We wonder why an Arab-speaking woman, in this case, a woman of Iraqi origin plays the role of an intermediary—we later on find out that she needs the money to take care of her rather sick child.

Saeed makes it clear that the horror of what the woman was subject to cannot be spoken of for two reasons: the interrogating officer shows her a picture of herself being carried in the arms of a giant soldier and notes tersely that she cannot cry rape, when she had surely consented to sex. Secondly, he notes that she was being paid a rather large amount of money for her services, and that she must know that this was not only on account of her translation skills. Rather gratuitously, the officer reminds her of her child. This calculus of loss and gain renders her speechless.

The violence done unto her contrasts with the torture carried out on the prisoner whose words she is called to interpret—that torture is equally sexual in that his genitalia are subject to extravagant violence, but this is achieved through precise instructions and contrasts with what was done to her, which remains hazy and shadowy in her memory but which is present as unbearable pain in her body. Interestingly the tortured prisoner, when told he must confess, repeats just this one line, ostensibly addressing her, 'Iraqi woman, how many children do you have?'

Saeed brings together two kinds of political violence: the deliberate sexual assault of a woman, which sexualizes her and on that account renders her vulnerable and complicit with a cruel system; and the violence of political torture that seeks to shore up this cruel system by maiming and finally murdering its alleged opponents. Sexual violence confronts the interpreter with hurt and shame that she cannot hope to transcend, whereas political violence, however cruel, has to reckon with the stubbornness of those who would rather die than 'confess'. While sexual violence produces a sexual victim who can be repeatedly tormented and abused, political violence causes death. The gendered equivalence that Saeed establishes between two sorts of violence is rather telling. Yet in the one, imposed on the interpreter, we see a triumphant masculinity at work, whereas in the other, for all its success at torturing a prisoner unto death, we see a thwarted politics, a failure.

Victims of torture indict the torturers, and their very persons, even if they die, bear witness to an abuse of authority and state violence; whereas survivors of sexual violence remain doomed to their inexorably 'sexual' status, and to silence. Even the melodramatic fact of the woman in the story doing this for her child recedes in the face of what she must endure.

In this context, it is clear that we need to render sexual violence as a crime that indicts the world and the perpetrator in no uncertain terms, in short a crime against bodily integrity, personhood, why our very humanity. This is not because it is the most terrible thing that can happen to a woman, but because it is seen as a sexual crime, and confounded with questions of shame and stigma, and not as a tormenting of the body and spirit. To communicate recognition of what women endure, therefore, we need to re-imagine personhood itself, in all its richness and with a keen feminist sensibility. For unless we are able to hold the experience of violence to account from within a shared and fraternal sense of social fellowship, we are unlikely to muster an acknowledgement of the victim survivor's suffering from society at large. And, such acknowledgement, so hard to come by in the sexual, caste and class worlds we live in, is ultimately the most important indictment of impunity.

REFERENCES

Copelon, Rhonda. 1994. 'Surfacing Gender: Re-Engraving Crimes Against Women in Humanitarian Law', *5 Hastings Women's Law Journal*, 5(2). http://repository.uchastings.edu/hwlj/vol5/iss2/4 (accessed on 22 November 2015).

Rowena, Jenny. 2012. *The 'Dirt' in the Dirty Picture: Caste, Gender and Silk Smitha*. http://roundtableindia.co.in/index.php?option=com_content&view=article&id=5283%253Athe-dirt-in-the-dirty-picture-caste-gender-and-silk-smitha&catid=119%253Afeature&Itemid=132 (accessed on 22 November 2015).

Saeed, Mahmood. 2012. 'Lizards' Colony', *World Literature Today*, November, http://www.worldliteraturetoday.org/2012/november/lizards-colony-mahmoud-saeed (accessed on 22 November 2015).

Acknowledgements

This book has a long history. It owes a great deal to the time I spent with the late K. Balagopal, in the 1990s, assisting him in editing fact-finding reports produced by the Andhra Pradesh Civil Liberties Committee in the first decade of its existence. As we sifted through the reports, most of which were written by Balagopal, I marveled at how each of them ended: on a note of hope that also gestured towards justice, even when the content of each, replete with descriptions of vile torture, mocked the possibilities of securing either. Later on, I asked Balagopal about that line of hope—and he wryly remarked that elusive as it might appear, it was yet an imperative. I have reflected on that statement many times over, and this book is a continuation of those reflections on 'foul, deceitful hope'. I wish Balagopal was here to help me continue the argument—while writing, his cherished memory chastised my despair.

I would like to invoke another dear departed friend: Ossie Fernandes, who involved me in the work he undertook with many others on reviewing and refining the Prevention of Atrocities against Scheduled Castes and Tribes Act, 1989. Thanks to him, I sat in on many a public hearing to do with the Act, and had the opportunity to learn from the witnesses that spoke in these tribunals, not only of their travails, but also of their struggles to secure justice. I remember with gratitude and respect an Irula (a scheduled tribe in Tamil Nadu) witness, Murugan, an epitome of ethical grace.

I must acknowledge here two judgements and judges that taught me a great deal about truth-telling and justice: the Vachathi Sessions court judgement, delivered by S. Kumaraguru, and the judgement delivered in the Naroda Patiya case, by Jyotsna Yagnik.

The shock of State impunity, its deliberate-ness, though depressingly familiar, proved particularly hard-hitting when Afzal Guru was hung. Anguished like many others, I wrote two plays on the subject of State violence, featuring resistant women—all those who worked on those plays, especially A. Mangai, who directed them and my young friends, Revathi, Ponni and Jeny who acted in them, taught me a great deal about representing and negotiating violence and sorrow, and the healing possibilities of art.

From the plays to this book—I did not intend that journey to happen. It did, thanks to Urvashi and Zubaan, who persisted in the face of my recalcitrance to do so, and got this volume out of me— even as they worked on their larger publishing project on impunity, State violence and sexual violence.

Along with me, many others have authored this book, in the most fundamental sense of the term: I have named some of them in these pages, as I cite their publications. But there are many others, who do not feature here, but whose lives and work have enriched my understanding of civil rights and feminism: K. Manoharan, Mythily Sivaraman, Fatima Burnad, Sandana Mary, Sharifa, Selvam, Subatra, Lucy, Anuradha, Jayanthi, Meena, Gita, Jayashree, Githa Ramaseshan, Anusha and Sneha. Thanks for everything.

Lastly, I would like to thank the trio of little girls in my life for existing: wondrous beings, unconditional in the love they dispense, Nila, Shayiri and Maitreyi.

A Note on References

Each chapter of this book comes with a set of references. Arguments in a particular chapter draw on the books or articles cited in the reference list appended to it. I have deliberately refrained from using footnotes, or internal referencing, except when I have quoted from a particular text—instead I have cited the author's name in the main body of the text, indicating I have drawn from her or his work.

People Involved in the Project

Advisors

Amena Mohsin
Hameeda Hossain
Kishali Pinto Jayawardena
Kumari Jayawardena
Mandira Sharma
Nighat Said Khan
Saba Gul Khattak
Sahba Husain
Sharmila Rege
Uma Chakravarti

Country Groups and Coordinators

Bangladesh: Ain o Salish Kendra
Amena Mohsin
Hameeda Hossain

India: Zubaan
Ishani Butalia
Laxmi Murthy
Meghna Singh
Satish Sharma
Shweta Vachani
Urvashi Butalia

Nepal: Advocacy Forum
Mandira Sharma

Pakistan: Simorgh
Hira Azmat
Neelam Hussain
Zahaid Rehman

Sri Lanka
Priya Thangarajah
S. Sumathy

Researchers and Writers

Abira Ashfaq
Afiya Zia
Amena Mohsin
Bani Gill
Bina D'Costa
Bishnu Maya Bhusal
Chulani Kodikara
Dhiraj Pokhrel
Dina Siddiqi
Divya Arya
Dolly Kikon
Essar Batool
Farzana Haniffa
Faustina Pereira
Gazala Peer
Hameeda Hossain
Hooria Khan
Huma Qurban Fouladi
Iftikhar Firdous

Ishita Dutta
Ifrah Butt
Jagdalpur Legal Aid Group
Jayshree P. Mangubhai
Jeannine Guthrie
Kabita Chakma
Kamala Visweswaran
Kavita Panjabi
Kishali Pinto Jayawardena
Laxmi Murthy
Maliha Zia
Mallika Aryal
Mandira Sharma
Meena Saraswathi Seshu
Meghna Guhathakurta
Munaza Rashid
Natasha Rather
Neelam Hussain
Neha Dixit
Noreen Naseer
Pranika Koyu
Pratiksha Baxi
Priya Thangarajah
Rajashri Dasgupta
Reshma Thapa
Rohini Mohan
Roshmi Goswami
Rubina Saigol
S. Sumathy
Sahar Bandial
Sahba Husain
Samreen Mushtaq
Sanjay Barbora

Sarah Zaman
Sarala Emmanuel
Seira Tamang
Shahidul Alam
Shobna Sonpar
Surabhi Pudasaini
Tanya Matthan
Uma Chakravarti
V. Geetha
Zainab Qureshi

Zubaan Team

Ishani Butalia
Laxmi Murthy
Meghna Singh
Satish Sharma
Shweta Vachani
Urvashi Butalia

IDRC

Navsharan Singh